The Story of the Giro d'Italia

A Year-by-Year History of the Tour of Italy

Volume Two:
1971–2011

Bill & Carol McGann

Published by McGann Publishing
P.O. Box 576
Cherokee Village, AR 72525
USA
www.mcgannpublishing.com

**McGann
Publishing**

ISBN 978-0-9843117-9-8
Printed in the United States of America

Cover photo: Stage 13, the queen stage, of the 2005 Giro d'Italia.

Look at them, as they pedal and pedal through the fields, hills and forests. They are pilgrims traveling to a distant city that they will never reach: they symbolize, in flesh and blood, as depicted in an ancient painting, the incomprehensible adventure of life. That's what it is—pure romanticism.

—Dino Buzzati

Contents

Map of Northern Italy

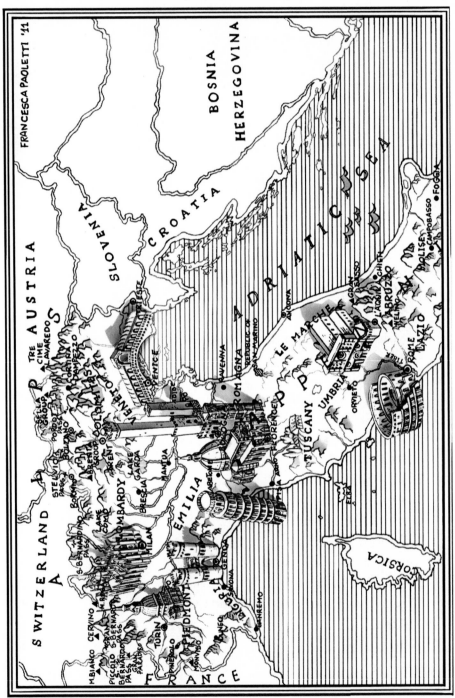

Map of Southern Italy

Preface and Acknowledgments

A few notes about the text

With its rich history, virtually unknown to English-speaking readers, writing the story of the Giro d'Italia was a labor of love. I wish I could have gone deeper into the individual stories of each rider, but since the text is already at two volumes, and fat ones at that, I had to stick to the plan of a year-by-year history, emphasizing the race itself.

I know many cycling fans dislike drugs being part of cycle racing narratives. But it is too important to be swept under the carpet; in the 1990s and early 2000s it is a sad and crucial part of our story. With riders dying and race results regularly affected by modern science inappropriately applied, a hard look at drugs is necessary.

Where a place or event has a commonly used English equivalent, I have generally used the English term, such as *Turin* for *Torino, Tuscany* for *Toscana* and *Tour of Lombardy* for *Giro di Lombardia*. When I use *Giro* (or its Italian plural *Giri*) alone in this book, it means the Giro d'Italia, even though there are many races in Italy with *Giro* in their titles. Likewise, *Tour* means the *Tour de France* and *Vuelta* means the *Vuelta a España*.

There is a glossary of both English and Italian cycling terms at the back of the book.

The unedited texts of our interviews are posted on our website: www.bikeraceinfo.com/oral-history.html

Acknowledgements

This book could not have been written without the generous assistance of several kind people who possess a deep love of cycling's history and culture. Larry Theobald, co-owner of CycleItalia bike tours, is a man mad about bikes and Italy. Larry sent me several precious, out-of-print reference books that were essential to this project and was kind enough to review this text and make valuable suggestions.

Valeria Paoletti conducted several interviews for me. Though a busy research scientist, she was always available when I couldn't figure out the meaning of some Italian passage.

Several gentlemen, James Witherell, Owen Mulholland, Les Woodland, and Gino Cervi, all with deep knowledge of cycling history, reviewed all or parts of this manuscript; all suggested improvements that were gratefully accepted. Steve Lubanski sent me several rare books that were of immeasurable value. Special thanks to Francesca Paoletti for the terrific map of Italy at the beginning of the book.

Any errors in this book are my own.

Many passages in this book are written in the singular, first person, usually expressing some opinion I hold, but Carol's contribution to this work easily equals my own; hence the author credit.

—Bill McGann

Introduction

Our Story So Far

The first volume of our Giro d'Italia history explains the Giro's origins in 1909 and tells the story of the Tour through 1970. In this volume we begin the story *in medias res*, jumping right in with the Giro's 1971 edition.

If the reader hasn't read the first volume, the following synopsis of the Giro's first 61 years will help make the narrative that follows understandable.

In the nineteenth century newspapers used a multitude of devices to increase their sales. Much of what both Charles Dickens and Alexandre Dumas wrote was serialized in newspapers. People breathlessly bought the next day's edition to learn how Oliver Twist or the Three Musketeers would get out of the fix the authors left them in at the end of the last installment. From 1895 to 1898, Darwin and Hattie McIlrath, sponsored by the *Chicago Inter Ocean* newspaper, took a 3-year trip around the world by bicycle while the paper printed weekly reports of their progress. Newspapers would often create their own news, for which they were the only suppliers in an era before radio and television.

Around 1862 Frenchman Pierre Lallement had the inspiration to connect pedals to a crank and the crank to a wheel, and with that brilliant invention the bicycle was born. In 1867 Pierre Michaux began manufacturing bicycles in Paris. Almost from that moment, the newspapers understood the magical appeal of men crossing great distances on these wonderful new machines and began promoting bicycle races. In 1869 *Le Vélocipède Illustré* sponsored the 130-kilometer Paris–Rouen race. Other papers jumped in and soon Europe was covered with races as people along the race routes eagerly bought papers that told the story of the race and listed the results. Both cycle racing and the papers thrived under this symbiosis.

In 1902 Henri Desgrange, the editor of the French sports newspaper *L'Auto*, was desperately searching for some way to drive competitor Pierre Giffard, and his newspaper *Le Vélo*, out of business. Desgrange's paper was the creation of right-wing industrialists who were upset with the liberal politics and high-priced advertising that characterized Giffard's paper.

At the suggestion of one of his writers, Desgrange took the audacious step of promoting a month-long bicycle race around France, a plan much grander than the one-day races that were the norm. His race would have the competitors ride six separate races, with rest days between each race, in a great tour of France. He then added up each rider's accumulated time for each race, or stage, called the General Classification. The winner was the rider with the lowest total elapsed time. This kind of multiple-race competition is called a stage race. This is the most glamorous and prestigious type of bicycle road racing, and we can credit Desgrange and his staff with its invention and refinement.

The first running of this Tour de France in 1903 was a smashing success. *L'Auto's* sales soared, driving *Le Vélo* out of business. Despite a few missteps, Desgrange and his Tour (and believe me, it was his Tour) went on to become first a French and then an international institution. Of the twelve Tours run before the First World War, four were won by foreigners.

As the fortunes of Desgrange's Tour and *L'Auto* waxed, newspapermen in Italy saw what promoting a national tour could do for sales. Learning that a competing paper planned to put on such a race in Italy, the struggling sports newspaper *La Gazzetta dello Sport* decided it had to take quick action. Throwing caution to the wind, the paper announced it would promote a *Giro d'Italia*, or Tour of Italy, in 1909. It was an audacious move because the struggling paper had trouble even making payroll, and coming up with the money to put on such a gigantic enterprise looked to be nearly impossible.

The Story of the Giro d'Italia

But the creative men at *La Gazzetta* hustled up and down Italy and found the funds to run their race and on May 13, 1909, the Giro's first peloton of 127 riders left from the Piazzale Loreto in downtown Milan for an eight-stage trip that went as far south as Naples before returning to Milan. In these early years the Giro calculated its standings on the basis of points (as had the Tour since 1905), the winner of a stage getting one point, second place, two points, etc. The rider with the lowest accumulated point total was declared the winner. In 1914 the Giro switched to making the winner the rider with the lowest accumulated time, and so it has remained.

Racing in those days was a brutal business. Each day's race or stage could approach 400 kilometers and take more than fourteen hours to complete, necessitating night-time starts. The riders spent long hours on unpaved roads that turned to mud when it rained. The bikes were single-speed, derailleurs not becoming common until the early 1930s. Before derailleurs, the rear hubs were double sided and could accommodate up to four cogs. When a rider wanted to change gears, he would dismount, remove the rear wheel, flip it around, remount it and be on his way.

The Giro d'Italia was a hit, making *La Gazzetta dello Sport* a profitable, widely read paper. As the years passed, bicycle racing became Italy's favorite sport. Unlike the Tour, which attracted competitors from all over western Europe, the Giro was basically an Italian race with no foreign winners until after the Second World War.

In the years surrounding the First World War, a man of astounding ability appeared. Costante Girardengo, plagued with bad luck and a fiery temper that held him to only two Giro victories, was nicknamed the *Campionissimo*, or Champion of Champions.

As Girardengo aged, another great talent emerged, Alfredo Binda, who became the first man to win the Giro five times and during one edition, took the lead in the first stage and held the lead to the end (as had Girardengo in 1919). The rivalry between Girardengo and Binda became the first of the great duels in Italian cycling. The Italian cycling fans, called *tifosi*, loved the disputes (*polemiche* in Italian) between the riders, and argued passionately among themselves as to which rider was the greater. That was the beauty of the sport in those days. Even the poorest farmer could stand on the side of the road and watch his hero whiz by and that afternoon he could join in the *polemica* while playing dominoes at the local bar.

In 1935 Gino Bartali, who could soar up mountains like no other, arrived on the scene. When the road became steep, he could leave the others behind at will. Never possessing a fine tactical or strategic sense, his raw talent and willingness to suffer (one of his nicknames was "The Man of Iron") made him one of the greatest riders in the history of the sport. Among his many victories, he won the Giro three times and the Tour twice. In the late 1930s he fought epic duels with a rider now largely forgotten outside Italy, Giovanni Valetti.

A skinny racer from Piedmont was hired in 1939 to help Bartali (a rider who is paid to help another win is called a *gregario* in Italy and a *domestique* in the rest of the world). After Bartali was injured in a fall in the 1940 Giro, the new rider, Fausto Coppi, became the youngest racer to win the Giro. Coppi turned into Italy's greatest-ever rider, and arguably the finest rider in the history of the sport. Coppi became the next *campionissimo*. He revolutionized the sport, applying science to his training and diet. He turned his cycling team into a machine dedicated to delivering Fausto Coppi to the finish line first.

But Bartali didn't give up his place in the sun without a fight. The Coppi/Bartali rivalry was the greatest ever in the history of cycling. Every *tifoso* lined up behind either Coppi or Bartali and passionately argued for his man. The competition between the two lifted the sport and made the two greater and richer than either of them would have been without the other.

Coppi won the Giro five times and became the first rider to win the Tour and the Giro in the same year. In fact, he did it twice. When Coppi died in 1960, even though Italy had often treated Coppi roughly over his disordered private life, the entire peninsula mourned his passing. As one writer said, "I pray that the good God will one day soon send us another Coppi."

One of the men working to launch the Giro back in 1909, Armando Cougnet, became the race's director, a position he held through 1949. In 1946 Cougnet began delegating responsibilities to Vincenzo Torriani, a young writer on the staff of *La Gazzetta*, and in 1949 Torriani became the Giro's sole director.

The 1950s were an exciting time for cycling. Probably no other era was so rich in talent and interesting personalities. It was also a time of ferment in the bicycle industry, which so far had been the sole support of the sport. As Europeans put aside their bikes and started traveling on mopeds and in cars, many bike factories faced with plunging sales could no longer support their race teams. In 1954, future three-time Giro winner Fiorenzo Magni saved his team by signing Nivea face cream to be his sponsor. The move was initially resisted, but today the lion's share of racing's money comes from outside the cycle industry.

Torriani created fearsome races with staggeringly difficult ascents. He was willing to run stages in the most appalling weather, creating several of the Giro's greatest legends. But Torriani knew the *tifosi* wanted an Italian to win the Giro, and his unfortunate legacy is one of bias against foreign riders. Despite his efforts, foreign riders still did well in the Giro, winning three Giri in the 1960s.

The final chapter of Volume One told of the arrival of a rider with an inexhaustible drive to win, Eddy Merckx. He stunned the cycling world with an attack on the steep Block Haus climb in the 1967 Giro that left the world's best behind. Merckx didn't win the Giro that year but in 1968 he triumphed with his first Grand Tour (three-week national stage race) win. In 1969 he was booted from the Giro with a doping positive that still has people scratching their heads. In 1970, fueled with the rage of his 1969 expulsion, he executed a perfect race, winning with an unusual economy. That made two Giro wins for the man nicknamed "The Cannibal".

And now, the 1971 Giro d'Italia.

one

1971–1978

The Giro Becomes an International Race and Foreigners Run Off with the Spoils

1971 "The Vikings have landed" trumpeted *La Gazzetta dello Sport* with the arrival of the Pettersson brothers. As the Swedish national team, Gösta, Sture, Erik and Thomas had dominated the now-discontinued 100-kilometer Team Time Trial World Championship. In 1964 (with Sven Hamrin instead of Thomas) they took a bronze at the Tokyo Olympics. In 1967, '68 and '69 they won gold medals at the World Championships as well as silver at the 1968 Mexico City Olympics. Gösta turned in a masterful performance in the 1968 Tour of Britain (then called the Milk Race), taking the lead in the first stage and holding it to the end. Offers to turn pro were plentiful, but the Petterssons turned them all down until 1970.

Gösta wanted to avoid the wild-west doping that prevailed among the pros (he also hated racing against the Iron Curtain teams, some of which had very advanced government-financed drug programs) and refused to even consider competing with the professionals until he felt competent drug testing had been implemented. Ferretti team manager Alfredo Martini finally prevailed and signed the four Swedes. Coincidentally the Ferretti kitchen equipment sponsor was owned by four brothers.

In his first year as a pro at the ripe old age of 29, Gösta won the Tour of Romandie and the Coppa Sabatini, came in sixth in the Giro and third in the Tour. It was a splendid way to begin a professional career.

For the 1971 Giro, Martini put three of the Petterssons in his lineup, Gösta, Erik and Sture. Gösta had shown good early-season form when he came in second to Merckx in Paris–Nice.

Spaniard José-Manuel Fuente turned pro in 1969 and made his Grand Tour debut in the 1970 Vuelta. His sixteenth place, 5 minutes 23 seconds behind winner Luis Ocaña, was considered a revelation. The talented climber signed to ride the 1971 season for KAS, one of Spain's greatest-ever teams. KAS brought their prodigy to the Giro along with Spanish hardmen Vicente López-Carril, Andrés Gandarias, Francisco Gabica and Domingo Perurena.

Eddy Merckx decided not to contest the Giro in 1971, choosing instead to ride the Dauphiné Libéré, which he won along with 54 other races that year, including the Tour and the World Championship.

Merckx had moved to Molteni where he wore the iconic brown and black jersey of the Italian sausage company from 1971 through 1976. Molteni's 1971 Giro team was anchored by Herman van Springel, who'd missed winning the Tour in 1968 by only 38 seconds.

SCIC (another kitchen equipment maker, as was Salvarani) assembled a first-rate squad with Franco Balmamion, Davide Boifava, Michele Dancelli, Giancarlo Polidori and Claudio Michelotto.

Italian observers thought (hoped?) Salvarani's Felice Gimondi and Gianni Motta would be the men to beat. Yes, these two ferocious opponents were on the same team, some said in order to find a way to beat Merckx. In fact, Gimondi was distressed when he learned that the Salvarani brothers had signed Motta in response to Gimondi's poor 1969 season.

Gimondi felt Motta's abilities and psychology made them natural competitors, not collaborators, and they had no business being on the same team. Motta initially turned out to be a poor bet, needing surgery in the spring of 1970 to correct an old problem from a crash in the 1965 Tour of Switzerland, making him unable to ride the Giro that year. But in 1971 he came back, winning the Tour of Romandie—the Swiss stage race that comes just before the Giro, often used by Giro contenders to put a fine edge on their form. Gimondi had no significant victories in the spring of 1971, his best result being a second place to Merckx in Milan–San Remo with Gösta Pettersson third.

The Salvaranis replaced team boss Luciano Pezzi with recently retired Vittorio Adorni. Adorni announced that for the Giro, Salvarani would have co-captains—Gimondi and Motta. That rarely works.

The Giro started off with a relay prologue at Lecce in Italy's boot-heel which, although Salvarani won it by three seconds over Molteni, did not count towards the General Classification. The first stage, won in Bari by Molteni's speedster Marino Basso, did count, making Basso the leader.

The next stage went through the hills of Puglia and Basilicata and Gimondi didn't enjoy it one bit. He was having a terrible day, trying to disguise his distress, riding in the middle of the peloton during what he hoped would be an easy, or *piano*, day.

But who attacked? None other than his teammate Motta, in fantastic condition after the Tour of Romandie. Motta's aggression got everybody's juices flowing, turning the day's racing red-hot. Gimondi, suffering his *giornata no* (a day when a rider has no strength), couldn't stay with the leaders as they surged ahead. To make things worse, Motta had told Franco Bitossi, Enrico Paolini, Dancelli and Pettersson ahead of time about his planned attack as a way to make sure his off-form teammate was put out the back door. Losing almost nine minutes meant Gimondi's Giro was over almost before it began. It turned out Salvarani's Giro was over now as well.

After coming in second to Paolini in that second stage, Motta was found to have an errant chemical in his system. The disfavor of the anti-doping control earned him a relegation to last place along with a ten-minute time penalty, enough damage to render him completely out of contention. Motta blamed the doping positive on a cup of herb tea. I would have paid good money to have been at the Salvarani team meeting that evening.

Paolini now took the Pink Jersey, which he kept until the stage five hilltop finish at Gran Sasso.

Vicente López-Carril, first to reach the top of the Gran Sasso, had suffered catastrophic time losses in the second stage, but sitting high in the standings was the day's sixth place, Claudio Michelotto, and not far behind were Aldo Moser and Ugo Colombo. Several of the main contenders—Pettersson, Fuente, Gimondi, and Zilioli—finished the stage ten minutes or more behind Lopez-Carril.

That made Colombo the *maglia rosa*:
1. Ugo Colombo
2. Aldo Moser @ 15 seconds
3. Claudio Michelotto @ 52 seconds
4. Silvano Schiavon @ 1 minute 17 seconds
5. Giancarlo Polidori @ 4 minutes 45 seconds

This was the fruit basket upside-down Giro. Several riders came back from the dead when Gimondi led an elite break of nine riders into the Tuscan coastal town of San Vincenzo. Gaining back more than six minutes were Pettersson, van Springel, Moser and Michelotto. Moser was the new Pink Jersey, with Michelotto a half minute back. Pettersson and van Springel were in the top ten, but more than eight minutes behind Moser.

Back into the Apennines. At the end of stage eight, where Moser had to give up the lead to Michelotto, the exhausted riders dribbled into Casciana Terme either alone or in small groups.

Stage ten gave the riders three good climbs to chew on, the last being to the top of Sestola Pian del Falco, not far from Abetone. Fuente showed why KAS had hired him when he was first over the Passo Radici before finishing alone, though Lino Farisato was only 3 seconds back. *La Gazzetta* called the stage win a "revelation", making it two Grand Tours where Fuente was revealed. I wonder if Merckx was paying attention.

The first of two time trials was held at Lake Garda where Pettersson and van Springel turned in excellent rides. Davide Boifava won the 28-kilometer race but Pettersson was fourth at 63 seconds, while van Springel was 13 seconds slower. Michelotto was 25th at nearly three minutes.

With the Alpine and Dolomite stages still to come, the General Classification was getting interesting. Riders who had suffered early race-killing time losses were coming back:
1. Claudio Michelotto
2. Aldo Moser @ 2 minutes 13 seconds
3. Gösta Pettersson @ 4 minutes 37 seconds
4. Ugo Colombo @ 5 minutes 36 seconds
5. Giancarlo Paolini @ 6 minutes 27 seconds
6. Herman van Springel @ 6 minutes 38 seconds

The Story of the Giro d'Italia

The standings remained unchanged as the Giro traveled to what was then Yugoslavia before heading into the Austrian Alps for a trip to the Grossglockner. Fuente made another attempt for mountain glory and was first to the top of the second major ascent but it was 1968 Olympic road champion Franco Vianelli who carried the day, climbing alone to the top.

Michelotto had been unable to stay with the main chase group containing Pettersson, van Springel, Gimondi and Colombo. He blew up at the Franz-Josefs Höhe where a friendly car door handle gave the leader an easy lift to within a minute and a half of the Pettersson group. The officials didn't think that was the way the race should be ridden and penalized him a minute. This was far less than he gained by cheating, and allowed him to stay in pink with Pettersson third at two minutes and van Springel fifth, four minutes behind. Michelotto had expected no punishment for his cheating and expressed astonishment at the one-minute penalty.

When Michelotto cracked on the Franz-Josefs, Pettersson and the other strongmen smelled blood. They weren't happy with his nominal penalty, but the next two days in the Dolomites weren't going to give the *maglia rosa* a moment's rest. Stage eighteen took the riders from Linz in Austria over the Tre Croci, Falzarego, Pordoi and Valles passes. Given that sprinter Marino Basso was the first rider over the Pordoi, one can assume that the pace for the first three ascents wasn't exactly white hot. But even that pace was too much for the Pink Jersey who must have been exhausted after riding well beyond himself defending the lead for more than a week. Indeed, Michelotto couldn't stay with the leaders on the Pordoi's ascent and while descending he flatted, rolled his tire and crashed.

With the better riders together on the final climb, Alfredo Martini drove up next to Pettersson in the team car and was distressed to find that his team captain, who didn't have a particularly aggressive personality, was content to sit in the pack. Martini knew Pettersson was riding into magnificent condition and also knew this was the time to make a move.

"Don't you know how strong you are?" he yelled, and screamed at the Swede to attack. The rest of the riders told Gösta to ignore Martini. At Martini's furious insistence Pettersson took off with several good riders for company, the move turning into a four-man break of Pettersson, Gimondi, van Springel and Francisco Galdós. Gimondi led them into

Falcade ten minutes ahead of Michelotto, who was sporting a bad head wound from his crash.

Michelotto was out of the Pink Jersey and, following his team doctor's advice, abandoned. Pettersson had quietly (if you ignore Martini's yelling) moved to the front of the line:

1. Gösta Pettersson
2. Ugo Colombo @ 1 minute 34 seconds
3. Herman van Springel @ 2 minutes 1 second
4. Francisco Galdós @ 3 minutes 29 seconds
5. Silvano Schiavon @ 5 minutes 19 seconds

The next stage had three ascents including the Passo Tonale. It didn't change things much, except that van Springel was able to sneak into Ponte di Legno 19 seconds ahead of Pettersson. With only the 20-kilometer final-stage time trial left to affect the standings, that could be a big deal. The gap between them was now only 102 seconds and both van Springel and Pettersson were good against the clock.

But, there was no way van Springel, as competent as he was, could take the Giro away from Pettersson, one of the world's best time-trialists. Ole Ritter won the stage while Pettersson was second at 39 seconds. Van Springel gave up 22 seconds to the Swede, but it was a good enough performance to move him past Colombo into second place.

Pettersson's director Alfredo Martini is given a lot of credit for Pettersson's careful, economical and measured climb to the lead. Pettersson didn't waste a single watt, winning a difficult Giro à la Balmamion, without winning a single stage. Martini said that if Pettersson had been a more aggressive rider, his talent would have allowed him far more victories during his short professional career.

Final 1971 Giro d'Italia General Classification:
1. Gösta Pettersson (Ferretti) 97 hours 24 minutes 3 seconds
2. Herman van Springel (Molteni) @ 2 minutes 4 seconds
3. Ugo Colombo (Filotex) @ 2 minutes 35 seconds
4. Francisco Galdós (KAS) @ 4 minutes 27 seconds
5. Franco Vianelli (Dreher) @ 6 minutes 41 seconds

Climbers' Competition:
1. José-Manuel Fuente (KAS): 360 points
2. Franco Vianelli (Dreher): 270
3. Franco Mori (SCIC): 190

Points Competition:
1. Marino Basso (Molteni): 181 points
2. Patrick Sercu (Dreher): 148
3. Felice Gimondi (Salvarani): 139

Winner Gösta Pettersson

Gimondi returned to good form in time for the World Championships where he and Merckx fought an epic duel. The two were alone together for the last twenty kilometers as the Italian withstood attack after attack from Merckx, with the Belgian prevailing in the final sprint. With each acceleration from Merckx, Gimondi would literally grit his teeth, so much so that during the intense final lap, Gimondi dislocated his jaw. Champions are different from the rest of us.

For much of the twentieth century, Italian sport was cycling. The newspapers sold millions upon millions of copies to the sports-mad Italians who gobbled up the news of their heroes.

But Italy had changed. Following the end of the Second World War, Italians desperate for work poured into the great manufacturing cities of the north, creating an enormous well of cheap labor that fueled Italy's post-war economic miracle. But big cities are poor venues for road racing. As a result soccer, a stadium sport better suited to city living, grew in popularity. Adding to bicycle racing's woes was television, which had gone from a rare luxury to an important part of western life. Televising the moving circus that is a road race is a complex, expensive and technologically demanding enterprise. In addition, no one really knows how long a bicycle race will take, making it a scheduling nightmare. Setting up television cameras in a soccer stadium, on the other hand, is a comparative piece of cake. By the 1970s, professional cycle racing was scrambling to find a way to remain important. To make things worse, over the following decades, the owners of the Giro regularly botched the sale of the Giro's broadcasting rights, costing it vital spectators when it needed them most. Even the Tour de France had become tawdry with exhausting transfers designed to maximize the number of stage towns paying for the privilege of a Tour visit along with countless awards, each with a sponsor chipping in a few francs.

1972 Eddy Merckx returned to contest the 1972 Giro. He was the reigning World Road Champion and the winner of the previous year's Tour. Giro director Vincenzo Torriani designed a mountainous race hoping to keep the man nicknamed the "Cannibal" from eating the rest of the competition alive.

The 100-man start list of riders would have to try to figure out some way to deal with the Merckx menace. This group included Gösta Pettersson, Italo Zilioli, Roger de Vlaeminck, Motta, Bitossi, Fuente and Gimondi. *La Gazzetta* thought de Vlaeminck, winner of that spring's Paris–Roubaix as well as the week-long Tirreno–Adriatico stage race, might be able to give Merckx a real challenge. Merckx would find plenty of trouble in this Giro, but it would come from elsewhere.

The man who holds the record for Giro participations (eighteen starts and sixteen finishes) almost didn't start the 1972 Giro: super climber Wladimiro Panizza was without a team until Zonca signed him at the last minute.

The Giro organizers had long wanted a Venice stage with the riders finishing in front of St. Mark's Cathedral. The Venetians had continually rebuffed plans for the riders to cross the canals over a series of temporary wooden bridges. In 1972 the city relented and agreed to the proposal, but at the last minute Venice changed its mind and the prologue was cancelled. Several other cities offered to host the prologue, but Torriani wanted his Venetian start. He did the best he could with a bad situation and had the riders attend mass in Venice's St. Mark's. Since he was the 1971 winner, Gösta Pettersson was awarded the Pink Jersey to start the next day's stage and the prize money that had been held for the prologue was distributed among the 100 riders.

The first stage left from Mestre, the mainland city across the lagoon from Venice, and traveled to Ravenna, onetime capital of the Roman Empire. The Giro settled into its normal rhythm of a *piano* pace in the stage's early kilometers. As the race got closer to the finish, the speed increased until the final 20 kilometers were nearly non-stop attacks. It came together for a bunch sprint with Marino Basso winning the stage and taking the lead. This year time bonuses weren't in play so the field was credited with same time as Basso.

The next day ended just inland from the Adriatic in Fermo, a hilltop city in Le Marche. The mild climb to the finish caused a selection that resulted in a sprint of champions. Gianni Motta won it from Bitossi, who was having gear troubles. Basso was third, followed by Merckx and de Vlaeminck. Basso kept his leadership in both points and the Overall.

The hilly third stage, still taking the riders through Le Marche, sparkled with hard attacks. Fuente, probably testing Merckx's legs, jumped away on a climb, only to have Merckx easily mark him and then counter-attack, forcing Fuente to dig deep. The finish showed why Franco Bitossi had the reputation of being one of cycling's finest tacticians. After another series of blistering attacks, the peloton regrouped, a time when the pack can become lazy while the riders hope for a chance to recuperate. Bitossi sent his teammate Ugo Colombo on a flier. Colombo made it stick, beating the Merckx-led pack by 15 seconds and becoming the new *maglia rosa*.

Now came the much anticipated stage four's 48-kilometer morning half-stage with its hilltop finish at Block Haus. It was here in 1967 that Merckx had sent shock waves through the cycling world when he dropped Adorni, Zilioli, Anquetil and Gimondi in his first Giro.

The climbing started just before the little town of Pretoro, the pack splitting almost immediately. Fuente's KAS team began probing and sending men up the road. Merckx didn't take the bait, knowing that it was Fuente he had to watch. With fifteen kilometers left, Fuente rolled the dice and off he went, leaving Merckx protected by only one teammate and surrounded by six good-climbing KAS riders.

The day would not be a replay of stage three. Fuente flew to the top, not bothering to look back at the damage he had done. Merckx and Motta came in 2 minutes 36 seconds later, while Gimondi lost almost four minutes. Bitossi, who had won the climber's crown three times (1964, '65 and '66) lost over seven minutes. Fuente had blitzed the mountain so fast that in those seventeen kilometers of climbing, twelve riders were eliminated because they had lost more than fifteen minutes, the time cutoff mandated by the rules. Because Basso, Patrick Sercu and Dino Zandegù were among the *squalificati,* the bunch sprints for the rest of the Giro would not be the same. Fuente was now the leader. Merckx said that Fuente was "virtually unbeatable on a short stage with a mountain finish." He also warned, "The Giro isn't over yet."

The Giro continued to head straight for the toe of the Italian boot as Fuente held his lead. The biggest animator of the next few stages was Bitossi, who kept trying to escape. He came close several times, but was always hunted down and caught.

Stage seven went through the rugged Sila Mountains of Calabria. While Fuente and the KAS team spent the time before the stage's start signing autographs, the Molteni squad did a hard warm-up. Merckx took off from the gun. Most of the peloton thought that with 151 difficult kilometers ahead, the Belgian was committing suicide. Fuente and his KAS teammate Santiago Lazcano were the only riders with Merckx after the first climb and they suffered horribly in the process. Over the top of Monte Scuro, Merckx descended like a fiend. The Spaniards, not having Merckx's downhill skills, had to let him go. Pettersson, who had been staying reasonably close to the trio, took terrible chances and managed to close the gap to Merckx on the descent. Fuente tried to bridge up to Merckx and Pettersson but gave up and waited for the bunch. Merckx let Pettersson take the stage and the field came in 4 minutes 13 seconds later.

The General Classification after stage seven:
1. Eddy Merckx
2. Gösta Pettersson @ 10 seconds
3. José-Manuel Fuente @ 1 minute 37 seconds
4. Miguel María Lasa @ 3 minutes 12 seconds

The Giro crossed the Strait of Messina for a Sicilian stage that made no change to the General Classification. The riders were given a rest day and transferred to Rome to head up the western side of the peninsula.

It wasn't unusual for the Spanish riders of the 1970s and '80s to sit in the back of the field during the *piano* sections of the race, but it is a tactic fraught with danger, and regularly the Iberians were caught napping. It happened to them during stage ten, going from Rome to Monte Argentario/Porto San Stefano. There was an intermediate sprint mid-way through the stage that caused a split in the pack. The Spaniards were forced to chase the Merckx-led front group, making contact just in time for the beginning of the climb up Monte Argentario. Italo Zilioli got away near the top and held his slender 15-second lead into Porto San Stefano.

Stage eleven, 242 kilometers up to Forte dei Marmi on the Tuscan coast, was a combative day with the Spaniards yet again playing catch-up. When Merckx saw Fuente wasn't near the front, he launched an attack. Merckx always tried to keep speeds high on the flat and rolling stages, feeling this caused the smaller climbers—whom he believed had lesser energy reserves—to suffer and arrive at the mountains exhausted. Fuente was able to bridge, but during the closing kilometers he was hit with even more bad luck. His tire developed a slow leak as the speeds had been whipped up, forcing him to ride the last fifteen kilometers on a low tire. He didn't dare stop to change his wheel and possibly never re-join the pack.

The ferocity of the racing in stage eleven had been a surprise, since a 40-kilometer time trial was the next day's race. Again Torriani showed his creativity. Instead of a single 40-kilometer run, the day had two 20-kilometer races spaced a couple of hours apart. Merckx won the first one with his teammate Roger Swerts and Gimondi 11 seconds behind. Swerts turned the tables on the second ride, beating Merckx by 11 seconds. The judges awarded the overall stage to Merckx, who was 26/100 of a second faster.

If you have ever wondered what it would take to ride like the pros, writer Peter Fretwell recorded the gear ratios the best riders used that day. Try to stay on top of gears like these:

Eddy Merckx: 55 x 13 for the first ride, 54 x 14 for the second
Roger Swerts: 54 x 13
Roger de Vlaeminck: 54 x 13 & 14

After the time trial, the General Classification stood thus:
1. Eddy Merckx
2. Gösta Pettersson @ 1 minute 32 seconds
3. José-Manuel Fuente @ 3 minutes 59 seconds
4. Miguel-María Lasa @ 5 minutes 41 seconds
5. Felice Gimondi @ 6 minutes 26 seconds

Stage fourteen featured two climbs, Sestriere and a mountain new to the Giro, the Jafferau, topped by the town of Bardonecchia. As the climb to Sestriere started to bite, the Spaniards started to dish out some pain to the slow-moving peloton. Almost instantly a front group of fourteen containing most of the big names (but missing Bitossi and de Vlaeminck) formed. After three attacks, Fuente managed to extract himself from this group and meet up with two teammates who were already off the front, López-Carril and Galdós. López-Carril was unable to withstand the pace and soon dropped off.

Merckx, who had met Fuente's first two attacks, decided to climb at his own pace and let Fuente go. Fuente crested the Sestriere climb with a 50-second lead on Merckx's nine-man group. This was a slim lead,

Eddy Merckx in action on stage fourteen.

but Fuente and Galdós pressed on into the valley where they found themselves fighting a headwind. Still, they arrived at the base of the Jafferau climb with a lead of about one minute on Merckx, who had waited for help. Merckx's group was now 28 men strong.

Once the climbing started, Galdós ran out of gas and Fuente was on his own. With four kilometers remaining of the ever-steepening climb he still had 1 minute 5 seconds. It wasn't enough. Merckx was on fire and as Fuente cracked in the final kilometer, Merckx steamed right on by. Panizza, the last man to come off Merckx's wheel, also went by the Spaniard.

Fuente said he had given everything, but Merckx had twice his strength. Merckx replied that Fuente was even stronger than Luis Ocaña. High praise indeed, Ocaña being the only rider who really challenged Merckx in stage races when the Belgian was at his peak.

Trusting that the Giro management would want to keep the stars in the race, several of the most famous riders blatantly hung onto cars or let themselves get pushed up the Jafferau. Their fame was an insufficient defense and Motta, Bitossi, Zilioli, Willy De Geest and Giovanni Varini were thrown out of the Giro. The day's cheating was so widespread that most of the others still left in the race were given some form of penalty. The teams threatened to quit if the riders weren't reinstated, but the race jury stood its ground and the teams stayed in.

The denouement of the Giro was at hand. Stage sixteen took the riders over two hard passes, the Foscagno and the Eira. The day's drama was supplied in a water bottle filled at a roadside stream by one of Merckx's *gregari*. As the racers began the Foscagno, Merckx began to suffer abdominal pains, thought to have been caused by the unclean water in his bottle.

Fuente attacked and was able to extract a slim lead that Merckx was able to erase on the descent. Merckx turned the day into another triumph when he came into Livigno 63 seconds ahead of the feisty Spaniard.

The General Classification at this point:

    1. Eddy Merckx

    2. José-Manuel Fuente @ 5 minutes 49 seconds

    3. Gösta Pettersson @ 5 minutes 52 seconds

    4. Vicente López-Carril @ 10 minutes 1 second

The next day was the Giro's *Cima Coppi* (a Giro's highest point), the Stelvio. The ascent was to be up the famous northern, or Trafoi side. Twelve kilometers from the summit Fuente launched his second attack and not even Merckx could resist. Fuente ascended the Stelvio using a mind-boggling 54 x 18 gear. It's said that only Coppi had been able to use such a huge gear on the Stelvio. Fuente nearly cooked himself, slowing near the top as he passed between walls of snow. He crossed the finish line at the top of the Stelvio 32 seconds ahead of his teammate Galdós and 2 minutes 5 seconds ahead of Merckx and Panizza. Merckx was still the Pink Jersey.

That was it. Fuente had thrown everything he could at Merckx every time the road rose to the sky. It was never enough. There were still two stages with climbing, but the contest was over. Merckx won the penultimate stage, an 18-kilometer time trial, extending his final lead over Fuente to more than five minutes.

While Torriani had been denied his dream of a Venetian prologue, he was finally granted another wish, a finish in front of Milan's giant white gingerbread cathedral, won by Paolini.

For the first time, the best-placed Italian rider was a lowly fifth. Merckx's Molteni team was the only squad to finish intact. That made three Giro victories for Merckx.

Final 1972 Giro d'Italia General Classification:
1. Eddy Merckx (Molteni) 103 hours 4 minutes 4 seconds
2. José Manuel Fuente (KAS) @ 5 minutes 30 seconds
3. Francisco Galdós (KAS) @ 10 minutes 39 seconds
4. Vicente López-Carril (KAS) @ 11 minutes 17 seconds
5. Wladimiro Panizza (Zonca) @ 13 minutes 0 seconds

Climbers' Competition:
1. José-Manuel Fuente (KAS): 490 points
2. Eddy Merckx (Molteni): 350
3. Francisco Galdós (KAS): 270

Points Competition:
1. Roger de Vlaeminck (Dreher)
2. Eddy Merckx (Molteni)
3. Miguel-Maria Lasa (KAS)

Showing how far cycling and the Giro had fallen, Italian television had dispensed entirely with live broadcasts of the Giro stages and was showing only highlights in the evening.

1973 Today, upcoming Giro routes are usually announced in November or December. Back in 1973 things were not settled that early, with the route being announced in early March. The route Torriani designed was different from previous Giri, placing the start in Verviers, Belgium, and having the riders spend a week working their way south in a Giro of the Common Market, through Holland, Germany, Luxembourg, France and then Switzerland before landing in Piedmont, Italy.

The Tour de France had, like the Giro, previously crossed into adjoining countries, but neither had scheduled such a far-ranging foreign adventure. The next year the Tour would have a single stage in Plymouth, England (a colossal failure) but would not venture wildly afield again until 1980 when it traveled deep into Germany.

A blue-ribbon peloton arrived in Verviers. Merckx, coming from a win over Luis Ocaña in the Vuelta that had ended only five days earlier, was there with his team of champions to try for a fourth Giro win. Hoping to at last get the better of the relentless Belgian was the formidable Spanish KAS team, with Fuente, Galdós, Gonzalo Aja, José Pesarrodona, Domingo Perurena and Santiago Lazcano. Filling out the roster of contenders were Gimondi, Panizza, Motta (now on the Zonca squad and no longer teamed with Gimondi, who had moved to Bianchi), de Vlaeminck, Pettersson, Francesco Moser, Bitossi, Zilioli, Olympic Champion Hennie Kuiper and a new face, Giovanni Battaglin, winner of the 1972 Tour de l'Avenir.

Torriani was never afraid to do things differently. Case in point, the 5.2-kilometer prologue was a two-man team time trial. In the 1972 Giro Merckx and his teammate Roger Swerts had shown that they were the best against the clock. As a team, they were, as expected, the winners. What wasn't expected were Fuente and his teammate Pesarrodona being only seven seconds slower. The prologue times didn't count towards the General Classification, but the win gave Merckx the first Pink and Swerts the first Purple Jerseys.

The next day the race finished in Cologne, Germany. Merckx, being Merckx, had no intention of giving up the *maglia rosa*. With twenty kilometers to go he put his men at the front of the pack and had them ride nearly all-out. From that platform he launched his own solo attack, but he couldn't stay away and the peloton was together in the final kilometer. And despite all of that work, he still led out the sprint, and incredibly, won it by a clear margin.

The stage into Luxembourg was ridden Giro-style, *piano* until the last 60 kilometers. But those final attacks were ferocious, with de Vlaeminck, Bitossi, Merckx and Panizza managing to get about a half-minute clear and finishing in that order.

The fourth stage went through the Mont Blanc tunnel and brought the Giro into Italy at last. Over the Colle San Carlo, Fuente tried his best to escape, but with a long descent after the summit (for which Merckx changed bikes to have a machine with huge gears for the downhill), he couldn't hope to stay away. There was a regrouping that allowed Merckx a third stage win.

So far Merckx's team had been tyrannically controlling the race, making sure that every break had a brown-clad Molteni rider in it.

Stage six, going from Milan eastward to Iseo, went over the Colle San Fermo. Both Merckx and Fuente sent their lieutenants up ahead to prepare for the coming attacks. Not waiting for Fuente to jump, Merckx attacked hard and only Panizza and Battaglin could answer the call. At the worst possible time, Fuente was crippled with cramps and had to get off his bike.

The Merckx trio had to dig deep, being pursued by a formidable group: Bitossi, Motta, Gimondi and former World Hour Record holder Ole Ritter. Try as they might, the group couldn't hold off the chasers, allowing Gianni Motta to take the stage. The unfortunate Fuente lost twelve minutes.

After stage six, with Fuente tossed and gored, the General Classification stood thus:

1. Eddy Merckx
2. Franco Bitossi @ 29 seconds
3. Wladimiro Panizza @ 37 seconds
4. Giovanni Battaglin @ 51 seconds
5. Ole Ritter @ 1 minute 6 seconds

After a boring trip across the pancake-flat Emilian Plain, the race went into the hilly countryside of Le Marche. On one of the early climbs of the day, Merckx escaped bringing Fuente along for company.

Foolishly, Fuente took his pulls with the powerful Belgian and after having burned his matches, was spit out the back.

Next Battaglin bridged up to Merckx and as the two sped over the hills they distanced themselves from the peloton. Merckx tried to drop Battaglin, but wasn't able to lose his young Italian companion until the top of the last climb. Merckx bombed down the hill and raced into Carpegna 45 seconds ahead of Battaglin and more than four minutes ahead of the first chaser, Zilioli.

At the stage's end Fuente was in such a bad state, he thought he needed a doctor. He was fine and the next morning was fit to start the next stage. Roger de Vlaeminck's hopes for a high placing were ruined as well after he lost nine minutes. They weren't the only ones losing big. Trying to cut down on the spectators' pushing riders up the hills, large fines were imposed on the riders who accepted the fans' help. The next day the threat of a riders' strike over the severity of the punishments came to nothing.

Stage ten took the race further down the Adriatic coast into Abruzzo where, at last, Fuente seemed to be finding his legs. He escaped, only to be caught by Merckx, who won the stage, his fifth stage victory so far. Putting on an extraordinary—I guess the better adjective would be Merckxian—show of aggression and power, he now held the lead in the General Classification as well as the points and mountains categories.

A crash early in stage eleven allowed Merckx to form a break that included de Vlaeminck, Gimondi and Motta. Battaglin was at the back of the field when he was hit with both bad cramps and Merckx's attack, and by the time he made his way up to the front, the big boys were gone. Battaglin got help from Hennie Kuiper and Francesco Moser (riding in his first Giro), but they had to concede three minutes, seeming to put the race out of the reach of everyone not named Merckx.

The General Classification as the Giro reached its most southern point, Benevento, northeast of Naples:

1. Eddy Merckx
2. Giovanni Battaglin @ 6 minutes 39 seconds
3. Felice Gimondi @ 7 minutes 27 seconds
4. Gianni Motta @ 7 minutes 56 seconds

As the race turned north and rode through Umbria and Tuscany, the standings didn't change significantly. At the Tuscan coastal city of Forte dei Marmi, for the first time in years, Merckx suffered a defeat in an individual time trial over 30 kilometers long. And the man who won the stage? Felice Gimondi beat the Belgian by 31 seconds. His superb ride moved him to second place, pushing Battaglin down to third at 9 minutes 34 seconds.

The next day Michele Dancelli was expelled from the race for using "intemperate language" on the race jury after the stage eight fines were imposed.

Two Dolomite stages were next. Stage eighteen, from Verona to Andalo went over the Bondone and the Paganella. The previous day it had rained hard on the miserable, huddled peloton and the prospect of a cold, snowy day on the Bondone scared both the riders and the organizers. But the sun came out and so did Merckx's Moltenis. Just as most of the riders were picking up their feedbags and the Bondone started to bite, Merckx's team gave it the gas, forcing many of the riders to forgo their musettes. The Spaniards, not expecting the attack, were already off the back before the hard work was expected to begin.

With a huge effort Fuente bridged up to the leaders. Upon making contact he attacked, and this drew out a select group of riders as they climbed the steepest part of the 27-kilometer ascent: Merckx, Fuente, Gimondi, Moser, de Vlaeminck and Lazcano. The last ten kilometers of the Bondone pass were unpaved and here Lazcano galloped away, taking Fuente with him. They crested with less than a minute's lead, and of course they were caught in a general regrouping on the descent.

On the far milder Paganella, Fuente attacked again, but his efforts on the Bondone climb had left him without punch. Now it was Merckx's time to go clear, Gimondi and Battaglin being the only riders able to keep him in sight. Merckx held on to a 46-second gap all the way into Andalo with Gimondi and Battaglin second and third. Fuente came in sixth, 3 minutes 30 seconds down.

The penultimate day had four major climbs: the Valles, Santa Lucia, the Giau (the *Cima Coppi*) and the Tre Croci. On the Passo Valles, Fuente jumped several times before getting clear. Still alone after the Santa Lucia, he tackled the Giau while Merckx was content to go at his own speed, topping the Giau with Battaglin for company, 2 minutes 25 seconds behind Fuente.

At the start of the Passo Tre Croci, Fuente's lead was two minutes. Moser and Ritter had tried to get up to Fuente but the Spaniard was on song and increased the gap on his chasers to 2 minutes 45 seconds.

There were 24 kilometers of mostly downhill to go and one might expect two superb big-gear men like Moser and Ritter would be able to reel in a small, exhausted climber. They couldn't. Fuente pulled off one of the great rides, being away for more than 130 kilometers and finishing 1 minute 6 seconds ahead of Moser, allowing Fuente to take the Mountains Classification lead away from Merckx.

Having suffocated his competition, Merckx had a commanding lead in the General Classification. The points and mountains classifications, however were still not completely settled as the Giro started the final stage into Trieste. Fuente scooted over the Passo della Mauria first and secured the mountain prize. De Vlaeminck made an attempt to win the stage and take the points prize from Merckx, but he was swamped when the Bianchi squad positioned world champion Marino Basso perfectly for the sprint.

Merckx now had four Giro wins. In winning the 1973 edition he did what no man had done since Alfredo Binda in 1927, taking the lead on the first stage and keeping it until the end. Moreover, along the way to winning his "sunrise to sunset" Giro he won six stages. It was a scintillating performance.

Final 1973 Giro d'Italia General Classification:
1. Eddy Merckx (Molteni) 106 hours 54 minutes 41 seconds
2. Felice Gimondi (Bianchi) @ 7 minutes 42 seconds
3. Giovanni Battaglin (Jolliceramica) @ 10 minutes 20 seconds
4. José Pesarrodona (KAS) @ 15 minutes 51 seconds
8. José-Manuel Fuente (KAS) @ 26 minutes 6 seconds

Climbers' Competition:
1. José-Manuel Fuente (KAS): 550 points
2. Eddy Merckx (Molteni): 510
3. Giovanni Battaglin (Jolliceramica): 180

Points Competition:
1. Eddy Merckx (Molteni): 237 points
2. Roger de Vlaeminck (Brooklyn): 216
3. Felice Gimondi (Bianchi): 146

1974

The Italian economic miracle of the 1950s and 1960s was uneven, leaving most Italians dissatisfied with many aspects of how Italian government and society in general were ordered.

The causes for the unease were many and there was a wide-spread belief that communist, specifically Maoist, thought held the solution to Italy's problems. As in much of the western world, student demonstrations in the late 1960s shook Italy badly. In most countries, left-wing unrest had calmed down by the early 1970s, but in Italy the demonstrations signaled more than just youthful anger. While Italy produced consumer goods in abundance, wages to buy these beautiful items remained low. Truly fearing revolution, industrialists and the government raised wages and gave workers more power. This real improvement in the Italian standard of living that took place over the next eight years left most of the Italian population reasonably content with their personal situation, even if still contemptuous of their government.

But the most militant of the left didn't want the populace to be satisfied with televisions and cars, they wanted a revolution, and through the 1970s they escalated their efforts. By 1974 over a hundred separate groups were engaged in murderous acts of terrorism against judges, police, journalists and industrialists, causing a severe reaction within and without the government. Right-wing groups with ties to the military and police formed and, trying to cause a public reaction against the leftists, bombed and murdered as well. Former prime minister Aldo Moro's 1978 kidnapping and murder generated a sweeping clamp-down on the revolutionaries and by the early 1980s, violence for the most part was suppressed.

One prominent victim of the Red Guards, the most famous of the violent communist revolutionary groups, was Emilio Bozzi, who owned the legendary Legnano bike company, sponsor of Binda, Bartali and Coppi. After Bozzi's 1974 assassination, his family sold the firm to Bianchi. In 2011, the Bozzi family reacquired the Legnano brand.

✢

Starting in the Vatican City, 1974's 22-stage Giro headed south down the Tyrrhenian coast, all the way to the instep of the Italian boot before heading east for Taranto. Then it traveled north along the Adriatic coast before heading inland to Modena. In the final week the Giro made a snaking journey around northern Italy for a final showdown in the Dolomites. The twentieth stage had the fearsome Tre Cime di Lavaredo for a hilltop finish and the next day the riders had to negotiate the Falzarego, Valles, Rolle and Monte Grappa climbs.

The Story of the Giro d'Italia

Fuente and his KAS boys came to have another go at Merckx, Fuente having been ill-prepared the year before and uncompetitive in the mountains until the final days. Using the form he gained in the 1973 Giro, he had gone on that year to win the Tour of Switzerland and come in third in the Tour. This year he was ready, having won the Vuelta earlier in the spring with two stage wins.

Merckx, on the other hand, for the first time since 1965 (his first year as a professional), did not win a single spring Classic.

The rest of the roster of contenders was mostly a list of the usual suspects: Gimondi, Panizza, Moser, Battaglin, Pettersson and Motta. There was one fresh face, Giambattista Baronchelli, who had won both the Tour de l'Avenir and the Girobio (the amateur or "Baby" Giro) in 1973. Hired by SCIC, he was in his first professional Grand Tour.

Gimondi was the current World Road Champion after winning the final sprint from Merckx, Luis Ocaña and Freddy Maertens. Gimondi still had the legs in March when he won Milan–San Remo, Coppi-style. He initiated an early break, battered it senseless and rode solo for 25 kilometers to finish nearly two minutes ahead of Eric Leman, the largest gap since Fausto Coppi beat Vito Ortelli by more than four minutes in 1949.

The first stage ended in a great rush that should have been a showcase for the big names in speed, Basso, Sercu, Bitossi and de Vlaeminck, but a man who had just turned pro upstaged them all: Wilfried Reybrouck zipped up the side of the road with 400 meters to go, holding off a hard-charging de Vlaeminck.

When Vittorio Adorni had needed a couple of Belgian *flahutes* for his Filcas squad, he asked Guido Reybrouck, an accomplished and well-known professional, for recommendations. Guido suggested his brother Wilfried. That's how an unknown neo-pro came to stun the cycling establishment when he donned the *maglia rosa*.

The next day ended in Pompei. A major strike didn't fulfill its threat to close the road through Naples, but the wary pack stayed together for security. Young Reybrouck kept his lead.

The hilly area of Sorrento gave the climbers their first chance to show their form in stage three. Fuente promised to make trouble for the others and was true to his word. He left them behind on Monte Faito, an eleven-kilometer climb with patches of eleven-percent gradient. Merckx wasn't able to stay with the first two groups of pursuers, but he was a good descender and connected with the second group of chasers, finishing 42 seconds behind stage winner Fuente, the new leader.

And Reybrouck? He got a hard lesson in the intensity of climbing in Grand Tours. Shelled on an early minor climb, he finished outside the time limit. One day he was a young hero wearing the coveted *maglia rosa*, the next day he was in tears packing his bags for home.

From there, the Giro went to the bottom of the peninsula and turned northward. Each day was almost a carbon copy of the previous one, the racers riding slowly until the final 50 or so kilometers and then winding the speed up to almost the limit of human performance before unleashing a wild sprint. The master of the last-minute escape, Franco Bitossi, managed to foil the sprinters at the end of stage six, holding off the hard-charging pack by two seconds. Through these stages, Fuente kept his lead and de Vlaeminck remained the points leader.

The next day stage nine ended with a climb and descent of Monte Carpegna in Le Marche, not far from San Marino. Once the pack reached the mountain Fuente came out of the saddle, gave his pedals a hard push and was gone. Merckx chased, but the Fuente of 1974 was a far better rider than the Fuente of 1973. Because of the hard rain, Merckx chose not to take any serious risks on the way down the mountain, allowing the Spaniard to add another 65 seconds to his lead.

The General Classification at this point:
1. José-Manuel Fuente
2. Eddy Merckx @ 1 minute 40 seconds
3. Felice Gimondi @ 2 minutes 12 seconds
4. Giovanni Battaglin @ 2 minutes 16 seconds
5. José-Luis Uribezubia @ 2 minutes 18 seconds

Big-time sprinters sometimes make public their plans to ride only a few flat stages before retiring from a Grand Tour, generally outraging the organizers. Patrick Sercu announced that he would retire from the Giro after stage fourteen in San Remo and prepare for the Tour de France. Torriani was especially enraged because Sercu told television audiences that his team boss had approved of the plan. Torriani called Sercu's sponsor, Giorgio Perfetti of Brooklyn chewing gum, telling him he must punish Sercu by sending him back to Belgium now. Perfetti refused, telling Sercu that he should win another stage before quitting, just to twist Torriani's tail.

Stage eleven's morning half-stage had a finish atop the steep Il Ciocco climb. Again Fuente jumped and no one could hold his wheel. Merckx chased, but could get no closer than 41 seconds. That afternoon Sercu won that third stage Perfetti asked of him.

The next day was a 40-kilometer individual time trial. In winning the stage, Merckx erased all but 18 seconds of the lead Fuente had spent almost 2 weeks accumulating. Feeling that a bullet had just missed his ear, Fuente said, "Today I won the Giro." With the Dolomite stages coming, he predicted that this year Merckx would see that Fuente was the superior rider.

The Giro's original plan was to have a rest day in San Remo after stage fourteen. But on the afternoon of stage twelve, news came of the outrage in Brescia. During an anti-fascist demonstration, the right-wing group *Ordine Nuovo* set off a bomb that killed six. The government declared a national day of mourning and the Giro decided to stay put and have its rest day two days early.

Stage fourteen, a run up the Ligurian coast using many of the same roads and climbs as Milan–San Remo, is a day famous in the history of racing. The weather was terrible with hard, pouring rain. The organizers, feeling that the Passo del Ceppo would be too dangerous in the wet, changed the day's route. It was extended by 24 kilometers, making it 189 kilometers and now included two ascents of the Ghimbegna.

After the first time over, a small group that included Fuente teammate López-Carril broke away. On the second ascent the remaining top riders, including Merckx, Gimondi and Fuente, separated themselves from the peloton. Fuente, having the lead, decided to ride the stage defensively. If Merckx wanted to win the Giro, he would have to take it away from Fuente on Fuente's own turf, the mountains.

Seeking the riders up the road, Baronchelli blasted away from the Merckx/Fuente group and after a short hesitation, Merckx and Gimondi took off after the Italian. Then fans watching the race got the shock of their lives. Fuente wasn't with Merckx and Gimondi, he was off the back! He quickly lost two minutes. Fuente was suffering a dramatic *défaillance*. His final time loss for the day was 10 minutes 19 seconds.

On the day he had planned to make the Giro his, Fuente lost the race. Why?

"I forgot the most important thing, which was to get plenty to eat. Perhaps it was because of the bad weather or because I had been feeling so strong…it was all well planned but I failed because I forgot to eat." It's not an unknown failing. Anquetil lost the Giro in 1959 because he didn't eat and Lance Armstrong got into trouble more than once for the same reason.

Merckx became the *maglia rosa*:
1. Eddy Merckx
2. Giambattista Baronchelli @ 35 seconds
3. Felice Gimondi @ 2 minutes 23 seconds
4. Francesco Moser @ 2 minutes 31 seconds
5. Roger de Vlaeminck @ 2 minutes 33 seconds

Stage sixteen finished at the top of the 1,209-meter-high Monte Generoso near Como, just inside the Swiss border. As he predicted and was expected, Fuente escaped on the lower slopes of the eleven-kilometer climb and no one was able to stay with him. But Merckx seemed worried. Midway through the stage he broke his left toe clip, but refused to get the defect repaired. De Vlaeminck rode up to him, advising Merckx to get his bike fixed, given the coming climb. But afraid to stop, Merckx pressed on, finishing fifteenth that day, 2 minutes 21 seconds behind Fuente. Gimondi had a fine day, coming in second, only 31 seconds behind the flying Spaniard. This moved Gimondi up to second place in the Overall.

The next day was also mountainous and again Fuente was on the hunt. He sent two of his men up ahead and eventually hooked up with one of them, Lazcano. The pair hot-footed it for the finish with Merckx, Gimondi, Moser and others in pursuit. The Spanish duo barely held their lead to the end with Fuente sitting up just before the line to let his hard-working helper take the stage. For the four hours of hard work Fuente had gained 13 seconds.

It was raining for the start of stage twenty with its ascent of the Forcella di Monte Rest followed by the milder Passo dell Mauria and then a finish at the top of the Tre Cime di Lavaredo. Merckx had grown disgusted with the help the *tifosi* had given the Italian riders on the climbs and worried that there might be a repeat of the 1967 episode on the same climb, where the riders had cheated so flagrantly that Torriani had annulled the stage.

Meanwhile, framebuilder Ernesto Colnago, supplier of frames to Merckx's Molteni team as well as Baronchelli's SCIC squad, had hatched a plan. Historian Beppe Conti explained that Colnago was good friends with Merckx, having built the special bike Merckx used to win the World Hour Record. Colnago suggested that Merckx let the young Baronchelli have a bit of glory on the Tre Cime climb, and after the young SCIC rider had made the *tifosi* happy with some time alone on the famous ascent, Merckx could close the gap and win the stage. Despite Baronchelli's high placing, Merckx is said to have agreed to the plan, largely because of his friendship with Colnago.

Ten kilometers from the top, Fuente unleashed a blistering attack. Merckx answered, with Baronchelli, Battaglin, López-Carril and Tino Conti coming along.

Then Baronchelli attacked. This might have been the most dangerous move of the entire Giro because Baronchelli was less than a minute behind Merckx in the General Classification. Merckx clawed his way back up to the young Italian and then Baronchelli went again. Had Merckx relaxed a bit at some point and let the Italian get a gap? It is written that he did, but I remain unsure. Baronchelli was riding far better than anyone anticipated.

Despite Merckx's desperate attempts to catch him, Baronchelli was well and truly gone. Fuente won the stage, his fifth this year and was now sitting in fifth place, 3 minutes 22 seconds behind Merckx. And Baronchelli? He was now in second, only 12 seconds behind Merckx.

The close standings made it likely that the twenty-first stage with its four climbs would be a rough day in the Dolomites. Fuente promised to make it so; it was his last chance to take the lead. It was on the final climb of the day, the 24-kilometer long ascent of Monte Grappa that the Giro was decided.

Fuente was desperate to get away and did three hard accelerations before he was able to drop Merckx's *gregari* Jos Huysmans and Jos de Schoenmaecker. Merckx bided his time, letting Baronchelli and Gimondi mount the chase. And still he waited. Finally Merckx went to the front of the chasing group and dragged them at a punishing pace to the top. When Merckx had started the chase Fuente had a lead of 2 minutes 40 seconds and at the summit it was down to just 35 seconds. With the long descent into Bassano del Grappa, Fuente's goose was cooked. Merckx won the stage and seemed to seal his Giro victory.

But not so fast, said Fuente. The final stage of a Grand Tour is usually a ceremonial promenade, but not this time. Fuente attacked hard and forced Merckx himself to mark him. Separated from the pack, Fuente did all the work with a concerned Merckx sitting on his wheel. After the lead had grown to 80 seconds, Merckx asked his director, Giorgio Albani, to have the Molteni team shut down the break. Merckx was worried that with a determined Fuente riding away from the peloton, a flat tire or some other difficulty might cause him to lose the Giro. Fuente was brought back, but the indomitable Spaniard tried two more times to get away. It was no use and the pack was together for a sprint on the Vigorelli velodrome.

The Giro was again Merckx's. This was his fifth, equaling the record of Alfredo Binda (1925, '27, '28, '29, '33) and Fausto Coppi (1940, '47, '49, '52, '53). It was a slim win, not gained with the dominating power of previous years. This was a terrific Giro, but Italian RAI television, fearing another boring, dominating Merckx march across Italy, chose to show only highlights from some of the stages.

While Merckx may have had a disappointing spring, his 1974 turned out to be historic. He won the Giro, the Tour of Switzerland, the Tour de France and the World Road Championship. No one before or since has done this. The closest was Stephen Roche when he won the Giro, Tour de France, Tour of Romandie and the World's in 1987. Merckx had one more good year in him, but never again would he win the Giro or the Tour.

Final 1974 Giro d'Italia General Classification:
1. Eddy Merckx (Molteni) 113 hours 8 minutes 13 seconds
2. Giambattista Baronchelli (SCIC) @ 12 seconds
3. Felice Gimondi (Bianchi) @ 33 seconds
4. Constantino "Tino" Conti (Zonca) @ 2 minutes 14 seconds
5. José-Manuel Fuente (KAS) @ 3 minutes 22 seconds

Climbers' Competition:
1. José-Manuel Fuente (KAS): 510 points
2. Eddy Merckx (Molteni): 330
3. Santiago Lazcano (KAS): 230

Points Competition:
1. Roger de Vlaeminck (Brooklyn): 265 points
2. Franco Bitossi (SCIC): 209
3. José-Manuel Fuente (KAS): 171

1975

There were ten riders missing at the start line in Milan. Eddy Merckx got sick at the Tour of Romandie and at the last minute he and his entire team withdrew from the Giro. Back-numbers one through ten had been reserved for Merckx and his Molteni wrecking crew but they wouldn't be needed this year, leaving a peloton of only 90 riders. For the Giro this probably wasn't bad news. Races regularly improve with a dominant rider absent; with more riders in actual contention, the ferocity of the competition grows.

But de Vlaeminck was peeved. With Merckx absent, many Belgian journalists stayed home as well. Hating Merckx's long shadow, de Vlaeminck vowed to make the Belgian sports writers regret missing the show he would put on.

Torriani's 1975 route sent the race from Milan south to the arch of the boot and then returned all the way back up to the Alps and the Dolomites as it had in the past, but it was the last stage that he hoped would be his masterstroke. The Giro ended at the top of the Passo Stelvio. No trip into Bormio, no final time trial, no promenade into Milan. On the final day, after crossing the San Pellegrino and the Costalunga passes, the race shot up the north face of the Stelvio and when the riders reached the top, their Giro was over.

The first two stages were flat, made for the sprinters. Sercu probably would have won the first except Marino Basso grabbed his jersey. Sercu broke loose only to have the Italian grab hold again. So good was Sercu that after all the tugging and squabbling, he still managed fourth place while Basso was buried back in the pack. Sercu righted things the next day by winning stage two.

The third stage traveled from Ancona to the top of the 1,450-meter-high Prati di Tivo, located near the Gran Sasso, northeast of Rome. The day's climbing amounted to a series of attacks by Spaniards followed by counter-strokes from the Italians. Near the top, Battaglin put in a hard acceleration and the Spaniards closed up to him. Battaglin had more where that came. Bam! He hit them again. No one could take it and the young rider beat Francisco Galdós to the finish by 21 seconds. Battaglin was the Pink Jersey.

De Vlaeminck, after having messed with his seat height the night before, couldn't follow the pace and lost almost four minutes, killing his chances of owning the *maglia rosa* in 1975. He repaired things a bit in stage four. Ridden over the rolling countryside of Abruzzo, it had three highly rated climbs and a technical finish in the town of Campobasso. De Vlaeminck won the stage, while behind him Battaglin was furiously chasing the peloton after a badly timed flat tire. He never regained contact and lost the lead to Galdós.

The General Classification stood thus:
1. Francisco Galdós
2. Giovanni Battaglin @ 23 seconds
3. Miguel Lasa @ 1 minute 32 seconds
4. Marcello Bergamo @ 1 minute 53 seconds
5. Fabrizio Fabbri @ same time

The race careened south into the bottom of the peninsula and turned north. The lead remained with Galdós and the stages were almost all taken in bunch gallops.

Before the start of stage eight, de Vlaeminck had a word with his *gregario* Marcello Osler. Telling him that he was as good as any of the other riders who were getting attention from the press, he asked Osler to perform an exploit: to do something big for the Brooklyn team's morale. Osler more than fulfilled his team captain's request.

Roger de Vlaeminck wins at Castrovillari in stage six.

He escaped early in the stage and at one point had built up a 23-minute lead over a listless peloton. Not being a classification threat, he was allowed plenty of freedom. Even with a final climb over Monte Faito before coming into Sorrento, Osler was able to beat the pack by almost nine minutes after having been away for almost 160 kilometers.

The Monte Faito ascent split up Osler's chasers and when Battaglin attacked the peloton, only Galdós, Fausto Bertoglio and Conti could answer, the quartet beating the pack led in by de Vlaeminck by about a minute and a half.

Now Bertoglio was in third place:
1. Francisco Galdós
2. Giovanni Battaglin @ 23 seconds
3. Fausto Bertoglio @ 1 minute 24 seconds
4. Tino Conti @ 1 minute 55 seconds
5. Miguel Lasa @ 3 minutes 7 seconds

Stage nine had a short climb before the finish in Frosinone, located southeast of Rome. Spaniard Javier Elorriaga flew away with de Vlaeminck and Paolini on his wheel. Elorriaga and de Vlaeminck worked together but Paolini (Italian Champion that year), confident that the trio would stay away, refused to help. When it came time for the sprint, Paolini sped away for the stage win, leaving de Vlaeminck livid. But before the reader feels too sorry for the Belgian, de Vlaeminck was guilty of using the same tactic himself when it suited him. Few riders in cycling history have been more ruthless than Roger de Vlaeminck.

Paolini's stage win wasn't important; it was how de Vlaeminck's anger colored the next few stages and their outcome that mattered.

The next day's stage was over the heavy (constantly climbing and descending) roads leading to Tivoli. Paolini was a good rider and tried valiantly to get away. After each of more than ten attacks, de Vlaeminck would pull the pack back up to him. After Paolini's fruitless battering at the peloton, Baronchelli and Battaglin took advantage of a moment when the pack relaxed a bit to get away. They did so without Paolini, but they did pull Galdós, Panizza, Gimondi, Conti and de Vlaeminck with them. De Vlaeminck won the stage and Galdós kept his lead. That made four stage wins for de Vlaeminck.

La Gazzetta's Rino Negri made a bet with de Vlaeminck. He asked de Vlaeminck if he would do better than Merckx had done in the Giro.

"That means seven stage wins. No, it's impossible for me," demurred de Vlaeminck.

"100,000 Lire?" persisted Negri. De Vlaeminck shook his hand and the bet was on.

Before the Giro started the next day in Rome, the riders went to the Quirinal palace to meet Italian president Giovanni Leone. Leone, like nearly all Italians, was following the Giro and asked de Vlaeminck if he were going to win the day's short stage to Orvieto. De Vlaeminck promised to try. Orvieto sits atop an ancient tufa mound and the ascent to the city center is nasty, brutish and short.

Paolini was at it again, pummeling the pack and again, to no avail. Others tried to escape and each time de Vlaeminck personally did the work of policing the front and closing the gaps. Then, just at the right moment, with about a kilometer to go, de Vlaeminck was gone. The rest were helpless as the man called "The Gypsy" took stage win number five. Gimondi was irritated and chewed out his team's sprinter, Rik van Linden, for coming off de Vlaeminck's wheel. Van Linden defended himself with the truth when he told his team captain, "When Roger goes, it's just like a hot bullet."

The race transferred north to Tuscany. Stage thirteen was a 38-kilometer individual time trial at Forte dei Marmi, imperiling Galdós' 23-second lead.

Galdós didn't have to wait until the end of his ride to find out he had lost the lead. Just after leaving the start chute he crashed, while Battaglin surprised everyone with a ride that made him the leader. Many were astonished that a rider who had so far never shown a talent for time trials had done so well. Panizza was particularly grumpy, accusing Battaglin of drafting a police motorbike for almost the entire distance. The race jury investigated and found that at times the dense crowds along the route had hindered the lead motorbike, forcing Battaglin to close in on the policeman. Panizza must have wondered why only Battaglin had this problem.

The General Classification was quite different now. The Jolliceramica squad had grabbed the top 2 places:

1. Giovanni Battaglin
2. Fausto Bertoglio @ 1 minute 42 seconds
3. Francisco Galdós @ 2 minutes 40 seconds
4. Felice Gimondi @ 3 minutes 20 seconds

Wounded by the accusations, Battaglin promised to prove that he had the chops the next day on the timed hill-climb up Monte Ciocco. Again, everyone was dumbfounded by the result. A third-year pro whose father was a fan of Fausto Coppi won. Fausto Bertoglio had not only won the stage, he had seized the *maglia rosa* from his team captain by six seconds.

The General Classification:
1. Fausto Bertoglio
2. Giovanni Battaglin @ 6 seconds
3. Francisco Galdós @ 2 minutes 0 seconds
4. Felice Gimondi and Giambattista Baronchelli @ 3 minutes 0 seconds

Battaglin understood the consequences of the stage and announced that he was still the number one rider on the team. The team director, Marino Fontana, didn't see things quite the same way. He must have been reaching for some stomach antacids as he said his Jolliceramica team now had two protected riders. As Alfredo Binda noted many years ago when he managed Coppi and Bartali on the same national Tour de France team, having two ambitious leaders on one team can be like putting a cat and a dog in a sack.

Fontana didn't have to worry too much about his abundance of riches. The next day took the race north and west up the hilly Ligurian coast where the weather turned ugly, very ugly.

On the ascent of the Foce Carpinelli, Felice Gimondi glanced at the man who said he was still Number One and saw a rider having a bad day. The man whose first name means "Happy" thought this would be a perfect time to ruin Battaglin's day, it being much easier to kick a guy when he's down. Gimondi and Bertoglio went full gas and took a lot of horsepower with them: Paolini and de Vlaeminck along with three other members of Paolini's SCIC team. Missing this move were Battaglin, Galdós and Lasa. Galdós and Lasa figured that the Giro was riding away, so they took off with Bitossi (who had tarried a while to keep an eye on Battaglin) and after a few kilometers, connected with the *maglia rosa* group. With every pedal stroke Battaglin was losing ground.

By the end of the day his catastrophe was complete. He came in almost 10 minutes after stage winner Bitossi.

The General Classification stood thus:
1. Fausto Bertoglio
2. Francisco Galdós @ 2 minutes 0 seconds
3. Felice Gimondi and Giambattista Baronchelli @ 3 minutes
   0 seconds

A couple of stages moved the race across northern Italy to the Dolomites. With only four stages left, snowplows were hurriedly clearing the Stelvio for the grand finale. Torriani had "Plan B" in his hip pocket: if snow should fall on the newly cleared road the Giro would finish instead atop Tre Cime di Lavaredo.

Stage eighteen with its ascent of Monte Bondone changed nothing, the leaders finished together. The surprise was that de Vlaeminck won the stage. He voiced regret that moving his saddle before stage three had cost him so much time.

That left Bertoglio with only two stages where his lead could be in danger. Stage twenty, the penultimate day, was a classic Dolomite stage with four big passes: Staulanza, Santa Lucia, Marmolada and the Pordoi. Not unexpectedly the peloton fell to bits on the Marmolada: it's a heartbreaking climb with long, straight uphill stretches that can seem endless. Here Bertoglio had only 12 riders with him, all of the contenders.

On the Pordoi the battle raged. Galdós attacked and de Vlaeminck countered. Oddly, Bertoglio, who had done such a fine job of monitoring the front and protecting his lead, mis-judged this move and let Galdós and de Vlaeminck, who was enjoying terrific form, move away with several others. On the descent Bertoglio, Gimondi and Giacinto Santambrogio closed to within 45 seconds, but then lost time from there to the finish. De Vlaeminck won the stage, his seventh for this Giro. With only the Stelvio stage left, Galdós' savvy move had pulled him to within 41 seconds of Bertoglio. This was a race!

Neither Bertoglio nor Galdós slept well that night, both knowing how quickly 41 seconds could evaporate on the Stelvio's 48 numbered switchbacks.

As the stage began, there was no action on either the San Pellegrino or the Passo di Costalunga, everyone was waiting for the Stelvio. A little after the town of Trafoi, well into the ascent, there were a few probing attacks that put Baronchelli out the back. Up the pass they went and with about eleven kilometers to go Galdós struck his first blow. Bertoglio and a few others were able to close up to him.

Galdós kept pouring it on and by six kilometers from the top it was Galdós off the front with Bertoglio on his wheel. Having the lead, Bertoglio needed only to stay with the Spaniard.

Over and over Galdós attacked and each time Bertoglio had no trouble matching the accelerations. Near the top Galdós tried again and this time Bertoglio counter-attacked. That was it. Galdós closed the gap and then attacked no more. Clearly Bertoglio was not going to lose the Giro on the Stelvio and he generously eased at the line to let his valiant opponent win the stage.

Italy was jubilant over Bertoglio's being the first Italian to win since Gimondi in 1969. This was the high point of Bertoglio's career. For all the brilliance of his Giro victory, he had only two other big career wins, the Tour of Catalonia and the Coppa Placci.

This was the first Giro won on a Pinarello bicycle. Giovanni Pinarello won a cash prize for being the last rider (then called the *maglia nera*) in the 1951 edition and used that money to start his famous frame building operation.

De Vlaeminck won his bet with Negri with a Merckx-beating seven stage wins.

Final 1975 Giro d'Italia General Classification:
1. Fausto Bertoglio (Jolliceramica): 111 hours 31 minutes 34 seconds
2. Francisco Galdós (KAS) @ 41 seconds
3. Felice Gimondi (Bianchi) @ 6 minutes 18 seconds
4. Roger de Vlaeminck (Brooklyn) @ 7 minutes 39 seconds
5. Giuseppe Perletto (Magniflex) @ 8 minutes 0 seconds

Climbers' Competition:
1. Francisco Galdós (KAS) and Andrés Oliva (KAS): 300 points
3. Fausto Bertoglio (Jolliceramica): 240

Points Competition:
1. Roger de Vlaeminck (Brooklyn): 346 points
2. Fausto Bertoglio (Jolliceramica): 159
3. Felice Gimondi (Bianchi): 154

1976

After failing to televise one of the most exciting races in Giro history, RAI brought its cameras back for the 1976 edition. There was so much to love about the 1976 Giro. It was contested by most of the great riders of the era and to list them brings to mind hand-built steel bikes equipped with Campagnolo Super Record components, silk tubulars and racers in wool jerseys and cloth caps. On the starting line at Catania in Sicily were Merckx, Gimondi, Bertoglio, de Vlaeminck, Panizza, de Muynck, Moser, Sercu, Basso, Galdós, Baronchelli, Joaquim Agostinho and Bitossi.

By the time the 1975 Tour had reached Paris, Merckx was a battered but defiant lion. A crash had broken bones in his face so that he could consume only liquid food and he had been viciously punched by a spectator, forcing him to take blood thinners and painkillers. Still, Bernard Thévenet was only able to beat him by 2 minutes 47 seconds. After that Tour Merckx was never the same rider. As the 1976 season began, he did win Milan–San Remo for a record seventh time as well as the Catalonian week. But that was it in the win column for the spring. He was second in Tirreno–Adriatico and sixth in both Paris–Roubaix and Liège–Bastogne–Liège. Coming to the Giro he was suffering from a nasty saddle sore.

As for Gimondi, the other giant, there was nothing in his spring to suggest that he was going to ride the Giro with exceptional form. Johan De Muynck probably looked the best, having just won the Tour of Romandie.

The route itself was suitable for a good all-rounder. It started in Sicily and wiggle-waggled up the peninsula, landing in the Alps before heading across to the Dolomites.

The Sicilian start was tragic. Juan Manuel Santisteban was helping his KAS teammate José Linares González rejoin the peloton after a puncture when he mis-judged a corner and ran headfirst into a steel guard rail. Santisteban was dead before he reached the hospital. When Sercu won the sprint and the year's first Pink Jersey he had no idea that there had been an accident.

The day after Tom Simpson died in the 1967 Tour, an Englishman was allowed to win the next stage. Torriani promised the Spaniards a similar neutral stage to commemorate their countryman, but no Spaniard was given an opportunity to roll across the finish alone immediately after Santisteban's death because the Classification times of nearly all of the peloton were separated by mere seconds. Letting a Spanish rider win a stage and gain the bonus time would mean giving up the Pink Jersey. The stage was contested with vigor, and won by the speedy Sercu for his second win on that split-stage day.

The Belgians continued to have their way with the Giro over the remaining Sicilian stages. Francesco Moser managed to win stage four, but it was a Pyrrhic victory for the Italians because the big prize, the *maglia rosa*, went over to Roger de Vlaeminck. Before crossing the Strait of Messina the General Classification stood thus:

1. Roger de Vlaeminck
2. Francesco Moser @ same time
3. Giambattista Baronchelli @ same time
4. Alfio Vandi @ same time
5. Felice Gimondi @ same time

De Vlaeminck was also the points leader while Merckx made the Belgian domination complete by carrying the Climber's Jersey over to the mainland.

After Francesco Moser had taken the stage four sprint from de Vlaeminck, Moser indulged himself in a little public gloating. De Vlaeminck told the young Italian that he would be waiting for Moser at the finish line in Cosenza.

The prediction came true, but not quite the way anyone wanted it to come out. As the sprint was winding up, Moser bumped Sercu, sending both flying. De Vlaeminck said he was sorry to win that way and looked forward to another chance to beat Moser in a clean sprint.

Stage six ended in Matera, an ancient city in the arch of the Italian boot. Originally Matera was a city of caves carved into the ancient rock 9,000 years ago and has been almost continuously occupied ever since. Being one of the oldest occupied sites in the world, the streets are narrow and none of them are straight. The Brooklyn team of de Vlaeminck and Johan de Muynck felt that the treacherous, hilly city had trouble written all over it. Their director told them to be sure to be at the front of the peloton when the pack reached the town.

Sure enough, they were at the pointy part of the pack as they blasted through Matera. But as de Muynck was negotiating a difficult descent, two non-Brooklyn riders on his wheel crashed, blocking the way and making a hash of everything. De Muynck won the stage and a fuming de Vlaeminck came in 21 seconds later. De Muynck was in pink and de Vlaeminck was miffed because he felt his teammates should have waited to help him win the stage. De Vlaeminck, already stiff-jawed over de Muynck's beating him in the Tour de Romandie, was so angry with his young *gregario*, that he decided to punish him, refusing him the team's support the rest of the race.

The first time trial at Ostuni in the heel of the Italian boot changed things. Merckx was thinking that a dead-flat time trial would be the perfect place for him to take the lead. He selected a 54 x 13 and ended up losing almost a minute because his gear was too small! Moser learned that a monster gear would be needed when his teammate Ole Ritter finished in time to tell him that even a 55 would be inadequate. Moser had his mechanic hurriedly mount a monster 56. Gimondi spotted Moser's mechanic racing to put on the big meat and had his wrench do likewise. Moser won the time trial with Gimondi only 7 seconds slower. The rest of the field lost a minimum of a half-minute. On such things great victories can rest.

The new General Classification:
1. Francesco Moser
2. Felice Gimondi @ 7 seconds
3. Johan de Muynck @ 40 seconds
4. Roland Salm @ 59 seconds
5. Roger de Vlaeminck @ 1 minute 1 second

When the next day dawned, Moser's *gregari* knew they would be in for a day of hard work defending his slim lead as the race hit the hills of Irpino, northeast of Naples. Their job would be doubly difficult because Moser's gut was acting up and the Belgians had not come to Italy for the sights, they came to win. As soon as the peloton reached the mountains, de Vlaeminck started breaking legs. He jumped away from the pack. He was brought back. Again he attacked and again he was brought back; each time Moser's men pulled the pack up to de Vlaeminck. Then de Muynck went. Again Moser's *gregari* dug deep and closed the gap. With this attack, the riders could see Moser was in trouble. Then one after another of de Vlaeminck's Brooklyn boys took turns slapping Moser around. First Ronny de Witte, then Willy de Geest hit the field and then finally Patrick Sercu got away.

Sercu was probably gone but de Vlaeminck was a hungry shark who could smell blood in the water and the blood was Moser's. Rather than let teammate Sercu take the stage win he had de Muynck deliver the *coup de grace*. De Muynck's hammer-blow was it. Moser couldn't take anymore. Others, sensing that the moment had arrived, piled on. Merckx, Gimondi, de Vlaeminck and Bertoglio bridged up to de Muynck. De Vlaeminck won the stage and Gimondi was now in pink, the first time since 1969, with de Muynck in second place, 33 seconds back. Moser was third at 52 seconds.

Nothing changed as the race went north to Tuscany. Now that the gesture was without cost, it was decided to let a Spaniard win a stage in memory of Santisteban. The peloton was happy to have a true *piano* day while Antonio Menéndez was allowed to take a solo flyer that began the moment the starting flag was dropped. The pack finished over twelve minutes after Menéndez, who was no threat in any of the classifications.

Stage thirteen presented the riders with a series of climbs in the hills near Lucca and Pistoia, the hilltop finish at Il Ciocco coming after the Prunetta, Abetone and the Radici ascents. The first three climbs whittled the pack down for the final selection, which started when de Muynck jumped with Panizza coming along for the ride. Up the little road they soared, but others were having a good day as well and it came down to six riders for the sprint. With Gimondi and Merckx a half-minute back down the hill, de Witte tried to lead out de Muynck but de Muynck's chain jammed. De Witte won the stage then crashed into a spectator who wandered onto the course. Even with his mechanical troubles, de Muynck had closed to within 16 seconds of Gimondi while Moser lost 17 seconds. Merckx claimed his saddle sores were so bad he could barely sit on the saddle and sleep was almost impossible.

De Muynck, in second place, was in a difficult position. He hinted, but would not state outright that his team was not behind him and that he felt he could be betrayed. De Muynck must have been walking on eggs because de Vlaeminck had already made that clear after the Matera stage.

Up to Piedmont and eastward to Veneto the race headed. Even though Gimondi had crashed hard twice, his second fall knocking him out for three minutes, the delicate sixteen-second balance between de Muynck and Gimondi remained. The reason? Both times the pack rode slowly and let the *maglia rosa* regain contact.

Stage nineteen had six rated climbs in only 132 kilometers: Staulanza, Santa Lucia, Falzarego, Gardena, Sella and a finish at the top of the Torri del Vajolet. One could reasonably expect this stage to disturb the equipoise that existed between De Muynck and Gimondi. Gimondi feared the steep, unpaved portion of the final climb, thinking the smaller climbers like de Muynck might scoot away from him.

De Vlaeminck had crashed in stage seventeen and was showing the effects on the Falzarego when he wasn't able to stay with the small group of Classification riders. Up ahead Spaniard Andrés Gandarias, who was too far down the standings to worry about, was having a brilliant day and eventually won the stage with a wonderful and mostly solo effort.

Behind Gandarias and unworried about him, de Muynck, Gimondi, Moser, Bertoglio and a few others crested the Sella. They then started the Vajolet climb which was so narrow and crowded with insane *tifosi* the follow cars couldn't accompany the riders. Both Bertoglio and de Muynck attacked and Gimondi grimly closed back up. They went again and this time Gimondi could not respond. Finally Bertoglio dropped de Muynck and beat him to the top by 18 seconds, with Gimondi 39 seconds behind de Muynck. De Witte was just 9 seconds slower than Gimondi.

De Muynck was the Giro's leader:
1. Johan de Muynck
2. Felice Gimondi @ 25 seconds
3. Fausto Bertoglio @ 32 seconds
4. Ronny de Witte @ 1 minute 48 seconds

Gimondi climbs the Vajolet in stage nineteen.

The next day had more climbing. Stage twenty went over a climb new to the Giro, the Passo Manghen, a dirt road with a stretch of eighteen percent gradient, followed by Monte Bondone. When de Muynck asked de Vlaeminck and his sidekick de Witte for assurance of their help if he came into difficulty, de Muynck said the two just laughed. On the Manghen, de Vlaeminck, still wearing the purple of the points leader, abandoned. Actually, he threw down his bike and ran into the woods. His *gregario* Ercole Gualazzini said he ran after him, fruitlessly calling the fast-running cyclocross champion back to the race. Later in the stage de Witte also quit. The Classification leaders all finished the stage together.

This left only a final mountain stage into Bergamo and a last time trial before the ride into Milan.

The next to last climb in the twenty-first stage was the Colle Zambla. Everyone was watching everyone else as they went over the top, and as the descent began, the pack ran into gravel where the road was being repaired. In an instant de Muynck was down. A few seconds later, groggy from the effects of the fall and all cut up, he screamed for his bike and remounted. Who should be coming down the road at that point? Eddy Merckx, one of the finest descenders to have ever turned a pedal. "Get on my wheel, Johan", he shouted to the wounded Pink Jersey. Before the descent was completed Merckx had de Muynck back up to the Gimondi group, which had taken it easy upon learning of de Muynck's fall. No one could get away on the final climb, the Selvino, so they came into Bergamo together.

De Muynck's hands were shredded from the crash. While de Muynck's director was trying to tell others that he would be fine for the time trial, Merckx thought otherwise. "With his hands as they are, he will not sleep more than an hour."

Writer Jan Cornand says that when de Muynck came to the line the next day for the time trial, he looked a wreck. As Merckx predicted, the pain from his wounds kept him up all night, killing his time trial. Merckx *gregario* Joseph Bruyère won the stage while Gimondi was able to beat de Muynck by 44 seconds. De Muynck lost the Giro by only 19 seconds and Gimondi had won his third Giro.

Belgian fans were so outraged at the lack of support given to de Muynck that angry protestors gathered outside de Vlaeminck's house. They felt that if de Muynck had received even a little help he would have won the Giro.

Final 1976 Giro d'Italia General Classification:
1. Felice Gimondi (Bianchi): 119 hours 58 minutes 15 seconds
2. Johan de Muynck (Brooklyn) @ 19 seconds
3. Fausto Bertoglio (Jolliceramica) @ 49 seconds
4. Francesco Moser (Sanson) @ 1 minute 7 seconds
5. Giambattista Baronchelli (SCIC) @ 1 minute 35 seconds
8. Eddy Merckx (Molteni) @ 7 minutes 40 seconds

Climbers' Competition:
1. Andrés Oliva (KAS): 535 points
2. Andrés Gandarias (Teka): 390
3. Francesco Moser (Sanson): 270

Points Competition:
1. Francesco Moser (Sanson): 272 points
2. Eddy Merckx (Molteni): 149
3. Felice Gimondi (Bianchi): 143

This was Eddy Merckx's last Giro. He admitted that his during his 1974 season there were signs of wear and tear and by 1975 he was unmistakably in decline. In 1971, his best season, he won 54 out of 120 races, a fantastic 45 percent. Driving himself ever harder he contested more races during the following four years but his winning percentage declined in two-year plateaus. In '72 it was 39 and in '73 it was 37 percent. Then in 1974, his brilliant banner year, he won 27 percent and in 1975 it was 25 percent. In 1976 he was about done, winning only (by Merckx standards) 15 races, a paltry 13.5 percent of those he entered. He wanted to go out with the same dramatic winning power he showed when he entered pro racing, but the insane drive to win probably accelerated his decline.

He would go on to ride the Tour in 1977, getting sixth place. He would never again win a major race. Merckx contested over 1800 road races and won 525 of them, almost a third, winning an average of one race a week for six years. He had flogged his magnificent body mercilessly, year round, and it had finally had enough. After riding only five races in 1978, he retired.

1977 RCS Media Group purchased *La Gazzetta dello Sport*, the sports newspaper that owned the Giro d'Italia. In

1927 Angelo Rizzoli had started magazine publisher RCS, then named Rizzoli Editore. Over the decades Rizzoli's firm grew and prospered, culminating in its 1974 purchase of Italy's most important newspaper, *Corriere della Sera*, leading to the firm's being renamed Rizzoli-Corriere della Sera (RCS).

The company's complicated financial history during the 1980s and 1990s—including involvement in a banking scandal that led to a 1982 bankruptcy—would make any green-eyeshade owner cross-eyed. The ultimate result is that RCS Media Group is now a hugely successful international enterprise owning magazines, newspapers, broadcasters and most important for bicycle racing, RCS Sport. This is the branch of the media behemoth that organizes the Giro as well as Milan–San Remo, Tour of Lombardy and other important Italian races.

༄

The Flandria squad brought Freddy Maertens, one of the most extraordinary riders in the history of the sport, to the 1977 Giro; extraordinary in that he won 54 races in 1976, including the World Road Championship and the points competition in the Tour, where he won eight stages. Maertens says that his 54 professional road wins is the greatest single-year total in cycling history, arguing that the 54 claimed for Merckx for 1971 is wrong because that number includes three track races. In 1977 Maertens would win 53 races, including Paris–Nice, the Vuelta (winning 13 stages in a flat edition that was probably designed for him), the Tour of Catalonia and Het Volk. Maertens possessed one of the finest sprints in the sport's history as well as a wonderful time trialing engine. He was formidable everywhere except in the high mountains.

But trouble followed the gifted Belgian like a lost dog looking for a home. He earned disqualifications for doping in the 1974 Tour of Belgium and the 1977 Flèche Wallonne. Maertens' positives didn't occur with greater frequency than they did with other good Belgians of his era, but the opprobrium seemed to stick to him when others seemed to slough it off.

For help in winning Giro stages Maertens brought along his good friend and loyal *gregario* Michel Pollentier, who would also become intimately acquainted with trouble. The short, powerful Belgian was one of the most styleless racers ever, but even with elbows out and knees flailing, he was a potent and feared rider. In 1976 he won the

Tour of Belgium and was second in the Tour of Switzerland. Fine help indeed for Mr. Maertens.

The age of Merckx and Gimondi had passed. After winning the Giro and Paris–Brussels in 1976, Gimondi would never again win a major race. The sport was owned by younger riders and the list of likely Giro winners included Baronchelli, Panizza, Battaglin, Bertoglio and the youngest of the racing Moser brothers, Francesco.

This 3,968-kilometer edition started with a 7.5-kilometer prologue at Monte di Prócida, west of Naples, which Maertens won. Moser was only 3 seconds slower, with de Muynck at 21 seconds and Baronchelli at 25 seconds. The prologue times counted this year towards the General Classification.

Maertens made it two in a row when he outsprinted the bunch in Avellino to win stage one. All the big men were clustered near the top of the standings with only a few seconds separating them, and it stayed this way day after day. Moser managed to gain a few seconds on Maertens and take over the lead, but by the end of the sixth stage at Gabbice Mare, the race was effectively unchanged.

The gloves came off during the seventh stage with its climb to San Leo and the Rocca delle Caminate before finishing in Forlì. As they raced over the hills of Le Marche, the big guns boomed, causing a group of six riders to form off the front. Just as the peloton had been breaking up, de Muynck and Magniflex rider Alfio Vandi crashed. At the end of the stage Maertens led in Moser, Panizza, Pollentier, Baronchelli and de Witte while Gimondi, de Muynck and Battaglin lost 71 seconds. For them the day was short of being a catastrophe, but Bertoglio lost almost six minutes and Baronchelli more than eight.

The standings at the top of the leaderboard remained tight:

1. Francesco Moser
2. Freddy Maertens @ 16 seconds
3. Giambattista Baronchelli @ 22 seconds
4. Wladimiro Panizza @ 26 seconds
5. Michel Pollentier @ 49 seconds

Maertens took his seventh stage win at Mugello in Tuscany. A second half-stage was held that afternoon on the Mugello motor raceway. Maertens thought the next day's time trial would see him back in pink. It didn't work out that way. He and Bianchi's crash-prone sprinter Rik van Linden collided in the final meters of the Mugello circuit race. Their handlebars tangled while they were traveling more than 60 kilometers an hour, sending both of them to the ground and then Maertens to the hospital with a broken wrist. Maertens' fabulous winning run was stopped cold.

Flandria *gregari* Marc de Meyer and Pollentier thought it would be best to go home and perhaps prepare for the Tour. Flandria director Guillaume Driessens wanted to remain. Torriani agreed with Driessens and thought it would turn out well for the team if they hunted for stage wins and looked for a way to take advantage of the growing feud between Moser and Baronchelli.

Flandria stayed, and with Maertens on his way home to Belgium, Pollentier was made team captain. The people who are paid to know about these things said that the race was now going to be between Moser and Baronchelli. The *tifosi,* and it's fair enough to say the two riders themselves, saw things that way as well. A rivalry was starting to grow between them, nothing like the Coppi–Bartali competition of years past, but the two riders waged a serious fight for the affection of the fans.

The stage nine Pisa time trial didn't clarify things much. Track pursuiting ace and time trial specialist Knut Knudsen won the stage with Moser second, a minute slower. But Quasimodo Pollentier tortured his bike into a fabulous performance and lost only 6 seconds to Moser.

That left things thus:
1. Francesco Moser
2. Michel Pollentier @ 55 seconds
3. Giambattista Baronchelli @ 1 minute 15 seconds
4. Wladimiro Panizza @ 2 minutes 16 seconds
5. Ronny de Witte @ 2 minutes 42 seconds

Pollentier managed to hook up with Wilmo Francioni and a trio of Spanish riders in the Ligurian hills without dragging Moser along. Stage twelve's result was a 22-second gap between Pollentier and Moser and a doping positive for the stage winner Miguel-María Lasa.

The stages taking the Giro to the Dolomites were for the fast men and when the race arrived at Conegliano for stage seventeen, the General Classification was unchanged.

Stage seventeen went up into nosebleed country with the Rolle, Pordoi, Falzarego and Drusciè passes. Baronchelli had a crisis on the Falzarego and ended up losing two minutes. De Muynck crashed yet again and was now down more than twelve minutes. Pollentier pulled off his coup when he and Moser *gregario* Mario Beccia (who was supposed to be riding with his captain, not buccaneering in search of stage wins, especially with his man narrowly holding first place) beat Moser into Cortina by 25 seconds, making Pollentier the *maglia rosa* by three seconds.

Moser was beside himself with rage over the narrow loss and nearly got into a fistfight with Beccia that evening. Driessens tried to smooth him over and told him not to worry, that Pollentier was not really an active combatant in the race. I wonder if he also told Moser the check was in the mail and that he would still respect him in the morning.

Stage eighteen had six Dolomite passes: Valparola, Gardena, Sella, Costalunga, Mendola with the finish atop Campo Carlo Magno. Baronchelli and Pollentier made common cause, extracting another 85 seconds from Moser, increasing the Flandria *ad hoc* captain's lead to 1 minute 28 seconds. Moser was a fabulously talented rider, but was a big man, a severe handicap when it came to dealing with the real climbers in the high mountains.

Pollentier's margin still needed to withstand two serious tests, the first being the final Dolomite stage: the nineteenth leg going over the Tonale, Presolana and Zambla passes on the way to its finish in San Pellegrino. Renato Laghi, a *gregario* who had labored for eleven years without a single professional victory, took off on a long solo flyer and after riding alone for 185 of the stage's 205 kilometers, arrived at the finish a minute and a half ahead of Giambattista Baronchelli's brother Gaetano, while Pollentier carved out another half-minute from Moser's flesh. This would be good insurance against Moser's fearsome reputation as a time-trialist with the penultimate stage being a 29-kilometer time trial, Pollentier's second test.

Pollentier surprised the pundits by winning the stage, riding 30 seconds faster than Moser. And that was the 1977 Giro; like 1975, won by a rider no one had considered a potential winner.

Final 1977 Giro d'Italia General Classification:
1. Michel Pollentier (Flandria) 107 hours 27 minutes 16 seconds
2. Francesco Moser (Sanson) @ 2 minutes 32 seconds
3. Giambattista Baronchelli (SCIC) @ 4 minutes 2 seconds
4. Alfio Vandi (Magniflex) @ 7 minutes 50 seconds
5. Wladimiro Panizza (SCIC) @ 7 minutes 56 seconds

Climbers' Competition:
1. Faustino Fernández Ovies (KAS): 675 points
2. Ueli Sutter (Zonca-Santini): 490
3. Michel Pollentier (Flandria): 320

Points Competition:
1. Francesco Moser (Sanson): 226 points
2. Pierino Gavazzi (Jolliceramica): 185
3. Luciano Borgognoni (Vibor): 183

Pollentier's amazing 1977 kept rolling along. Seemingly unstoppable, that spring and summer he also won the Tour of Switzerland and the Belgian Road Championship. In 1978 he took the Dauphiné Libéré and a second Belgian Championship (Merckx could do it only once). In the Tour he became the Yellow Jersey after a brilliant solo victory atop l'Alpe d'Huez, but that evening he was caught trying to cheat the dope controls and was sent packing. Of course, after l'Alpe d'Huez, the Italians wondered out loud if Pollentier had been able to beat the doping controls in the 1977 Giro. Maybe. But given the ubiquity of doping in professional cycling, it hardly mattered.

Pollentier still had some good kilometers left in him. He won the 1980 Tour of Flanders and was second in the 1982 Vuelta, but the man who came seemingly out of nowhere to seize the 1977 Giro was long gone.

Both Maertens and Pollentier trusted their money to others who lost it all for them. Maertens ended up broke and now works at a cycling museum in Belgium, and Pollentier opened a garage selling tires. Belgian Classics legend Rik van Steenbergen generously summed up Pollentier as "the last of the real stone-hard characters of Flanders."

That September Moser won the World Road Championship in San Cristobal, Colombia.

1978
The 1978 route was laid out in a 3,610.5-kilometer figure eight with an average stage length of 180 kilometers. Starting in Aosta, it crossed to the east, just north of the Arno and went only as far south as Ravello before turning north, taking seven stages to get to the Dolomites. With plenty of climbing and three individual time trials totaling 82.5 kilometers (not

counting the prologue), a good all-rounder should triumph again in Milan.

To avoid a conflict with soccer's World Cup, the Giro start was moved up two weeks, running into the end of the Vuelta. Because of this, only the Teka squad represented Spain. Not a single French rider came to contest what the French saw as an Italian race jiggered to allow Italians to win (they should have asked Pollentier). The Belgians were the only other nationality represented in any number to break up the Italian party.

Dietrich "Didi" Thurau won the two-kilometer prologue with Moser second at almost the same time. Since the prologue didn't count towards the General Classification, it mattered only for show and to award a first Pink Jersey.

It was stage three, ridden in Tuscany from La Spezia on the coast to Cascina, that may have decided the Giro. On the final climb, before the descent into Cascina, the contenders seemed to be content to mark each other. While Moser, Thurau, Giuseppe Saronni and the others were comfortable knowing that each had the other in sight, Johan de Muynck, now riding for Bianchi with Gimondi as *gregario di lusso,* motored off the front. Although de Muynck had placed second and nearly won the 1976 Giro, he didn't seem to worry the others. De Muynck cruised across the finish line with a 52-second lead over the Moser-led pack.

The slightly built Belgian was just barely able defend his lead the next day in a 25-kilometer time trial. Thurau was his usual superb self when it came to riding against the clock but he could only beat de Muynck by 44 seconds, leaving de Muynck in pink.

The General Classification stood thus:
1. Johan de Muynck
2. Didi Thurau @ 8 seconds
3. Francesco Moser @ 15 seconds
4. Knut Knudsen @ 18 seconds
5. Roger de Vlaeminck @ 20 seconds

After stage seven was finished rolling through the hills of Campania, the list of contenders was reduced by one. Thurau tried to escape early in the stage and ran out of gas. Completely. He finished 4 minutes 17 seconds after Giuseppe Saronni led in a twenty-man group that included de Vlaeminck, Moser, de Muynck, Baronchelli and Battaglin.

Thurau's quest for victory was over and after crashing in stage ten, he abandoned.

Stage eight ended on the Sorrento Peninsula south of Naples and revealed a new dimension to Italy's young wonder Giuseppe Saronni. On the climb to the finish line in Ravello, the 20-year-old racer attacked and got clear, showing that he was more than a sprinter.

With Thurau out of contention and Saronni's abilities visible, the General Classification after stage eight stood thus:

1. Johan de Muynck
2. Francesco Moser @ 15 seconds
3. Giuseppe Saronni @ 26 seconds
4. Roberto Visentini @ 1 minute 8 seconds

As the race headed north through Umbria, Tuscany, and Le Marche to Veneto for the start of the real climbing, Wladimiro Panizza, Baronchelli and Battaglin were able to move up in the classification while de Muynck steadfastly maintained his narrow lead.

Now came the Venice time trial, which required the construction of a floating bridge so that the riders could cross the Grand Canal and finish in St. Mark's Square. Moser won the stage. Panizza, who had been sitting in second place in the General Classification, a half-minute behind de Muynck, lost another half-minute. With a rest day before the Dolomites stages, de Muynck's position was looking a little bit more comfortable:

1. Johan de Muynck
2. Wladimiro Panizza @ 1 minute 3 seconds
3. Giambattista Baronchelli @ 1 minute 33 seconds
4. Francesco Moser @ 1 minute 45 seconds

The riders were lashed by nasty snowy weather during their days in the Dolomites. Stage fifteen had the year's *Cima Coppi*, the Passo Valles, where Baronchelli attacked with Moser and de Muynck on his wheel. There was some regroupment before the final climb, the San Pellegrino, where Moser cracked and lost over a minute to the lead trio of Baronchelli, Alfio Vandi and de Muynck. Though the *tifosi* had generously pushed Moser up the hill, the judges gave him only a nominal penalty of a few seconds. Baronchelli's stage win moved him up to second in the Overall, but de Muynck remained as steady as a rock, holding on to what was now a 93-second lead.

A 45-kilometer individual time trial at Cavalese, near Trent, over a highly technical course that included a hard climb, presented a serious danger to de Muynck. Moser, the hometown boy, won the day, beating de Muynck by 2 minutes 18 seconds. Baronchelli closed in as well.

The race was now a three-man fight:
1. Johan de Muynck
2. Francesco Moser @ 45 seconds
3. Giambattista Baronchelli @ 52 seconds
4. Alfio Vandi @ 6 minutes 11 seconds

Still in the Dolomites, stage seventeen finished at the top of Monte Bondone. It was too much for Moser—probably still tired from his time trial effort—he lost about two and a half minutes. Panizza won the stage alone, but about a minute behind him, de Muynck finished with the rest of the good climbers and two seconds ahead of Baronchelli.

Stage eighteen was the last day of climbing and things didn't change, except the grudge between Moser and Baronchelli deteriorated into a fistfight. The grand old man of the peloton, Felice Gimondi, intervened.

The organizers had tried to keep the racing challenging up until the penultimate stage, but bad weather and resignation kept the peloton from seriously contesting the minor climb into the city of Como. With de Muynck's unshakable racing combined with his powerful team's ability to protect his lead, the others probably thought there was no point in attacking the capable Belgian. The 1978 Giro was his.

For a second time Baronchelli had lost the Giro to a Belgian by less than a minute. Baronchelli may not have won the Giro but he expressed satisfaction that he had at least come ahead of Moser, whom he detested.

Final 1978 Giro d'Italia General Classification:
1. Johan de Muynck (Bianchi) 101 hours 31 minutes 22 seconds
2. Giambattista Baronchelli (SCIC) @ 59 seconds
3. Francesco Moser (Sanson) @ 2 minutes 19 seconds
4. Wladimiro Panizza (Vibor) @ 7 minutes 57 seconds
5. Giuseppe Saronni (SCIC) @ 8 minutes 19 seconds

Climbers' Competition:
1. Ueli Sutter (Zonca-Santini): 830 points
2. Giambattista Baronchelli (SCIC): 520
3. Claudio Bortolotto (Sanson) and Pedro Torres (Teka): 345

Points Competition:
1. Francesco Moser (Sanson): 229 points
2. Giuseppe Saronni (SCIC): 209
3. Giambattista Baronchelli (SCIC): 134

ℵ

It was 118 kilometers into the Tour of Emilia on October 4 that Felice Gimondi and his good friend Franco Bitossi undid their toe straps together and climbed off their bikes. Bitossi remembered, "I was 38 years, 1 month, and 3 days old. I started my career at the Tour of Emilia of 1961, the 4th of October and I finished my career at the Tour of Emilia of 1978, the 4th of October. After 17 years one has to know when to say, '*Basta*.'" The two of them ended their careers on the spot.

Bitossi had won 147 races including the Tour's Points Jersey and the Giro's Climbers' and Points Jerseys. Gimondi had won the Tour, the Giro, the Vuelta, the World Road Championship, Paris–Roubaix, Milan–San Remo and a host of other races totaling 135 professional victories. Both men could win almost any race on a given day and raced the whole professional calendar year after year. Theirs was a dying breed.

two

1979–1986

Moser and Saronni, the Last Great Cycling Rivalry

1979 With the exception of Gimondi's and Bertoglio's victories, the 1970s had been difficult for the *tifosi* to endure. Belgians (Merckx, Pollentier and de Muynck) and a Swede (Pettersson) had been sweeping in from the north for a decade, sacking and pillaging their race, ruining the afternoon games of dominos at the local bars. Pollentier, Pettersson and de Muynck struck the Italians as excellent but dull racers. Where were the *polemiche*, where was the excitement?

Now Torriani had two terrific Italian racers who were delighting their countrymen with victories all over Europe. SCIC had contemplated bringing Giuseppe Saronni to the 1977 Giro, his first year as a pro, but a crash in the Tour of Romandie a few days before the Giro's start kept the nineteen-year-old racer from being subjected to a Grand Tour well before he was ready. That year he still won Tour of Veneto and the Tre Valle Varesine. In 1978 he won the Tirreno–Adriatico, and three Giro stages, coming in fifth in the Overall.

Francesco Moser had added to his list of prestigious victories by taking Paris–Roubaix. This was the year Moser and de Vlaeminck, both riding for Sanson, confounded their competitors' expectations. Instead of aiming for Paris–Roubaix, which de Vlaeminck had already won a record-setting four times, he took Milan–San Remo while Moser completed the unintentional trade and won the cobbled Classic in front of de Vlaeminck by attacking at the precise point de Vlaeminck had planned on making good his escape.

While Moser and Saronni were amassing their victories, the *tifosi* split their allegiance in what so far was the last great Italian rivalry. While both were excellent time trialists, they were vulnerable in the high mountains. Moser had tried the Tour de France in 1975, winning the prologue time trial and keeping the Yellow Jersey until stage six. He finished in seventh place, more than 24 minutes behind winner Bernard Thévenet, but he never returned, finding the Tour's climbing not at all to his liking.

What was Torriani to do? Easy. Design the flattest postwar Giro and put in five (that's right, five) time trials. The two stars could flog each other on terrain suited to their gifts and the *tifosi* could go nuts. While Torriani may have been particularly overt in designing this Grand Tour for these two particular riders (some writers say Torriani had only Moser in mind), all three Grand Tour organizations have designed races for preferred riders.

Indeed, Torriani knew his boys. After the smoke had cleared from the eight-kilometer prologue time trial in Florence, Moser was in pink with Saronni just three seconds back. The game was afoot.

South to Naples for the third stage time trial, this one 31 kilometers long, giving Moser enough distance to create a significant gap— 26 seconds over Saronni in the stage and 29 seconds in the General Classification. Moser had been accused of letting his form slip a bit after an excellent spring Classics season, but his 49.56 kilometers per hour says that there was still plenty of good stuff left in his legs.

De Muynck and two-time Tour winner Bernard Thévenet had their hopes crushed in the next day's 210 kilometers of hilly roads through Campania and Basilicata, both losing more than seven minutes. Bertoglio's two-minute loss probably put his name in the no-hoper column as well while Moser and Saronni finished together.

The *tifosi* had marked the stage eight time trial from Rimini to the top of San Marino on their calendars as a bellwether day, and Saronni rode the 28 kilometers like a rocket. Moser lost a minute and a half and the *maglia rosa*. Historian Sandro Picchi dates the real beginning of the Moser/Saronni rivalry from that hot day in May.

The General Classification now stood thus:
1. Giuseppe Saronni
2. Knut Knudsen @ 34 seconds
3. Francesco Moser @ 1 minute 2 seconds
4. Michel Laurent @ 2 minutes 59 seconds
5. Bernt Johansson @ 3 minutes 4 seconds

Viral conjunctivitis was bedeviling many riders in the peloton. Moser was infected; Battaglin and his Inoxpran squad were so badly hit the team withdrew before the Giro's start.

The next episode in this Giro of big-gear time trial power tests was in the Ligurian town of Lerici, and the Vikings were back. Norwegian Knut Knudsen won the stage, bringing him to within eighteen seconds of Saronni, who in turn had taken about a half minute out of Moser.

When he designed the flat 1979 route, Torriani wasn't completely without shame. Stage fourteen ended at the top of the Bosco Chiesanuova climb, just outside Verona. Bernt Johansson was first to the summit, but Moser dug deep and finished just 2 seconds behind the Swede. But even that superhuman effort did him little good—Knudsen and Saronni were only a second behind him.

The two non-climbers would settle this during the three days of racing in the Dolomites.

Day one: Saronni beat Moser into Pieve di Cadore by 6 seconds after the peloton climbed Monte Rest and the Mauria. Half of the Norse threat was neutralized by Luciano Pezzi, manager of Johansson's Magniflex team, when he hit Knut Knudsen with the team car.

The rivalry between Saronni and Moser was starting to get a bit raw. Moser told Saronni that he would try to make him lose the Giro. Moser's mother scolded him for such unsportsmanlike sentiments. The dislike Saronni and Moser felt for each other was real. Saronni was quick with a biting riposte and seemed to enjoy getting a rise out Moser.

Day two: the two major climbs, the Falzarego and Pordoi came many kilometers before the finish, allowing twenty riders to coalesce before the sprint, probably exactly as Torriani had planned. Moser won the trip to his hometown of Trent with Saronni finishing just with him. Saronni prudently decided to let Moser have the stage and shut down his own sprint in the town that loved Moser best.

Day three: stage eighteen had the Tonale and Aprica climbs, but again they came far too early in the stage to allow the real climbers to gain time. The uphill drag to the finish in the small Alpine town of Valsássina, north of Milan, failed to bust things up, Saronni beating Moser by 3 seconds. Saronni now led Moser by 1 minute 48 seconds.

That left the fifth and final time trial, a run into Milan from the suburb of Cesano Maderno. At 44 kilometers, if Moser were having a good day he might have a chance. Saronni was having an even better

Saronni wins the 1979 Giro.

day. He won the stage, beating Moser by 21 seconds. Saronni, 21, became the third youngest Giro winner after Fausto Coppi and Luigi Marchisio. Saronni also took the cyclamen Points Jersey, beating Moser by a single point. Ouch.

Final 1979 Giro d'Italia General Classification:
1. Giuseppe Saronni (SCIC) 89 hours 29 minutes 18 seconds
2. Francesco Moser (Sanson) @ 2 minutes 9 seconds
3. Bernt Johansson (Magniflex) @ 3 minutes 13 seconds
4. Michel Laurent (Peugeot) @ 5 minutes 31 seconds
5. Silvano Contini (Bianchi) @ 7 minutes 33 seconds

Climbers' Competition:
1. Claudio Bortolotto (Sanson): 495 points
2. Beat Breu (Willora-Piz Buin-Bonanza): 330
3. Bernt Johansson (Magniflex): 300

Points Competition:
1. Giuseppe Saronni (SCIC): 275 points
2. Francesco Moser (Sanson): 274
3. Bernt Johansson (Magniflex): 260

1980

Bernard Hinault had won the Tour twice and the Vuelta once but the Giro remained unconquered. Before him only Anquetil, Merckx and Gimondi had won all three Grand Tours and Anquetil remained the only French Giro winner. In the spring of 1980, Hinault, nicknamed "The Badger", was in excellent form, having already won Liège–Bastogne–Liège and the Tour of Romandie. He was on track for another remarkable year, and for Hinault, unquestionably the finest rider alive at the time, the Giro was his to lose.

Not accepting that proposition were Saronni and Moser. Moser was the reigning World Road Champion and, by 1980, the winner of countless single-day as well as several shorter stage races. Also, his spring had been superb, with victories in Paris–Roubaix and Tirreno–Adriatico. But so far the big guy hadn't been able to translate his remarkable cycling talent into a Grand Tour win.

The other force to be reckoned with was climber Wladimiro Panizza. For a decade he had consistently placed in the top ten in the Tour and Giro, making it all the way to fourth once in each of them. Other contenders included Giovanni Battaglin, Tommy Prim and Giambattista Baronchelli.

The 1980 route was a perfect tough-guy race course. There were two hard mountaintop finishes and two others ending at less-severe hilltops. The Stelvio was defanged a bit by having the finish come well after the descent, in Sondrio. With 93.4 kilometers of time trialing, the pure climbers must have looked at the route map and shuddered. This was a race for a complete racer, one who could do it all.

The race opened in Genoa with a 7-kilometer prologue. Moser was the fastest rider on the port city's wet, slippery streets, taking chances as he aggressively raced over the flat course. Hinault rode his specialty time trial bike with care, conceding six seconds to Moser in the interest of avoiding a crash.

Saronni's sprinting legs were ready to race. He won the first three road stages, all in mass romps. While they were competing on the road, Saronni and Moser also fought a verbal battle in the press accusing each other of nothing of any particular importance, making an excellent *polemica*.

Again the weather turned wet in time for a time trial. Jørgen Marcussen, one of Battaglin's *gregari*, won the stage five time trial in Pisa. But Hinault, at second, performed a vivisection on the rest of the contenders over the flat, 36-kilometer route finishing in Pisa. Hinault was now in pink.

The General Classification stood thus:
1. Bernard Hinault
2. Knut Knudsen @ 32 seconds
3. Francesco Moser @ 54 seconds
4. Jørgen Marcussen @ 1 minute 1 second
5. Roberto Visentini @ 1 minute 20 seconds
7. Giuseppe Saronni @ 2 minutes 3 seconds

The next day Moser announced that he and Saronni should ally themselves against Hinault. The surprise isn't that riders would join forces against a dangerous rider, especially a powerful foreigner. Moser's request was odd in that it was made so openly.

After a day of racing on the island of Elba, stage seven headed south to Umbria with a finish in ancient Orvieto. As the peloton raced over the Apennines, all the contenders took turns attacking Hinault. Having brought a weak team to Italy, Hinault was forced to do a lot of the neutralizing himself. He made sure Saronni and Moser were in sight or behind him the entire stage. Eventually a break with Visentini, Panizza and Battaglin got away, beating the Hinault group by 3 minutes 14 seconds. Visentini took over the lead and Hinault was now eighth, almost three minutes back. There were several able men sitting between Hinault and the *maglia rosa*, yet Hinault swore that even with the Italians combining against him, he would triumph in Milan.

The next day's stage ending in Fiuggi showed that Hinault would have to dig deep if he wanted to defend himself against the combined efforts of the Italian riders. Six of his *gregari* were unable to finish with the leading group, the only rider on his team who had the strength to help him when the peloton was under severe stress was Jean-René Bernaudeau.

As the race headed for Italy's instep with a hilltop finish in Campotenese, the façade of Italian unity against Hinault broke down and the Giro became a more open race. During this eleventh stage, a dangerous escape that included Baronchelli and Panizza scared the contenders enough to work together, the break being caught just at the line, resulting in no significant changes to the standings.

The next day's racing was complicated enough to require a book of its own to tell the story completely. Halfway through the stage, as a result of an intermediate sprint, a break formed containing most of the big guns, but lacking race leader Visentini as well as Contini and Prim. Hoping to extract more than a pound of flesh from the three important missing riders, the break got itself organized and started motoring down the road. Contini buried himself and was able to claw his way up to the front group, but Saronni punctured. The sympathetic judges let one of the cars in the caravan motorpace Saronni back up to the peloton. Visentini and Prim finally made it up to the hard-charging Moser/Hinault break before the stage ended.

Contini crashed just 200 meters before the one-kilometer-to-go sign, meaning he would have to accept the time loss. The judges did some re-measuring and amazingly found that the sign had been placed 200 meters too close to the finish, allowing Contini to get the same time as the Moser/Hinault group and thus keep his second place in the General Classification. Finishing with the pack, Saronni lost 1 minute 16 seconds, dimming any hope of his gaining the *maglia rosa*.

During stage fourteen, Hinault decided to assert his sovereignty over the others. The stage had several major climbs including the final ascent to Roccaraso. Bernaudeau was sent off on the second climb, the Macerone. A racer of his ability could not be ignored, so the peloton was shredded trying to bring back the fast-moving Frenchman. After sitting in on the chase for a while, Hinault blasted off and only nine riders made it to the top of the Macerone with him. On the penultimate climb, the Rionero Sannitico, Hinault again hit hard and by the top he had Moser, Saronni, Prim, Baronchelli and Panizza for company. As the small lead group climbed to Roccaraso, Hinault was generous enough in handing out pain that all were dropped but Panizza. Hinault took the stage, and the surprising Panizza, a member of Saronni's Gis team, found himself in pink. The day was a disaster for Visentini and Contini who both lost over lost six minutes.

The new General Classification:
1. Wladimiro Panizza
2. Bernard Hinault @ 1 minute 5 seconds
3. Faustino Rupérez @ 1 minute 49 seconds
4. Giambattista Baronchelli @ 2 minutes 35 seconds
5. Giovanni Battaglin @ 2 minutes 40 seconds

The standings stayed just that way during the flat stages that took the Giro to Sirmione, a city on a spit of land that protrudes about four kilometers into Lake Garda.

Next came the stages that would decide the Giro. Stage eighteen was the first, going over the Duran and landing at Pecól in the Val Zoldana.

Part way up the Duran, Battaglin did a testing attack to see what sort of stuff the others were made of. Whatever it was, it was not the stuff of chasers. With no one along for company, Battaglin decided to continue, the others probably thinking it was too early in the hilly, 239-kilometer stage to make a successful move. He maintained his lead on the descent and managed to grow it to a minute as he continued to Pecól.

Back in the peloton, everyone seemed frozen, afraid working might help a rival. Prim and then Panizza finally decided to bring back the fleeing and dangerous Battaglin, but it was too little, too late. Battaglin won the stage by 1 minute 15 seconds over Panizza and had done himself a world of good, moving up to third place at 1 minute 25 seconds. It was a magnificent ride.

The day's hard racing ruined the hopes for two more contenders. Rupérez, exhausted after winning the Vuelta a few weeks earlier, struggled in eight and a half minutes after Battaglin. Moser, who had been looking tired during the last few stages, lost 2 minutes 34 seconds to Panizza. He announced his intention to quit the Giro and rest up for the coming Tour in July. Neither Moser nor his team were in Frankfurt for the Tour's start in July.

Even though Battaglin tried his disappearing act again the next day with the Tre Croci and Mendola passes, the pack finished together. *Status quo ante bellum.*

Hinault's director Cyrille Guimard had planned his set-piece assault on the Giro for the twentieth stage with the Passo Palade followed by an ascent of the north face of the Stelvio. The pack went over the Palade together. At Merano, 50 kilometers east of the start of the Stelvio climb, several riders escaped after an intermediate sprint, three of them from Hinault's Renault team. Why the pack let them go when everyone had to know Guimard would try something is a mystery, but escape they did and it was game on. At Spondigna the route turned left for the road that would become the Stelvio pass. The break was still away, now by six and a half minutes.

The Stelvio climb proper is generally considered to start at Prato allo Stelvio and here Bernaudeau was able to ride away from the others in the break. Back in the pack, Hinault was chasing down any escape attempts, keeping things together. The six-man break, less Bernaudeau, was soon caught by the fast moving peloton.

When his group arrived at Prato allo Stelvio, Hinault just about ripped the bars out of the stem in an attack that dropped everyone but Panizza, Prim and Battaglin. As the four raced up the mountain, Hinault put in three more hard attacks. The third was more than Prim and Battaglin could take, but pink-clad Panizza, 37 and in the twilight of his career, hung on like grim death.

Again, Hinault was out of the saddle attacking the *maglia rosa*. The last hammer blow was too much for even Panizza, and Hinault took off to catch Bernaudeau, now only three minutes up the pass. The catch was made and they raced for the finish.

Stelvio stages that don't end at the top usually finish in Bormio, the city at the bottom of the south face. Not this time: the French pair had to ride about 80 kilometers further to Sondrio. The Renault riders did a two-man time trial and extended their lead with every pedal stroke, arriving in Sondrio four and a half minutes before Panizza, Prim, Baronchelli and Battaglin. Hinault let Bernaudeau take the stage while Hinault took the lead. With only a time trial in the way of Hinault's march to victory, it looked like Guimard's guidance had allowed Hinault to use his strength to maximum advantage.

The new General Classification:
1. Bernard Hinault
2. Wladimiro Panizza @ 3 minutes 14 seconds
3. Giovanni Battaglin @ 4 minutes 39 seconds
4. Tommy Prim @ 7 minutes 28 seconds
5. Giambattista Baronchelli @ 8 minutes 25 seconds

The 50.4-kilometer time trial at Saronno on the outskirts of Milan was the penultimate stage and the last one that could affect the outcome. Normally Hinault was almost unbeatable in a time trial and he was certainly superior to any of the riders close to him in the General Classification.

Hinault didn't win the time trial. But he didn't have to. Saronni, Gregor Braun and Knut Knudsen were the day's podium while those high in the standings lost still more time to the Badger.

Hinault became the second Frenchman after Anquetil to win the Giro, and the first racer in history to win all three Grand Tours on the first attempt. Partial credit has to be given to Hinault's director, Guimard, who might be cycling's greatest-ever tactician. As Lucien van Impe, whom Guimard directed to victory in 1976 Tour said, "Cyrille was one of the best *directeurs sportifs* that I ever met…he always knew when to go after a break or to let it go. And everything he predicted at the morning briefing came true later in the race."

Final 1980 Giro d'Italia General Classification:
1. Bernard Hinault (Renault-Gitane) 112 hours 8 minutes 20 seconds
2. Wladimiro Panizza (Gis Gelati) @ 5 minutes 43 seconds
3. Giovanni Battaglin (Inoxpran) @ 6 minutes 3 seconds
4. Tommy Prim (Bianchi-Piaggio) @ 7 minutes 53 seconds
5. Giambattista Baronchelli (Bianchi-Piaggio) @ 11 minutes 49 seconds

Climbers' Competition:
1. Claudio Bortolotto (Mobilificio San Giacomo-Benotto): 670 points
2. Wladimiro Panizza (Gis Gelati): 400
3. Bernard Hinault (Renault-Gitane): 350

Points Competition:
1. Giuseppe Saronni (Gis Gelati): 301 points
2. Giovanni Mantovani (Hoonved-Bottecchia): 215
3. Tommy Prim (Bianchi-Piaggio): 179

Hinault had planned to make 1980 the year of his Giro/Tour double. As the Tour progressed he began to suffer terrible knee pain and after stage twelve, abandoned, allowing Joop Zoetemelk to win the Tour on his tenth attempt. Hinault recovered from his bout of tendinitis in time to win the World Road Championship that fall.

1981

Giovanni Battaglin had been knocking on the door of greatness for almost a decade. Winner of the Girobio in 1972, he turned pro in 1973. In his first year as a pro he was third in the Giro; only Merckx and Gimondi could beat him. The next year he spent a couple of days in pink, but his promise dwarfed his results. Luciano Pezzi (Gimondi's old director) is given a lot of the credit for reviving Battaglin's career when Pezzi formed the Inoxpran team in 1979. That year Battaglin won the climbers' prize in the Tour as well as several important late-season single-day races in Italy.

By the end of the season his form still held as he raced the World Championship road race in Valkenburg, Netherlands. He remains emphatic that he would have won the rainbow jersey if Jan Raas had not run him into the barriers in the sprint, a belief far from universally held among those who watched the race that day. In 1980 he came in third in the Giro and again won several significant single-day races.

In 1981 it all seemed to come together. Feeling that Saronni was the likely winner of the Giro, the Inoxpran team targeted the Vuelta, held in April at that time, which Battaglin won. Then, with only three days between the Vuelta's end and the Giro's prologue, he recalled, "The Vuelta ended on the Sunday and then the Giro started with a prologue time trial three days later. I came home from Spain, changed my suitcase and saw my wife and then we set off for the Giro. Can you imagine doing that today?"

Bianchi considered the Giro the core of its season and brought a lot of firepower to the race, including Baronchelli, Contini and Prim. Like the Petterssons a decade before, Prim had an extended career as a top amateur before turning pro late in 1979. He started his professional career with a bang, coming in fourth and winning the young rider's jersey in the 1980 Giro, and just before the start of the 1981 Giro he won the Tour of Romandie.

Bianchi team director Giancarlo Ferretti decided to make all three riders protected team leaders, bringing to mind Frederick the Great's aphorism, "He who defends everything defends nothing."

If the 1979 Giro had been designed to create a Saronni/Moser dogfight, the 1981 edition with more good, hard climbing, but with three individual time trials (plus a prologue time trial), had Saronni written all over it. Battaglin and many other riders agreed that with all the time bonuses (30 seconds to the stage winners, even those of the time trials) skewing the race towards the rider who could mix it up in the sprints, the Giro organization had built a race for Saronni.

When the dust had cleared after the first two days of racing—a short prologue in Trieste, a 100-kilometer half-stage and a fifteen-kilometer team time trial—Moser was in pink by four seconds over Famcucine teammate Gregor Braun. Almost immediately Moser and Saronni were scrapping in the press. The dispute turned almost pathological when the judges took hours to decide who came in second in stage five, Moser or Swiss rider Serge Demierre. If Moser were second, he would gain the bonus time and keep the lead. Otherwise, the *maglia rosa* would migrate to, gulp, Saronni. Since the television cameras were waiting, both were awarded pink jerseys without waiting for the judges. The two had to share the podium and, of course, both bellowed and filed protests. Eventually Moser was awarded the second place and kept his lead. Nothing freshens up a Giro like a good *polemica*.

As the Giro raced down the eastern side of the peninsula, Battaglin's criticism seemed to be validated. By the end of stage six in Bari, Saronni had won three stages, snarfing up a minute and a half of bonus time, putting him in the *maglia rosa* 24 seconds ahead of Moser.

The riders arrived in Reggio Calabria at the toe of Italy after three more days of racing, the standings more or less unchanged, even though the roads were hilly with no shortage of good, but less than epic climbs.

Stage ten, though, shook things up. After a transfer to Rome the race went over the Terminillo and then the less difficult Forca di Chiavano, a few kilometers from the finish in the remote Umbrian hill town of Cascia. Moser crashed descending the Chiavano, losing more than five minutes, while up ahead Baronchelli was winning the stage. Battaglin and Prim finished only a few seconds behind him but too far back to get any time bonuses. Saronni lost almost a minute on a day the climbers had taken control of the race.

The General Classification now:
1. Giuseppe Saronni
2. Claudio Bortolotto @ 12 seconds
3. Giambattista Baronchelli @ 31 seconds
4. Alfio Vandi and Silvano Contini @ 49 seconds
6. Giovanni Battaglin @ 50 seconds
7. Tommy Prim @ 1 minute 4 seconds
9. Roberto Visentini @ 1 minute 32 seconds

Knut Knudsen won the stage thirteen time trial in the Tuscan spa town of Montecatini, but the second-place rider who came in a full minute behind Knudsen became the Pink Jersey. Sammontana rider Roberto Visentini had enjoyed a scintillating amateur career before turning pro in 1978. Now he had the *maglia rosa* by seven seconds over Contini with Prim just 22 seconds behind and Saronni 23 seconds back. *La Gazzetta* thought Bianchi had the race firmly in its fist.

Moser blew the race up the next day when it went over the Apennines to another spa town, Salsomaggiore. After being away for 173 kilometers, he soloed across the line more than a minute ahead of the Contini-led chase group containing Prim and Battaglin. Visentini's group came in twelve seconds later but the remaining time bonuses were long gone, and gone to two of his main threats, Contini and Battaglin. Contini was back in pink with Visentini second, 25 seconds down.

Coming just before the Dolomites, stage seventeen was a transition stage with four rated climbs that broke things up. Prim squeezed out a half-minute from Saronni, Visentini, Contini and Battaglin, putting the Swede within 10 seconds of the Pink Jersey before stage eighteen's ascents of the Vivione and Tonale.

Instead of losing his lead to the hungry sharks, Contini came in to the finish at Dimaro a half-minute ahead of the other contenders with a second place that also gave him a 20-second time bonus. Contini had nearly a full minute's breathing room with two more brutal Dolomite stages to go.

The Palade was stage nineteen's appetizer for the Furcia Pass, where Battaglin successfully attacked. First over the top, he held his lead for the five kilometers into San Vigilio di Marrebe. Saronni and Prim were only 10 seconds behind and Visentini another 7 seconds back. But Contini was getting ragged. He still held the lead, but after losing a minute he was in trouble. Battaglin had closed to within 3 seconds and Prim was just 8 seconds behind.

The race was a virtual tie going into the *tappone* (a Giro's hardest stage), a crossing of the Tre Croci and a finish atop the Tre Cime di Lavaredo. Battaglin wasn't going to mess around with mountains like these; he had his mechanic fit a triple crankset on his Pinarello for the Tre Cime ascent.

Swiss climber Beat Breu was first both over the Tre Croci and to the top of Tre Cime di Lavaredo. Fifty seconds later Battaglin made it to the top with Saronni fourteen seconds slower and Prim a half minute back. Baronchelli, who had announced his arrival at the top ranks of cycling on the Tre Cime ascent in 1974, lost over seven minutes.

With a 42-kilometer time trial in Verona left to ride, the Dolomites had decided little. The top four riders seemed to be nearly equal in ability, with most observers thinking Saronni the likely final victor:

1. Giovanni Battaglin
2. Tommy Prim @ 50 seconds
3. Giuseppe Saronni @ 59 seconds
4. Josef Fuchs @ 1 minute 10 seconds
5. Silvano Contini @ 1 minute 44 seconds

Davide Boifava, Inoxpran's director for the Giro, was worried that things might not exactly go according to Hoyle during the final time trial, especially since the *tifosi* were desperately hoping Saronni would win the Giro at the last moment with a fabulous ride. Boifava told Torriani that he had nothing against him, but he was going to have a car with a video camera follow Saronni. That way, Boifava said, if Battaglin were to lose, the loss would be a fair and just one. It leads one to believe Boifava, an experienced and knowledgeable pro, had neither faith that Torriani would keep his hands off the final results nor belief that Saronni's Gis Gelati team would behave themselves.

As he had in Montecatini, Knudsen won the Verona ride against the clock. Prim took second, Battaglin was 2 seconds slower than the Swede and Saronni just a single second behind him.

Battaglin had won the Giro d'Italia and did what so far only Merckx had done: win the Vuelta and the Giro in the same year. Battaglin's victory was a time-bonus win, Prim's actual elapsed time was shorter than Battaglin's.

American George Mount had electrified American cycling with his sixth place in the 1976 Olympic road race. At the invitation of Mike Neel, an American racing in Italy, he eventually signed with the Sammontana team of Roberto Visentini and Moreno Argentin. In Visentini's service he rode to a commendable 25th place.

Final 1981 Giro d'Italia General Classification:

1. Giovanni Battaglin (Inoxpran) 104 hours 50 minutes 36 seconds
2. Tommy Prim (Bianchi-Piaggio) @ 38 seconds
3. Giuseppe Saronni (Gis Gelati) @ 50 seconds

4. Silvano Contini (Bianchi-Piaggio) @ 2 minutes 59 seconds
5. Josef Fuchs (Cilo-Aufina) @ 3 minutes 19 seconds
25. George Mount (Sammontana) @ 39 minutes 20 seconds

Climbers' Competition:
1. Claudio Bortolotto (Santini-Selle Italia): 510 points
2. Beat Breu (Cilo-Aufina) 300
3. Benedetto Patellaro (Hoonved-Bottecchia): 290

Points Competition:
1. Giuseppe Saronni (Gis Gelati): 215 points
2. Tommy Prim (Bianchi-Piaggio): 133
3. Giovanni Mantovani (Hoonved-Bottecchia): 127

A few months after reaching cycling's heights, Battaglin's career lay in shambles. In April of 1982 he crashed badly, breaking his collarbone, shoulder, hip and a vertebra. He said he should have taken a long time off in order to recuperate. Instead, just 20 days after the crash, he had the plaster casts removed and was soon racing, trying to get ready for the Tour. "I had to do it because the Inoxpran team was built around me and it could have folded if I hadn't ridden the Tour."

He said that instead of getting physiotherapy and making a proper recovery, he rushed back into the sport and was never the same again. After catching hepatitis during the 1984 Giro, he threw in the towel and retired to concentrate on his eponymous bicycle company.

1982 For years the Tour de France had been staving off financial ruin by accumulating myriad sponsors of various inconsequential awards, such as "friendliest rider", but at the time, the Tour was swimming in money compared to the Giro. The Giro's owner, RCS, was broke and would eventually undergo and emerge from bankruptcy. It had no money to give to Torriani. In a gamble reminiscent of the Giro's origins, at the last minute Torriani and his new right-hand man Carmine Castellano cobbled together the finances to run the 1982 Giro. It was a close-run thing, Torriani having to put up a personal financial guarantee before the Giro could go forward. They found the money to put on the Giro by first getting RAI to televise the race and then securing Coca-Cola, which was just introducing "Sprite" into Italy, as a major sponsor. The race was saved.

Many of the same faces from the 1981 Giro were on the starting line to begin the 16-kilometer prologue team time trial in Milan: Baronchelli, Contini, Prim (all three on the Bianchi team), Saronni, Moser and Visentini. The 500-pound gorilla in the room was the returning Bernard Hinault. He had attempted the Giro/Tour double in 1980 and after a smashing Giro victory, his knee failed under the added strain of the Tour. He didn't have a stunning spring, but with assaults planned on both the Giro and the Tour, I'm sure he didn't want his form to peak too soon.

The 22-stage, 4,010-kilometer Giro route looked to visit as much of Italy as possible. After the prologue in Milan, the route went south on the Tyrrhenian side of the Apennines all the way to the toe of the boot and then over to Sicily. Then the race headed north to the Dolomites and west to the Alps. The final stage was a 42.5-kilometer individual time trial in Turin.

On paper Hinault's Renault team looked to be one of the weaker squads, but a team time trial is as much an exercise in precision and teamwork as it is of power. Renault won the opener, giving Hinault the first Pink Jersey, Moser's Famcucine team being two seconds slower. The teams of Prim, Contini, Baronchelli and Saronni all finished about a half-minute back.

Each day over the next three stages the Pink Jersey changed hands, but always within the Renault team. Stage one gave it to Renault *gregario* Patrick Bonnet. The next day, Laurent Fignon became the leader after a second place to Michael Wilson, who became the first Australian to win a Giro stage.

Stage three was a 37-kilometer individual time trial going from Perugia up to Assisi via a short, moderate climb. Hinault won the stage with Prim second at 11 seconds, retaking the *maglia rosa* and keeping it until Moser won the seventh stage into Diamante on the boot's instep. With a rest day and a transfer to Sicily, the General Classification stood thus:

1. Francesco Moser
2. Bernard Hinault @ 1 second
3. Silvano Contini @ 14 seconds
4. Tommy Prim @ 27 seconds
5. Giuseppe Saronni @ 49 seconds

The three Sicilian stages had some brilliant sprinting at the stage ends, but nothing happened to affect the overall standings.

If the organizers thought that the race might get hot after transferring to the mainland, where the riders had to cross the Sila mountains (part of the southern Apennines), they were wrong. A small break of non-contenders stayed away and the first chase group's pace up to Camigliatello Silano wasn't fast enough to drop Moser, so he retained his lead over the second rest day. From here, there would be eleven straight days of racing.

Stage twelve raced through the Molise region to its finish at Campitello Matese, a village high enough to have a ski lift. On the final climb Tommy Prim went too fast for almost the entire peloton. Hinault stayed with him and then lifted the speed still higher. Near the top, Mario Beccia attacked and Hinault decided to come along for the ride. They traded pace until they were close to the finish where Hinault dropped Beccia to claim the stage win, the 30-second time bonus and the *maglia rosa*.

The next day's racing through the hilly Abruzzo region showed again what a skilled tactician Renault had in Cyrille Guimard. On the day's major climb, Contini escaped with three other riders. Hinault chose not to go with the move, fearing being isolated and getting worn down by the others in the break. So he let them go and waited for help. When the last climb had been negotiated, Hinault and his team set about using the remaining 50 kilometers to reel in the Contini quartet, now three minutes up the road. During the infernal pursuit the gap was reduced to 64 seconds, letting Hinault keep his lead. Contini had done himself a lot of good, he was now only 31 seconds behind. Moreover, Hinault's Renault team was showing some wear and tear with the Dolomites and Alps still to come. But, through intelligent patience and clever use of a weak team, Hinault's leading position had been preserved.

Stage sixteen ended with a hilltop finish at San Martino di Castrozza after 243 kilometers that also took in an ascent of Monte Grappa. Hinault, feeling that Contini was fragile and could be dealt with in the Alps, worried instead about the man he thought the real danger, Prim.

The descent of Monte Grappa was a disaster for many of the riders, an 8-kilometer section having lost its asphalt in the winter storms. Several riders flatted, including Prim and Hinault's lieutenant Laurent Fignon, delaying both riders badly. Hinault tried to wait for Fignon, but when the ascent to San Martino arrived, he had to go with the leaders and without a teammate. Hinault wasn't concerned with winning the stage and unworried that Contini was glued to his wheel. He wanted

Bernard Hinault in stage sixteen.

above all, to put time between himself and Prim. At the stage's end he had put the Swede another two minutes back.

The General Classification stood thus:

    1. Bernard Hinault
    2. Silvano Contini @ 26 seconds
    3. Mario Beccia @ 1 minute 40 seconds
    4. Francesco Moser @ 2 minutes 16 seconds
    5. Tommy Prim @ 3 minutes 9 seconds

In stage seventeen it again came down to the final climb, the Passo Croce Domini. Baronchelli leaped away. Then, seeing that Hinault appeared to be a bit over-geared for the climb, Prim escaped, quickly followed by his teammate Contini as well as Metauro Mobili riders Marco Groppo and Lucien van Impe.

Hinault had two Spanish riders with him who refused to help, while the break made up of five strong riders (three Bianchi and two Metauro Mobili riders) formed a smooth-working machine that rode powerfully into the headwind they encountered after the descent. They extended their lead over the chasing Hinault group to more than two minutes. Contini won the stage and was now the Pink Jersey, leading Hinault by 2 minutes 14 seconds.

Stage eighteen was only 85 kilometers long, with a hilltop finish on Montecampione. As the climb started, Hinault went to the front and just went fast. He liked to ascend mountains at a steady speed without unsettling changes in pace and as he put the screws to the field, Contini came off. Prim, in an act of misguided team spirit, went back for him. Contini immediately sent him back up the road to make sure Bianchi wouldn't lose everything on a day when Hinault was throwing high heat. Hinault finished at the top of Montecampione alone with Contini 3 minutes 25 seconds back. Hinault was again the Giro's leader.

After stage eighteen the General Classification stood thus:
1. Bernard Hinault
2. Silvano Contini @ 1 minute 41seconds
3. Tommy Prim @ 1 minute 53 seconds
4. Lucien van Impe @ 2 minutes 47 seconds
5. Giambattista Baronchelli @ 3 minutes 49 seconds

The final mountain showdown was run on as dramatic a course as could be imagined. Stage twenty-one was 254 kilometers going from Cuneo, south of Turin, over five major Alpine mountains: the Maddalena, Vars, Izoard, Montgenèvre and Sestriere, ending in Pinerolo. This was the same route used in stage seventeen of the historic 1949 Giro where Fausto Coppi had displayed extraordinary superiority, beating Gino Bartali by 12 minutes and third-place Alfredo Martini by almost 20 minutes. Hinault said he had no intention of trying to equal Coppi's wonderful solo ride into history. He only wanted to make sure Prim didn't win the Giro.

The first three climbs weren't ridden aggressively, but they took their toll, only thirteen riders remaining together in Briançon for the start of the Montgenèvre. Bianchi had all three of its top guns, Prim, Contini and Baronchelli there while Hinault was completely isolated. With all of those fine cards in their hand, Bianchi did nothing. The front group went over the final two climbs almost intact, at no point was Hinault put under pressure. Saronni won the sprint, Hinault was second followed by Prim and Contini. Giancarlo Ferretti, the director of the Bianchi team is nicknamed *Il Volpone* ("the Fox") for his tactical astuteness. I wonder why.

The General Classification with the climbing completed but before the final 42.5-kilometer time trial stage in Turin:

1. Bernard Hinault
2. Silvano Contini @ 1 minute 56 seconds
3. Tommy Prim @ 2 minutes 3 seconds
4. Lucien van Impe @ 3 minutes 7 seconds
5. Giambattista Baronchelli @ 4 minutes 22 seconds

Hinault delivered a fabulous time trial, the second fastest in Giro history so far, giving him two Giri. That summer he also won the Tour de France, at last getting his double and joining Coppi, Anquetil and Merckx.

It looked as if Ferretti had made the same mistake in 1982 that he made in 1981. By not putting his powerful team solidly behind Prim, he had squandered two opportunities to win the Giro. Over and over again Hinault was alone, without teammates, and vulnerable to attack. But Ferretti, like the Giro itself so often, wanted an Italian to win the Italian race.

Final 1982 Giro d'Italia General Classification:

1. Bernard Hinault (Renault) 110 hours 7 minutes 55 seconds
2. Tommy Prim (Bianchi-Piaggio) @ 2 minutes 35 seconds
3. Silvano Contini (Bianchi-Piaggio) @ 2 minutes 47 seconds
4. Lucien van Impe (Metauro Mobili-Pinarello) @ 4 minutes 31 seconds
5. Giambattista Baronchelli (Bianchi-Piaggio) @ 6 minutes 9 seconds

Climbers' Competition:

1. Lucien van Impe (Metauro Mobili-Pinarello): 860 points
2. Bernard Hinault (Renault): 380
3. Silvano Contini (Bianchi-Piaggio): 290

Points Competition:
1. Francesco Moser (Famcucine): 247 points
2. Giuseppe Saronni (Del Tongo): 207
3. Bernard Hinault (Renault): 171

1983

The 1983 edition went easy on the climbing (and the rouleurs), with only one hard day in the mountains, stage twenty out of the twenty-two scheduled. It was assumed that the route had been crafted with both Giuseppe Saronni's superb sprinting and tolerable ascending skills and Moser's big gear mashing and poor climbing in mind. Of the 162 riders who showed up in Brescia on May 12 to begin the race for the Pink Jersey, there were only a few true contenders. The odds-on favorite had to be Giuseppe Saronni, the reigning World Road Champion. Since winning the Rainbow Jersey in Goodwood, England in late 1982, he had gone on to win the Tour of Lombardy, Milan–San Remo and had come in second in Liège–Bastogne–Liège.

Roberto Visentini (who replaced Battaglin as the leader of the Inoxpran team, which was riding Battaglin bikes) and Tommy Prim were also high on the list of possible winners. Prim was saddled with his Swedish nationality, so far a handicap on the Bianchi team. Bianchi, an Italian company wanting to sell oodles of bikes in Italy, had preferred an Italian winner. Ironically, Bianchi is now owned by Grimaldi Industri, a Swedish company.

The Giro was supposed to start with a prologue individual time trial. The riders were suited up and the first man to ride, Jesus Ibañez, was on his bike. But then he had to wait, and wait some more. Striking workers were blocking the road and the police, not wanting to make a bad situation worse, didn't interfere. The prologue was cancelled.

They moved on to the next stage, a 70-kilometer team time trial going from Brescia to Mantua, which Prim's Bianchi squad won. And, surprisingly, Bianchi's director Ferretti had Prim cross the line first, letting the Swede become the first 1982 *maglia rosa*. The team's times didn't count towards the General Classification except for the time bonuses given to the top three teams, putting Saronni, whose Del Tongo team came in fifth, in thirty-first place at 40 seconds.

The next two stages let the sprinters show their speed. Fifteen kilometers before the end of the third stage there was a crash, taking about twenty riders down. Trapped behind the pile-up were Saronni and Moser. Capitalizing on the situation, Baronchelli and Battaglin hammered all the way to the finish line in Fano, beating the unlucky riders by 27 seconds.

The first hint as to who could climb came in stage four, with its six-kilometer ascent to Todi in Umbria. Lucien van Impe had driven the field hard up an earlier, more modest climb and had split the pack. Saronni out-sprinted the surviving 40 riders. By virtue of sprint time bonuses, Paolo Rosola was leader and Saronni was in fifth place.

The next day Saronni generated near panic when he got into a fast moving break on the road to Vasto because many of the big names had missed the move, including Prim, Moser and Baronchelli. Ferretti showed his intentions when he made Contini slow the break while Prim didn't do any work helping the pack chase the escapees. The break was caught after more than 100 kilometers of pursuit, mostly because of Moser's long, hard stints at the front of the chase. Then another break went and this time it was Saronni and his teammate Didi Thurau who did most of the work of shutting down the escape. But Eduardo Chozas had slipped away from the break to win the stage, keeping just 21 seconds of what had been a four-minute lead, plus a 30-second time bonus, after 60 kilometers of hard work.

Rosola had missed the important moves and Contini, despite Ferretti's favoring Prim, was the *maglia rosa*.

Stage six ended with the first hilltop finish of the year. Spanish rider Alberto Fernández made a series of in-the-saddle attacks and after the third, he was clear with six kilometers to go to the top of Campitello Matese. Saronni, with Franco Chioccioli and van Impe right with him, finished 23 seconds behind. The day was a disaster for Prim and Moser, who both lost more than two minutes.

The race continued heading for the western side of Italy with another day in the Apennines. There were two rated climbs that allowed van Impe to get clear with Marino Lejarreta and Jostein Wilmann. With only a few kilometers to go into Salerno, all three crashed, allowing a big sprint finish to settle things. Moreno Argentin won the stage, but Saronni's third place gave him enough bonus seconds to take the lead and don his twentieth Pink Jersey.

After stage seven and a week of racing, the General Classification stood thus:

1. Giuseppe Saronni
2. Silvano Contini @ 8 seconds
3. Wladimiro Panizza @ 45 seconds
4. Didi Thurau @ 48 seconds
5. Giovanni Battaglin @ 58 seconds

As the race turned northward, the next few stages didn't affect the standings, with Saronni keeping his slim lead. Visentini seemed to be the only rider who consistently challenged Saronni. He got into a good-looking break in the hilly stage eleven in western coastal Tuscany, but the move, less one rider, was reeled in with a few kilometers to go. It was 37-year-old Lucien van Impe who surprised everyone when he shot off the front of the dying break, winning the stage seven seconds ahead of the surging pack.

Saronni blitzed the Parma time trial, beating Visentini, also an excellent man against the clock, by 30 seconds. Moreover, by turning in such a good time, Saronni delivered a serious setback to the specialist climbers who were looking forward to the coming high mountain stages, but who now had an imposing time gap to close. Van Impe lost over two minutes.

The last stage of the second week took the riders out of Emilia-Romagna and into Liguria and the coastal road used by the Milan–San Remo race. The day's riding was perky enough to have Saronni put his Del Tongo team (most notably Thurau) at the front of the pack to bring a few wayward riders back to the peloton. Saronni's position was vastly improved because Battaglin was suffering from stomach problems and lost a half-hour.

After fourteen stages and two weeks of racing, the high mountains were only two stages away. The General Classification stood thus:

1. Giuseppe Saronni
2. Roberto Visentini @ 2 minutes 20 seconds
3. Didi Thurau @ 2 minutes 34 seconds
4. Silvano Contini @ 3 minutes 8 seconds
5. Lucien van Impe @ 3 minutes 16 seconds

Battaglin, sick and well down on the Classification, abandoned at the start of stage sixteen.

Stage 16b went over the Roncola Pass on the way to Bergamo. Van Impe did what van Impe did best: he attacked on the climb, but Saronni was able to stay with him while Contini was dropped. They came together on the descent for the nearly inevitable Saronni sprint win. So far, at no point in this Giro had Saronni been in trouble.

The next day was a short 91-kilometer stage with a hilltop finish on the Colle San Fermo. Once the pack hit the 1,067-meter-high mountain, van Impe was off the front again. Saronni kept him in sight while Alberto Fernández caught and dropped the Belgian. Saronni tried to hold a surging Visentini's wheel but couldn't. The damage was manageable, as there was only 15 seconds between them.

After Paolo Rosola won the sprint into Vicenza for his third stage victory, there was another rest day. There were two mountain stages and a time trial left to affect the outcome.

Stage nineteen up to Selva di Val Gardena, into the heart of the Dolomites, could have been a challenging climbing stage. It wasn't. The organizers looked for and found the easiest gradients into town. There was a climb at the end but van Impe didn't participate in the final rush for the line. Hoping to lighten his load for the climb, he had tossed his musette with food and later came down with the hunger knock. It was a strange error for one of the most experienced and finest riders ever to turn a crank. His teammate Alfio Vandi caught up to him and revived van Impe with his own food. The Belgian was able to repair a lot of the damage, but he wasn't able to attack on a day that he had planned to gain real time. Mario Beccia led Lejarreta across the finish line and Saronni and Visentini finished just 17 seconds behind them.

Stage twenty was the only real day in the mountains, a race on the sinuous and beautiful road around the Gruppo Sella massif with ascents of the Campolongo, Pordoi, Sella, and Gardena passes, and then up the Campolongo again. Alessandro Paganesi rode an epic race by escaping on the first ascent of the Campolongo and holding his lead all the way to the end. It was heroic, but did not affect the outcome of the Giro.

What did matter was Visentini's attack on the Pordoi, the *Cima Coppi* for the 1983 edition. Saronni didn't jump to close the gap, continuing instead to ride at his own measured pace, keeping Visentini in sight. By the top of the Pordoi, Visentini was a minute ahead of Saronni. Over the Sella, the gap remained unchanged. As they climbed the Gardena, Visentini appeared to be weakening and at the top, the gap was down to 40 seconds. Both riders were tiring. After the final ascent of the Campolongo they flew down the hill to Arabba and at the end of this titanic pursuit through the Dolomites, Visentini had managed to hold off Saronni by 29 seconds.

The flat penultimate stage could have given Saronni and his wonderful ability to sprint a chance to gain to bonus seconds, but others beat him, leaving him with a two-minute cushion on a man most thought to be the superior time trialist.

"Expect a surprise," Visentini predicted.

With only the final 40-kilometer time trial stage left, the General Classification looked like this:

1. Giuseppe Saronni
2. Roberto Visentini @ 1 minute 56 seconds
3. Alberto Fernández @ 2 minutes 50 seconds
4. Mario Beccia @ 4 minutes 1 second
5. Marino Lejarreta @ 5 minutes 9 seconds

Looking stylish and elegant on his bike, Visentini did win the stage, but took only 49 seconds out of Saronni, not nearly enough to wrest the Pink Jersey.

When I visited Italy that fall for the Milan bike show I heard unbelievable stories about an attempt to sabotage Saronni's time trial ride, but half-doubted them as gossip. It turns out they were true. Visentini rode Battaglin bikes equipped with FIR rims and the owner of FIR, Giovanni Arrigoni, was a little too eager for a Giro victory on his equipment. Signor Arrigoni traveled to the hotel in Gorizia where Saronni's Del Tongo team was spending the night before the time trial and tried to bribe two of staff to put Guttalax, an extremely powerful laxative, in Saronni's food. Despite the offer of two million lire (about $1,500), the alarmed hotel employees called the police and the press and Arrigoni was arrested. Saronni's food was safe. It was a strange move for a well-liked man whose company was enjoying extraordinary worldwide success in the rim market and who had contracted to have Saronni use his wheels the following season.

Final 1983 Giro d'Italia General Classification:
1. Giuseppe Saronni (Del Tongo-Colnago) 100 hours 45 minutes 30 seconds
2. Roberto Visentini (Inoxpran-Lumenflon) @ 1 minute 7 seconds
3. Alberto Fernández (Gemeaz Cusin-Zor) @ 3 minutes 40 seconds
4. Mario Beccia (Malvor-Bottecchia) @ 5 minutes 55 seconds
5. Dietrich Thurau (Del Tongo-Colnago) @ 7 minutes 44 seconds

Climbers' Competition:
1. Lucien van Impe (Metauro Mobili-Pinarello): 70 points
2. Alberto Fernández (Gemeaz Cusin-Zor): 43
3. Tie between Marino Lejarreta (Alfa Lum-Olmo) and Pedro Muñoz (Gemeaz Cusin-Zor): 27

Points Competition:
1. Giuseppe Saronni (Del Tongo-Colnago): 223 points
2. Moreno Argentin (Sammontana-Campagnolo): 149
3. Frank Hoste (Maria Pia-Europ Decor-Dries): 139

Visentini complained that his actual riding time was less than Saronni's and without the time bonuses, he would have won the Giro. Saronni won 3 minutes 20 seconds in bonuses compared to Visentini's 1 minute 25 seconds. By my arithmetic Visentini rode the 1983 Giro 48 seconds faster. But, them's the rules Roberto, and that's how the game is judged.

The 1983 Giro being run over such an easy course, probably the least challenging postwar route to date, was raced at the then record pace of 38.937 kilometers per hour, finally beating 1957's record 37.488 kilometers per hour held by Gastone Nencini. 1957's Giro was fast not because the course was easy, but because the competition that year was nothing less than savage.

1984

Torriani was acutely aware that his countrymen were passionate about wanting to have an Italian winner. In 1984 the best Italian stage racers were still thought to be Moser and Saronni. So Torriani again laid out a rather flat course, in the words of racing historian and journalist Pierre Chany, "to favor either Saronni or Moser." Racer Mario Beccia, the leader of the Malvor team and a competent climber, echoed those thoughts. Even Moser had reservations about the generous time bonuses in play for stage wins in the 1984 edition. Moser himself was in top form, having won the most coveted of all single-day Italian races, Milan–San Remo; and even more extraordinary, using an aerodynamic bike, he had smashed Eddy Merckx's world hour record. It was an impressive career renaissance. Only later did the world learn that Moser had blood-doped (reinjecting his own saved blood), not a banned practice at that time, to beat the hour record. And the other races he won during his late-career bloom, who knows? He was being trained by Francesco Conconi and we'll have more about Signor Conconi later.

The man who could offer the greatest challenge to the two Italian gentlemen was Frenchman Laurent Fignon, nicknamed "The Professor" because he had attended college for a while and wore glasses, both rarities in the 1984 peloton. Fignon won the Tour in his first attempt, in 1983. Not only had Fignon won it, he won it with startling ease. He had stalked Pascal Simon, the leader for much of the race, who was suffering from an extremely painful broken shoulder blade, waiting for him to abandon, which he eventually did. Moreover, Fignon was both good against the clock and an excellent climber, a true *passista-scalatore*.

This Giro and the accusations that the organizers (meaning Torriani) took an active part in influencing the outcome of the 1984 Giro has been the subject of spirited (meaning shouting and bulging veins) discussion ever since the winner was given his final *maglia rosa*.

We'll start with the route itself. It had a healthy 140 kilometers of individual time trialing, which worked to Moser's advantage. On the other hand there was a team time trial, where the Fignon-led Renault riders could be expected to do very well. And the climbing, where Fignon enjoyed a marked superiority over Moser, leaned to Fignon's advantage because of a planned ascent of the Stelvio in stage eighteen.

The other major climbing stage, with the short climbs around the Gruppo Sella in the Dolomites, was unlikely to allow Fignon to permanently dispatch Moser. On paper then, it looked that Fignon's only chance to win would involve a heroic climb up the Stelvio, but because of the way the stage was designed, even that looked iffy.

No other rider on the start list seemed to be on the level of Fignon and Moser. 1984 wasn't Saronni's year and he couldn't be expected to time-trial or climb well enough to beat the two favorites. Neither Baronchelli (still riding reasonably well) nor Battaglin (in his last year as a pro) were on the level of these two at this point. Van Impe was the Belgian Champion and had finished fourth in the 1983 Tour, a big improvement over his ninth in the 1983 Giro, but his fourth place was to Fignon.

The race started in Lucca and Moser, as expected, won the 5-kilometer prologue time trial, with Fignon eighth at 16 seconds. Fignon's well-drilled Renault squad won the team time trial the next day, but the team time trial's real times did not count towards the General Classification, though first place was good for a 2 minute 30 second bonification. Moser's Gis team was third, their bonus being 2 minutes 10 seconds, netting Fignon 20 seconds over Moser and the lead, by 4 seconds.

He slightly increased his lead in stage three, a circuit race in Bologna that included a stiff little climb that let Fignon put another 16 seconds plus a 15-second time bonus for second place between himself and Moser.

An American team, Linea Italia-Motta (run by professional cycling's first-ever female manager, Robin Morton), was entered, and a member of the squad, Karl Maxon, managed to become the virtual Pink Jersey in stage four when he gained 22 minutes in a solo break. Saronni's efforts to leave Fignon for dead when the Frenchman crashed enlivened the field and kept Maxon from winning the stage.

Stage five should have been Fignon's chance to hammer Moser back down the standings because it finished at the top of Block Haus. For a while it looked like Fignon, who was leading the front group, was going to do something special, but about four kilometers from the summit he was done in by hunger knock and struggled to the top. Moser, on the other hand, was having a terrific day and narrowly lost the stage win to Moreno Argentin. Fignon had to concede 88 seconds and the lead to Moser.

There was a crash on a badly marked corner during a descent in stage seven. The riders were incensed over the dangerous oversight and rode slowly the rest of the way to the finish. Almost all the riders, that is. Swiss sprinter Urs Freuler, seeing an easy stage win, jumped ahead of the striking riders.

The Giro reached the arch of the boot at the end of stage seven and headed up the western side of Italy. Still, Moser remained the *maglia rosa* with nothing happening to change the top ranks of the standings, which remained close. The first 25 riders were all within five minutes of Moser.

At the start of stage nine, Murella withdrew its team from the Giro to punish its stage seven striking riders, taking out Baronchelli. The Murella riders announced they would continue riding the Giro, even at their own expense. To prove their worthiness, the Murella riders rode the stage like fiends with Baronchelli attacking hard several times and finally setting up his teammate Erik Pederson for the stage win. Having proven himself to be a master manipulator (I'm sure he would have considered "motivator" to be a more accurate term), team director Luciano Pezzi concluded the Murella soap opera by ending his threat to withdraw.

But the *polemiche* were not finished. Felice Gimondi had resigned as president of the Italian Professional Riders Association to protest what he thought was a stupid strike, and vice-president Vittorio Adorni joined him. Incensed that their organization hadn't stood with them, the riders decided that future officers must be currently racing to hold office.

There was much noise, but the racing over unchallenging roads generated little heat. The race was back in northern Italy for the stage fifteen time trial going from the Certosa di Pavia to Milan. Before the 37-kilometer stage was run, the General Classification stood thus:

1. Francesco Moser
2. Roberto Visentini @ 10 seconds
3. Moreno Argentin @ 34 seconds
4. Laurent Fignon @ 39 seconds

Moser won the time trial, beating Visentini by 53 seconds and Fignon by 88 seconds, yielding the following standings:

1. Francesco Moser
2. Roberto Visentini @ 1 minute 3 seconds
3. Moreno Argentin and Laurent Fignon tied @ 2 minutes 7 seconds

Fignon and Visentini started to divide up the Giro's spoils, both expressing confidence that the coming mountain stages would surely be the scene of Moser's downfall. Yet, Fignon later wrote that with each passing day he could see that Moser was getting stronger and more confident.

Cue ominous background sound of cellos playing minor chords. News came that the Stelvio was blocked with snow, but would be ready for stage eighteen. After stage seventeen was completed, the word was the Stelvio was not yet passable.

Now here's where it gets complicated. Torriani had photos proving that it would be easy to clear the Stelvio and said he badly wanted the race to go over the pass. It was said that a government worker in Trent (Moser's home town) refused to allow the Giro to go over the Stelvio. Who, in writer Samuel Abt's words, evaporated the stage? I don't know.

To substitute, the race went over the Tonale and Palade Passes. Visentini, believing that the fix was in, quit the race after the stage. Fignon felt that even with the Stelvio eliminated, there was enough climbing left to give him a fair shot at the race.

Fignon tried to get away on the Tonale, but couldn't. He did cause Moser to get dropped, however. But Moser, a fine descender, got back on and apparently Fignon did not attack on the Palade.

The French erupted with white-hot fury after the stage was over. Fignon's director Cyrille Guimard said that Moser had been pushed by both spectators and riders and that when he had been dropped, he had been allowed to draft follow cars to regain contact. Moser didn't directly deny the charges, and there was no adjustment to Moser's time, as the Giro had done in decades past. To rub salt in the wound, the race jury penalized Fignon twenty seconds for taking food outside the feed zone. Cynics noted that this was a hard mountain stage that, strangely, had 46 riders finish within 5 seconds of stage winner Bruno Leali.

Stage nineteen was run without drama. Fignon left Moser 49 seconds behind going into Selva di Val Gardena. This tightened things up, and with the five-pass stage coming next, here were the standings:

1. Francesco Moser
2. Laurent Fignon @ 1 minute 3 seconds
3. Moreno Argentin @ 1 minute 7 seconds
4. Marino Lejarreta @ 1 minute 8 seconds
5. Mario Beccia @ 3 minutes 55 seconds

The twentieth stage was the last chance for the climbers, with the Campolongo, Pordoi, Sella, Gardena and again the Campolongo passes. The 169-kilometer stage wasn't the pure climber's play because this classic loop of shorter, hard climbs can give a good descender a chance to regain contact before the next climb hits. Fignon escaped on the Pordoi and no one was able to catch him. He sailed into Arabba 2 minutes 19 seconds ahead of Moser, who came in eighth. Fignon took the lead, 1 minute 31 seconds ahead of Moser.

The 1984 Giro d'Italia came down to the final time trial, 42 kilometers from Soave to Verona. Moser won it riding a road version of his aerodynamic World Hour Record bike with the remarkable time of 49 minutes 26 seconds. Fignon came in second, 2 minutes 24 seconds slower. Moser had gone at a blistering 50.977 kilometers an hour, the fastest-ever time trial longer than 20 kilometers.

That remarkable time trial ride gave the 1984 Giro to Moser.

The recriminations over this Giro continue to this day. There are three areas of controversy: the biased officiating that allowed Moser to be pushed up the mountains and draft the caravan cars, the elimination of the Stelvio climb, and problems with the final time trial.

It would appear that Moser did benefit from officials who turned a blind eye to the illicit help he received, yet they were quite willing to penalize others. Without a doubt, Fignon was hometowned.

The Stelvio question remains a muddle. Was the pass closed? The French magazine *Vélo* published pictures showing

Francesco Moser in pink.

the Stelvio was open. If the Stelvio did have snow, it wasn't much and clearing the summit would have been simple. The Giro organization seemed to be quite happy to save the big, muscular Moser the trouble of going up the mountain.

It is not clear to me that Fignon would have been able to take a lot of time out of Moser if the Stelvio had been run. The stage was scheduled to be run from the less challenging south-facing side, not the legendary 48-switchback Trafoi climb. After cresting the pass, the riders would have had a long technical descent and then a 50-kilometer flat run-in to Merano. Would Fignon have been able to hold a large gap on the descent and the road to Merano from Moser who was both a skilled descender and the superior time trialist? It's all conjecture but in my opinion if Fignon had been able to create a gap on the ascent, it probably would have been erased by the time the he arrived in Merano.

The final time trial where Moser took the Pink Jersey from Fignon has problems, unless you are Francesco Moser. As Fignon told historian Les Woodland in a *Procycling* magazine interview, "In the time trial, just get out the tapes from the television and see for yourself. It's very clear. The television helicopter was flying just behind him. You can see from the images. They are all from low down and behind him, so that the blades of the helicopter were pushing him along. Then look at the pictures of me and they're all taken from in front of me, so that while the helicopter was pushing Moser along, it was pushing me back." Fignon later said the turbulence from the helicopter came close to knocking him off his bike a couple of times. Furthermore, Moser rode the time trial strangely, staying in the center of the road, even in the corners where shooting the apex would have shortened his distance, which all professional riders normally do.

Moser countered, "Listen, the helicopter simply could not have flown that low. It would have had to have been just above our heads to make a difference. The story is so stupid because it's just impossible."

Clearly irritated by what he sees as French disinformation, in another interview he said, "One must remember the *crono* was in Verona on roads lined with trees and buildings." He further said that the helicopter was flying around all day, filming most of the riders but that he only noticed it in the last 100 meters or so. He said that even if it was trying to blow him along, it wasn't around long enough to make any difference. Further, it must be noted that Moser had soundly trounced Fignon in the stage fifteen time trial by a solid 88 seconds. He was the better man against the clock and Fignon said Moser was getting stronger as the Giro progressed.

The president of the race jury, a Belgian, said he followed Moser and that the helicopter in no way aided the Italian. He further remarked that he had never seen a rider go so hard in a time trial.

Moser is adamant that he won the race because he was the strongest while Fignon died believing he was robbed of victory in the Giro.

Final 1984 Giro d'Italia General Classification:
1. Francesco Moser (GIS-Tuc Lu) 98 hours 32 minutes 20 seconds
2. Laurent Fignon (Renault-Elf) @ 1 minute 3 seconds
3. Moreno Argentin (Sammontana) @ 4 minutes 26 seconds
4. Marino Lejarreta (Alfa Lum-Olmo) @ 4 minutes 33 seconds
5. Johan Van der Velde (Metauro Mobili) @ 6 minutes 56 seconds

Climbers' Competition:
1. Laurent Fignon (Renault-Elf): 53 points
2. Flavio Zappi (Metauro Mobili): 40
3. Moreno Argentin (Sammontana): 30

Points Competition:
1. Urs Freuler (Atala-Campagnolo): 178 points
2. Johan Van der Velde (Metauro Mobili): 172
3. Francesco Moser (GIS-Tuc Lu): 166

Winning a Grand Tour can require perfection in all the details. Fignon's final deficit was less than the 88 seconds he lost by not eating enough on the way to Block Haus. He did, though, go on to deliver a splendid performance in the Tour, easily beating Bernard Hinault by over ten minutes.

1985 Was the Giro organization stung by the harsh criticism of the Giro routes of the early 1980s, which seemed to be made for Italy's non-climbing stars? It seems there was some reforming going on with the announcement of the 1985 course. It had climbing starting from stage three, somewhat challenging mountains in the middle of the schedule and a couple of hard stages near the end.

The field was big, both in numbers and quality. There were 180 entrants spread over 20 teams, including all of the Italian professional teams and one from the USA. The list of formidable riders included Moser, Contini, Lejarreta, Visentini, van Impe, Saronni, Johan Van der Velde and two from La Vie Claire, Hinault and Greg LeMond.

Fignon could not ride. Although he started the season well, winning the Coppi-Bartali Week in Italy and taking a third in the Flèche Wallonne, an inflamed Achilles tendon required surgery, keeping the gifted Frenchman out of both the Giro and the Tour.

Greg LeMond had come in third in the 1984 Tour and the breach between Hinault and LeMond that began with the 1985 Tour was still in the future. For now, Hinault was the world's most potent racing machine, LeMond was a fast-rising, extraordinary talent and they were on the same team. If Moser wanted to repeat his 1984 win, he would have to ride extraordinarily well.

The 6.65-kilometer prologue in Verona went to an obviously in-form Moser with Visentini second at 7 seconds and Hinault in sixth place, 15 seconds slower. Moser got to start where he left off the previous June, in pink.

He didn't get a chance to get comfortable in the leader's jersey because stage two was a team time trial, won by Saronni's Del Tongo squad, giving Saronni the lead. The aerodynamic revolution had come to the professional peloton. Many of the teams sported disc, or as they were then called, lenticular wheels, as well as cow's horn handlebars and sloping top tubes.

Stage four went into the Dolomites via the Passo Costalunga to soften the legs before a hilltop finish at Selva di Val Gardena. Things were together for the final climb when Lejarreta dropped the hammer hard. Hinault reached deep into his reserves and managed to join the Spaniard, as did Baronchelli, Visentini and Hubert Saiz. The break stuck, with Saiz winning the sprint and Visentini becoming the new leader. Moser finished two minutes back while Saronni's Giro was already over after he lost more than four minutes. LeMond showed the La Vie Claire one-two punch by winning the field sprint, coming in sixth, 1 minute 20 seconds back.

The next day, after one of his riders was relegated for dangerous sprinting, Malvor's director Dino Zandegù threatened to withdraw from the Giro in protest. As usual, it was an empty threat and the team remained in the race.

The Giro then headed down the Adriatic side of Italy. La Vie Claire rode at the front, constantly attacking and harassing the peloton. Visentini declared in a press conference that the Hinault of this Giro was not the rider of years past and that Hinault was doing well only by virtue of his team's efforts.

With the stage twelve 38-kilometer individual time trial in Capua, just north of Naples, the Giro started in earnest. Here were the standings before the Capua stage:

1. Roberto Visentini
2. Bernard Hinault @ 28 seconds
3. Marino Lejarreta @ 1 minute 16 seconds
4. Francesco Moser @ 1 minute 36 seconds
5. Greg LeMond @ 2 minute 9 seconds

Hinault, having used the first two weeks of the Giro to ride into shape, won the time trial with Moser second at 53 seconds and LeMond third at 58 seconds. Visentini was sixth, 1 minute 42 seconds slower than Hinault. That gave a new General Classification and cause for Roberto to have a little bit more respect for Hinault:

1. Bernard Hinault
2. Roberto Visentini @ 1 minute 14 seconds
3. Francesco Moser @ 2 minutes 1 second
4. Greg LeMond @ 2 minutes 30 seconds

Stage fourteen finished atop the Gran Sasso, where Hinault seemed to be having an off day and let Moser gain a small gap on him on the final climb.

The next day Ron Kiefel, riding on the 7-Eleven team, became the first American to win a Giro stage when his squad chased down a fleeing Gerrie Knetemann, allowing Kiefel to cross the line in Perugia two seconds ahead of the former World Champion.

Stage seventeen, with the Prunetta and Abetone climbs, produced no real changes. When a break of good journeymen riders was allowed to gain over twenty minutes, the peloton left it up to the race leader and his team to bring them back. Hinault told the others that he and his team would not do it alone and rather than drag the entire peloton along, he would let the virtual *maglia rosa*, José-Luis Navarro, win the Giro. That got the chase going, cutting the break's lead to about ten minutes at the end.

If observers felt that perhaps Torriani was going to offer a course so hard that it might put an Italian victory in doubt, they were to be sorely disappointed. Stage nineteen had the Simplon and Gran San Bernardo Passes, and at the unveiling of the route, the entire Gran San Bernardo Pass was to be climbed. When the day's route maps were passed out, it turned out that Torriani had removed the steep final section of the top of the Gran San Bernardo from the day's schedule, stopping at the entrance to the tunnel, six kilometers from the summit. Hinault was livid over the change. The result? Moser led in 53 riders at the end of what should have been a tough Alpine stage, allowing Moser to pocket the 20-second time bonus.

For stage twenty, a short, 58-kilometer stage going uphill to Valnontey, near Aosta, La Vie Claire had LeMond pound away at the front for almost the entire stage, trying to make Moser work hard defending his second place and perhaps tire him a bit before the coming time trial. The result, after the peloton broke up, was a second American victory, this time by Andy Hampsten, beating Reynel Montoya and Marino Lejarreta, excellent climbers both, by a minute.

That left only the final time trial. Moser won the stage, but he was only able to beat Hinault by 7 seconds, not enough. As in the 1984 Fignon-Moser time trial, the French accused the television helicopter of carefully flying behind Moser to push him along. The alleged assistance enraged Hinault's sponsor, Bernard Tapie, who threatened to send up a private plane to intercept the helicopter. Tapie went on to spend six months in jail in 1997, not for aerial combat, but for financial irregularities in one of his companies.

That gave Bernard Hinault three Giro wins, only the second foreigner to do it (Merckx being the other, with five).

Final 1985 Giro d'Italia General Classification:
1. Bernard Hinault (La Vie Claire-Wonder-Radar) 105 hours 46 minutes 51 seconds
2. Francesco Moser (Gis Gelati-Trentino Vacanze) @ 1 minute 8 seconds
3. Greg LeMond (La Vie Claire-Wonder-Radar) @ 2 minutes 55 seconds
4. Tommy Prim (Sammontana-Bianchi) @ 4 minutes 53 seconds
5. Marino Lejarreta (Apilatte-Olmo-Cierre) @ 6 minutes 30 seconds

Climbers' Competition:
1. José-Luis Navarro (Gemeaz Cusin-Zor): 54 points
2. Reynel Montoya (Pilas Varta-Café de Colombia-Mavic): 47
3. Rafael Acevedo (Pilas Varta-Café de Colombia-Mavic): 38

Points Competition:
1. Johan Van der Velde (Vini Ricordi-Pinarello-Sidermec): 195 points
2. Urs Freuler (Atala-Campagnolo): 172
3. Francesco Moser (Gis Gelati-Trentino Vacanze): 140

1986

Torriani still played to the galleries of Saronni and Moser fans with a flattish parcours. Merckx called it "decapitated" and one writer lamented that a country of magnificent hills and mountains had shortchanged its national tour.

As in 1976, the Giro's Sicilian start was tragic. The first road stage had a mass crash and among the fallen was Emilio Ravasio of the Atala squad. The doctor took a quick look at him, thought he was fine and let him get back on his bike. He finished with several of the other fallen riders, about seven minutes behind stage winner Sergio Santimaria, who became the *maglia rosa*. Ravasio later fell into a coma and died about two weeks later. The tragedy brought to mind Portuguese rider Joaquim Agostinho who remounted after crashing during the Tour of the Algarve in 1984 and later fell into an irreversible coma, and Fausto Coppi's brother Serse, who thought he was fine after crashing in the Tour of Piedmont and later succumbed to head injuries.

There were more crashes. Just a few kilometers before the stage two finish in Catania a big smashup took down La Vie Claire's Giro captain Greg LeMond, costing the American rider more than a minute and a half. Some blamed the continual pileups on the high speed racing over the narrow Sicilian roads. In the peloton, riders would shake their fists at the television helicopters which they said were flying so low the rotor wash was blowing the riders around.

Before the Giro left Sicily there was a 50-kilometer team time trial. Saronni's Del Tongo squad took a nine-second victory over Moser's Supermercati Brianzoli team. LeMond's La Vie Claire squad, already a man short due to crashes, lost over a minute and a half. Racing had barely started and LeMond was down almost three and a half minutes.

The General Classification seemed like old times:
1. Giuseppe Saronni
2. Francesco Moser @ 10 seconds
3. Didi Thurau @ 12 seconds
4. Claudio Corti and Giambattista Baronchelli @ 16 seconds

A day later Baronchelli used the hills of Calabria to jet away from the pack, leaving teammate Moser to lead the field into Nicotera 18 seconds later. For all his high placings in the Giro, including two seconds and a third, Baronchelli had not yet spent a day in pink. Finally, in the thirteenth year of his pro career, he pulled on the *maglia rosa*. It must have been sweet for the man who had won the Baby Giro way back in 1973.

The next day LeMond squirted off the front in the final kilometers, soloing into Cosenza with a Saronni-led pack just 2 seconds behind.

Saronni seemed to be enjoying a renaissance. In the early 1980s, he had been one of the world's dominant riders but his legs had grown quiet. But when Visentini soloed into Potenza, Saronni was 11 seconds back, good enough to once again be the Pink Jersey with Baronchelli 8 seconds behind in the Overall.

Saronni couldn't be budged from his position at the top of the standings and the 46-kilometer time trial in Siena allowed him to increase his lead. LeMond might have done better than his fifth place, but he let himself get distracted. He had the fastest intermediate time, so fast that he caught Gianni Bugno and Stefano Colage. The two riders knew a good thing when it went by and drafted the steaming American. Infuriated by the Italians glued to his wheel, LeMond complained to the officials and got so rattled he used the wrong gear in the uphill finish in Siena.

Visentini, excellent against the clock, had crept up to third place, a minute and a half behind Saronni.

Could Saronni keep his lead in the Alps? Stage fourteen was the first test and after the hilltop finish in Sauze d'Oulx, Visentini gained another 21 seconds on Saronni, while Baronchelli lost a half-minute.

Torriani wanted to cancel the ascent of the San Marco pass, scheduled to be the major climb before the finish at the ski town of Foppolo, saying that with snow on the road it would be a difficult climb. This from the man who engineered stages like the famous Monte Bondone climb in 1956, where dozens of frozen riders, including the *maglia rosa*, quit in icy misery. LeMond, smelling a fix coming that would lock in Saronni's lead, got ugly. Arguing it was one of the few chances for him and the other climbers to challenge Saronni, he raised enough stink that Torriani kept the climb. It was good for Torriani and the Giro that the ascent was retained because it was truly memorable.

The Story of the Giro d'Italia

LeMond and Visentini hit the base of the climb at full gas. The peloton exploded as the contenders scrambled to get up to the flying pair. At the crest it was still LeMond and Visentini at the front, but Baronchelli, Pedro Muñoz, Claudio Corti and Franco Chioccioli had dragged themselves up to the duo. Further back, Saronni and Moser were already two minutes in arrears.

On the ascent to Foppolo, LeMond and Muñoz separated themselves from the other four with the Spaniard winning the stage. Twenty seconds later Visentini came into town, Baronchelli arriving another minute later, Moser and Saronni needing still another minute to arrive. Visentini was in pink and Moser was in high dudgeon. Moser and his director Gianluigi Stanga accused Baronchelli of betraying his teammate Moser by selling his services to Visentini.

After the Alps the General Classification looked like this:
1. Roberto Visentini
2. Giuseppe Saronni @ 1 minutes 6 seconds
3. Giambattista Baronchelli @ 1 minute 54 seconds
4. Greg LeMond @ 2 minutes 5 seconds
5. Claudio Corti @ 3 minutes 24 seconds
6. Francesco Moser @ 3 minutes 54 seconds

The next day Baronchelli abandoned, citing stomach problems.

Moser might have found the stiff climbs of the San Marco not quite to his liking, but a flat time trial where he could beat anyone alive was very much to his taste. The stage eighteen chrono to Cremona was just such a ride and Moser pulverized the competition, taking more than a minute out of anyone in the hunt for a high placing. LeMond, normally good against the clock, lost 1 minute 41 seconds, giving up third place to Moser.

That left the second to last stage, a trip through the Dolomites. Even with the Rolle, Pordoi, Campolongo and Gardena passes, the standings stayed where they were. LeMond gave it a desperate go, but he couldn't shake the others. The race was Visentini's.

Final 1986 Giro d'Italia General Classification:
1. Roberto Visentini (Carrera): 102 hours 33 minutes 56 seconds
2. Giuseppe Saronni (Del Tongo) @ 1 minute 2 seconds
3. Francesco Moser (Supermercati Brianzoli) @ 2 minutes 14 seconds
4. Greg LeMond (La Vie Claire) @ 2 minutes 26 seconds
5. Claudio Corti (Supermercati Brianzoli) @ 4 minutes 49 seconds

Climbers' Competition:
1. Pedro Muñoz (Fagor): 54 points
2. Gianni Bugno (Atala-Ofmega): 35
3. Stefano Giuliani (Supermercati Brianzoli): 32

Points Competition:
1. Guido Bontempi (Carrera): 167 points
2. Johan Van der Velde (Panasonic): 148
3. Paolo Rosola (Sammontana-Bianchi): 115

Carrera director Boifava had to be thrilled with his team's results. In addition to winning the General Classification, Guido Bontempi won five stages on his way to winning the points competition.

Using the form he gained riding the Giro, fourth placed Greg LeMond went on to win the Tour that July. This was Moser's last Giro. He accumulated an eloquent list of important single-day race wins including three consecutive Paris–Roubaix victories, yet for all of Torriani's attempts to help the big man, Moser won only that one troubled 1984 Giro.

three

1987–1991

The Giro Delivers Some of the Most Exciting Races in Its History

1987 Before the 1987 Giro started it was thought that this edition was going to be a battle between Roberto Visentini and Giambattista Baronchelli. This Giro was in fact contested by Visentini, the 1986 Giro champion, and Stephen Roche, both members of Boifava's Carrera team. It is strange that such a vicious intra-team rivalry was allowed to occur just after the 1985–1986 La Vie Claire bloodletting between Greg LeMond and Bernard Hinault that made those Tours de France such soap operas.

Roche had suffered his ups and downs. In 1981, not long after winning Paris–Nice, a blood disorder stalled his career. As he was starting to hit his stride, he crashed in the 1985 Paris Six-Day, badly injuring his knee. His 1986 was forgettable (probably not to the people paying his salary), prompting him to have knee surgery. The repaired Stephen Roche was a new man. In early 1987 he showed good form with firsts in the Tours of Valencia and Romandie and seconds in Liège–Bastogne–Liège and the Critérium International.

Visentini was the returning Giro champion but had attained no notable successes that spring. Writer Beppe Conti observed that the two riders were much alike, terrific in time trials and on the climbs and both difficult to manage. Roche in particular didn't get along with his directors and he didn't get along with Visentini. Visentini reciprocated the Irishman's dislike.

The official line from the team was that Carrera had two leaders and that team support would go to the rider most worthy of help. As far as Visentini was concerned, the team had only one leader and that was Roberto. Roche was resentful of what he saw as a loaded deck of cards. He was supposed to be available to support Visentini, but during that spring, Visentini had never turned a pedal to help Roche. Roche felt this arrangement was unfair because he was riding wonderfully well, bringing in high-value wins and placings for Carrera while Visentini so far had nothing to show for the season.

Visentini argued that Roche was focusing on the Tour and that he would be happy to help Roche win in France in July. But…Visentini had already booked a July vacation and Roche knew it. Roche had no plans to sacrifice his own chances to help a man who refused to reciprocate. Furthermore, Visentini hated riding the Tour.

The air was poisonous even before the race began. Visentini let it be known that if necessary to win the Giro, he would attack Roche. Now let's be fair. Visentini was the reigning Giro champion returning to defend his title and fully expected to have a unified team help him. He certainly had every right to that expectation. The failing was Carrera's in creating this dilemma.

Roche was almost completely isolated on the team, having his dedicated Belgian friend and *gregario* Eddy Schepers and mechanic Patrick Valcke as his only trustworthy support.

Visentini drew the first blood by winning the 4-kilometer prologue in San Remo. The next day Erik Breukink won the 31-kilometer half-stage, a ride from San Remo up to San Romolo, beating the pack by 19 seconds. Breukink was now in pink. That afternoon Roche won the 8-kilometer downhill San Remo time trial, beating Breukink by 6 seconds and Visentini by 7. Breukink remained the leader with a 14-second lead over Roche.

The Giro headed south via the Ligurian coast. At Lido di Camaiore, the Carrera team showed that they had the most horsepower when they won the 43-kilometer team time trial, beating second-place Del Tongo by 54 seconds. Baronchelli crashed near the end of the event, finishing well after his team, putting him out of contention.

After stage three the General Classification stood thus:
1. Stephen Roche
2. Roberto Visentini @ 15 seconds
3. Davide Cassani @ 52 seconds
4. Erik Breukink @ 53 seconds

The race continued its southward march with Roche in the lead. According to Roche, rather than acting as a loyal teammate, Visentini just rode on Roche's wheel, highlighting the adversarial relationship. In the rush to Montalcino in Tuscany, the Irishman was able to pad his lead a little, to 32 seconds.

By stage nine, the race had reached its southernmost point, Bari, and still it was Roche in the lead with Visentini at 32 seconds. Scottish climbing ace Robert Millar, riding for Panasonic, with Breukink and Phil Anderson for teammates, had been first over the majority of the rated climbs, earning him the green climber's jersey.

In three leaps the race made it to Rimini on the Adriatic coast for the first big event in the drama, an individual time trial up Monte Titano to San Marino. Visentini won the 46-kilometer event and took the lead. Roche's ride was dreadful. Blaming race jitters and a crash three days before, he came in twelfth, losing 2 minutes 47 seconds.

The new General Classification:
1. Roberto Visentini
2. Stephen Roche @ 2 minutes 42 seconds
3. Tony Rominger @ 3 minutes 12 seconds
4. Erik Breukink @ 3 minutes 30 seconds
5. Robert Millar @ 4 minutes 55 seconds

At this point everyone except Roche and Eddy Schepers thought the Carrera family fight, if not the Giro itself, was over. Visentini again announced that he would work for Roche in the Tour de France.

Roche, an intensely driven man, was burning with indignation and ambition and with Schepers he planned his revolt. They picked stage fifteen to put their plan into action, the first mountain stage with its three major ascents: Monte Rest, Sella Valcalda and a finish at the top of the Cima Sappada.

The story of the Sappada stage is one of the most famous in the modern history of the Giro. An aggressive descent of Monte Rest allowed Roche to separate himself from the pack, taking along Ennio Salvador and

Jean-Claude Bagot (whose loyalty had been purchased earlier when Schepers helped him win a stage). Boifava knew immediately what Roche was up to and was having none of it. He drove alongside the fleeing Irishman and told him to stop the attack. Roche refused, telling Boifava that if the other teams didn't mount a chase, he would win the stage by ten minutes and Carrera would win the Giro. Boifava was unmoved and ordered the Carrera team to bridge up to Roche. The Carrera squad buried itself working to close the gap and Visentini, a high-strung rider, seemed to be having an off-day and suffered badly during the pursuit.

The team chased like fiends, and finally, exhausted, they dropped out of the chase while Roche kept his escape going, leaving Visentini alone to try to salvage his jersey. Eventually a small group caught Roche, but Visentini was not among them. Phil Anderson and Jean-François Bernard were among those who did make the connection, then unsuccessfully tried to get away.

Johan Van der Velde won the stage with Roche in the second chase group, 46 seconds behind. A broken Visentini came in 58th, 6 minutes 50 seconds after Van der Velde. Roche now had a slender 5-second lead over neo-pro Tony Rominger while Visentini was sitting in seventh place, 3 minutes 12 seconds down.

All Italy erupted with fury. The Italian papers blared what they believed was Roche's betrayal of a teammate who was in pink and who had deserved the unstinting support of all members of the Carrera team. Moreover, Roche had been insubordinate. He had been given a direct order by his director to stop the break and Roche had refused. Carrera management was furious and threatened to keep Roche out of the Tour if he insisted upon winning the Giro. That evening team director Boifava, beside himself with anger over Roche's buccaneering, reminded Roche that before the stage, Carrera had a five-minute lead on Rominger, now they had only five seconds (thanks in no small part to Boifava's chasing the Roche break).

Visentini told the papers that someone (meaning Roche) was going home that evening and Boifava ordered Roche not to speak to the press. Roche ignored the command, feeling that if he didn't speak, no one else would present his case.

Roche's taking the Pink Jersey so enraged the *tifosi* that Roche was given police protection. He even went on television to plead for sanity.

He later wrote that he was frightened as the fans spit on him and even hit him. Because of the inflamed passions, that day after the Sappada stage is called the "Marmolada Massacre". It had five big climbs, the final one being the Marmolada, also called the Passo Fedaia. Visentini tried to get away, but Roche marked his every move. While Roche was obviously protecting his lead, another day of what appeared to the Italians of riding against his teammate cost Roche dearly in the eyes of the Italian fans. Second place Rominger lost time that day, but there was no other serious change to the standings.

On the big climbs that followed the Sappada stage, Millar stayed with Roche, riding at his side to protect him from assault while Eddy Schepers did the same. Visentini tried to make Schepers crash, even boasting about his attempted mayhem. The feelings on both sides were raw.

Stage seventeen was the last day in the Dolomites and again, the situation was unchanged. Heading to the Alps and the final time trial, the General Classification stood thus:

1. Stephen Roche
2. Erik Breukink @ 33 seconds
3. Robert Millar @ 2 minutes 8 seconds
4. Flavio Giupponi @ 2 minutes 45 seconds
5. Marco Giovannetti @ 3 minutes 8 seconds
6. Marino Lejarreta @ 3 minutes 12 seconds
7. Roberto Visentini @ 3 minutes 24 seconds

During this Carrera family fight, Torriani and the Giro management were reasonably impartial. Roche said the Giro boss whispered encouragement to him when they would meet. In any case, the incredible drama was selling papers and riveting everyone's attention to his race. Torriani probably couldn't believe his good fortune.

The equilibrium remained over the Alpine climbs of stage nineteen and Roche's slim lead held. It was the twenty-first stage to Pila that Roche showed he was deserving of the *maglia rosa* when he, Robert Millar and Marino Lejarreta broke clear and arrived in Pila over two minutes ahead of the first group of chasers. This moved Millar into second place. Visentini, suffering a terrible loss of morale, lost another six minutes.

The 1987 Giro ended with a 32-kilometer time trial. Visentini didn't start, having broken his wrist in a fall in the penultimate stage. Roche won it, cementing his ownership of the lead. While his Carrera team had been deeply divided, especially after Roche's attack on the Sappada stage, the squad slowly came around to the fact that he would probably win the Giro and therefore yield a good payday for all of them. Roche says that in the final stages he had plenty of support from the team.

Stephen Roche (right) in stage twenty-one.

But he didn't get it from the *tifosi*. To this day the Italians speak bitterly of Roche's betrayal of Visentini.

Final 1987 Giro d'Italia General Classification:
  1. Stephen Roche (Carrera) 105 hours 39 minutes 40 seconds
  2. Robert Millar (Panasonic) @ 3 minutes 40 seconds
  3. Erik Breukink (Panasonic) @ 4 minutes 17 seconds
  4. Marino Lejarreta (Orbea-Caja Rural) @ 5 minutes 11 seconds
  5. Flavio Giupponi (Del Tongo-Colnago) @ 7 minutes 42 seconds

Climbers' Competition:
  1. Robert Millar: (Panasonic) 97 points
  2. Jean-Claude Bagot (Fagor): 53
  3. Johan Van der Velde (Gis Gelati): 32

Points Competition:
1. Johan Van der Velde (Gis Gelati): 175 points
2. Paolo Rosola (Gewiss-Bianchi): 171
3. Stephen Roche (Carrera): 153

Visentini began his racing career by going from one triumph to another, including being Amateur Italian Road Champion and Amateur World Time Trial Champion, his promise being fulfilled with his 1986 Giro win. After the Sappada stage he never again won an important race. He retired to run the family funeral home in 1990 and has had little contact with the cycling world ever since.

Roche, on the other hand, had a brilliant 1987. For all of his trouble with Carrera, Roche, with grudging and equivocal support from his team, was the leader of their Tour de France contingent and raced to a brilliant win. He capped the Giro/Tour double with victory at the World Championships. He joined Merckx as the second rider in cycling history to win the Giro, Tour and World Championship in the same year.

Early the next year he re-injured his knee and from that point he was never a contender for overall victory in Grand Tours. He won several important shorter stage races before retiring in 1993.

1988

The 1988 Giro is memorable in no small part because it was a tough course contested by an excellent field. Great races are not made by watering down the route to favor particular riders. From the dawn of stage racing, Henri Desgrange worked to make the Tour great through hard but objectively-officiated racing. In 1988, the Giro rose to the call.

The 3,579-kilometer route was run without a single rest day, a schedule that would be against today's rules which require a Grand Tour to have two rest days.

The previous year Greg LeMond was nearly killed in a hunting accident. Hit with 40 shotgun pellets, he suffered a collapsed lung and lost three-quarters of his blood. Anxious to resume his career, he was already back on the bike and racing. He signed with PDM and was going to try to ride the Giro a little more than a year after he was shot.

The real contenders included Jean-François Bernard (third in the 1987 Tour with two stage wins), Gianni Bugno, Urs Zimmermann (third in the 1986 Tour), Erik Breukink (third in the 1987 Giro), Pedro Delgado (second in the 1987 Tour) and Andy Hampsten (winner of the 1986 and '87 Tours of Switzerland).

A secondary list should include Tony Rominger (second in the Tirreno–Adriatico earlier in the year) and the dedicated and determined Franco Chioccioli. Chioccioli was troubled by too many chiefs on his team: he was sitting third on Del Tongo's totem pole below Saronni and Flavio Giupponi. Twelve of the twenty teams entered were foreign, showing the Giro's slow change from important Italian race to one which had enough international presence to give the foreign sponsors the publicity they craved.

Starting in the hilly city of Urbino with a 9-kilometer individual time trial, Jean-François Bernard took the first Pink Jersey with Tony Rominger second at 3 seconds. None of the other big names lost serious time except Greg LeMond, who was struggling and already down 1 minute 27 seconds.

The race headed south down the Adriatic side of Italy. During stage four, while the peloton seemed to be happy riding *piano*, Cyrille Fancello and Massimo Podenzana went off in search of adventure. Podenzana dropped his companion and rode in for a solid five-minute victory over the lackadaisical peloton, making Podenzana the leader with Bernard second, 4 minutes 32 seconds behind.

A 40-kilometer team time trial was ridden that afternoon. In this Giro, the teams' real time counted in the General Classification. Del Tongo won it with Carrera second at 11 seconds. Podenzana's Atala team came in seventeenth, 2 minutes 36 seconds back, but still good enough to leave Podenzana in pink.

The race headed west and then north up Italy's western side. After stage five finished in Santa Maria Capua Vetere, near Naples, LeMond called it quits. It was too soon after his accident to be contesting a Grand Tour.

Stage six drew the first blood by going over central Italy's Apennines, with a hilltop finish at Campitello Matese. Franco Chioccioli soared to the top of the mountain, beating the chasing pair of Hampsten and Zimmermann by twelve seconds. A group with Bernard, who was marking Visentini, came in at 35 seconds. Chioccioli's attack brought him up to second place.

The new General Classification:
1. Massimo Podenzana
2. Franco Chioccioli @ 45 seconds
3. Urs Zimmermann @ 1 minute 18 seconds
4. Roberto Visentini @ 1 minute 40 seconds
8. Andy Hampsten @ 2 minutes 38 seconds

The top standings remained unchanged over next five stages, the only excitement being the cancellation of stage eleven when a group of demonstrators blocked the finish line.

Stage twelve had four rated climbs with a finish at the top of the Selvino. The days in the high mountains had begun. Del Tongo's manager Pietro Algeri decided to gamble on Chioccioli's excellent form and had Saronni and Giupponi keep the speeds high during much of the stage, bringing the best riders to the base of the final ascent together. Once on the climb, Hampsten scooted away with Delgado. They clawed out a fifteen-second gap on the group containing Breukink, Zimmermann, Bernard, Visentini and Chioccioli. Hampsten won the stage and Chioccioli took the Pink Jersey. Podenzana, too big to be playing in the hills with these boys, lost 16 minutes 5 seconds.

The General Classification:
1. Franco Chioccioli
2. Urs Zimmermann @ 33 seconds
3. Roberto Visentini @ 55 seconds
4. Flavio Giupponi @ 1 minutes 10 seconds
5. Andy Hampsten @ 1 minute 18 seconds

This takes us to the legendary 120-kilometer stage fourteen of the 1988 Giro d'Italia with its crossing of the Aprica, a trip partway up the Tonale and then a left turn up the south face of the Gavia pass with a final steep, technical descent into Bormio. The day was wet and cold. Until the start Torriani had been considering an alternate route because of the possibility of bad weather. It would end up being, in the words of *La Gazzetta*, "the day the big men cried."

Over the first two climbs, the cold, wet riders stayed together. When they began ascending the Gavia with its patches of fifteen percent gradient (back then, only the Gavia's switchback turns were paved), it began to snow and as the riders continued up the pass, it got ever colder.

Johan Van der Velde, in just shorts and short sleeves, was first over the top. He was followed a few seconds later by Breukink, Hampsten and then by Chioccioli and Marco Giovannetti.

Breukink and Hampsten had dropped the Italians well before the summit and crested together. The conditions were appalling; the road was frozen and when the riders began the descent, their brakes wouldn't work on the frozen rims. Some had their gears jammed up with ice. Van der Velde gave up, dismounted his bike, waited for warmer clothes

Hampsten in the snow

to be brought from the team car and descended the steepest part of the pass on foot. He lost 47 minutes that day.

Hampsten and Breukink pressed on down the steep, icy descent and into Bormio where Breukink won the sprint and Hampsten donned the *maglia rosa*.

The new General Classification:
1. Andy Hampsten
2. Erik Breukink @ 15 seconds
3. Franco Chioccioli @ 3 minutes 54 seconds
4. Urs Zimmermann @ 4 minutes 25 seconds
5. Flavio Giupponi @ 4 minutes 55 seconds

Let's look at some of the important riders and what happened to them on that harrowing descent. Chioccioli is still bitter about that day, saying he was only 40 seconds behind Hampsten when he reached the top, but he was wearing shorts and a short sleeve jersey. He was still the virtual *maglia rosa*, yet, incredibly, the team car was back with Giupponi; Chioccioli said he had to make it to Bormio with no hat or even warm gloves. Feeling abandoned by his team, Chioccioli's morale was shattered and after the Gavia stage he stopped riding offensively for the rest of the Giro.

Breukink had to take both feet out of the pedals to balance his bike on the descent. Hampsten had been descending ahead of him and Breukink only saw him in the final kilometers of the stage. He closed the gap and seeing that Hampsten was at his limit, out-sprinted him for the stage win.

Most of the teams were unprepared for the terrible conditions, even though they knew the weather was going to be rough at the top of the Gavia. The directors may not have expected the dantesque conditions they met, but the slovenly way most of the directors took care of their riders was deplorable.

Mike Neel, Hampsten's 7-Eleven team director, was ready with warm drinks and clothes to give the riders at the summit. Also, Neel had a 25-tooth rear sprocket mounted on Hampsten's bike while the others were thrashing 23s. In many ways, Hampsten's leadership in the Giro was one of preparation meeting opportunity. Even with Neel's foresight, 7-Eleven rider Bob Roll went to the hospital with hypothermia. He recovered quickly and was on the starting line the next day.

Unfairly, many in the press and the peloton thought Hampsten's position the result of good fortune rather than careful riding by a man who could climb as well as any in the world. The next day he got his first test as the new owner of the Pink Jersey. The fifteenth stage was originally scheduled to start in Bormio and go up the south face of the Stelvio with the finish at the Merano 2000 ski station.

It was snowing at the top of the Stelvio, so Torriani had the race start over the hill in Spondigna, just beyond the Stelvio descent. The riders faced a slightly downhill roll along the valley into Merano followed by a stiff climb to the ski station. Bernard went away at the base of the ascent with Urs Zimmermann for company until Zimmermann couldn't take the Frenchman's searing pace. Alarmed by the growing gap, Hampsten chased, but only hard enough to keep Bernard in sight, managing to gain a little time on Breukink in the process.

Bad weather continued to harass the riders. Stage sixteen, to Innsbruck in Austria, went over several difficult passes in cold and snow. The riders stopped a couple of times, hoping that Torriani would cancel the stage. Not this Giro. Breukink's director Peter Post had his team ride hard, causing a split that left only Hampsten and Breukink of the highly placed riders in the front group. The chasers nearly caught the leaders and the day's result was a few seconds added to the gap Hampsten and Breukink had on the rest of the contenders.

Hampsten had the same problem as many of the best pure climbers, questionable time trial skills. With a 40-kilometer individual test coming in the final stage, Hampsten had to pad his lead, otherwise he'd get run over by Breukink, a more complete rider.

He did get the bit of insurance he needed in stage eighteen, an 18-kilometer uphill time trial. Hampsten won the stage while Breukink was fifth, 64 seconds slower. Hampsten also pocketed the 20-second stage winner's time bonus. Bernard, feeling that he had lost the Giro, abandoned, hoping for better in the Tour. He didn't finish the Tour either.

The General Classification stood thus:
1. Andy Hampsten
2. Erik Breukink @ 1 minute 51 seconds
3. Franco Chioccioli @ 11 minutes 29 seconds
4. Marco Giovannetti @ 14 minutes 40 seconds
5. Pedro Delgado @ 14 minutes 51 seconds

It almost all came undone for Hampsten in stage nineteen. Zimmermann and Stefano Giuliani blasted away from the pack and carved out a large lead. The alarms went off in the peloton because Zimmermann, a racer not to be toyed with, was now the virtual *maglia rosa* and was cruising to victory. By the end of nearly three weeks of racing, Hampsten's team was a wreck. Instead, Breukink's Panasonic riders and the Del Tongo squad, looking after the interests of both Flavio Giupponi and Chioccioli, took up the chase. Giuliani and Zimmermann weren't seen until the stage's end, but the gap was narrowed enough to keep Hampsten at the top of the standings. Zimmermann was now second.

Now only the final stage's 43-kilometer individual time trial stood between Hampsten and final victory. Bad weather had dogged the riders this year and the final stage was ridden in the rain. Breukink was tiring and came in fifth, beating Hampsten by only 23 seconds.

Hampsten's victory was clear-cut. He not only won the General Classification, he took the Climbers' prize and was third in the points. For the second year in a row, there were no Italians on the podium.

Final 1988 Giro d'Italia General Classification:

1. Andy Hampsten (7-Eleven-Hoonved) 97 hours 18 minutes 56 seconds
2. Erik Breukink (Panasonic-Isostar) @ 1 minute 43 seconds
3. Urs Zimmermann (Carrera Jeans-Vagabond) @ 2 minutes 45 seconds
4. Flavio Giupponi (Del Tongo-Colnago) @ 6 minutes 56 seconds
5. Franco Chioccioli (Del Tongo-Colnago) @ 13 minutes 20 seconds

Climbers' Competition:

1. Andy Hampsten (7-Eleven-Hoonved): 59 points
2. Stefano Giuliani (Chateau d'Ax-Salotti): 55
3. Renato Piccolo (Gewiss-Bianchi): 49

Points Competition:

1. Johan Van der Velde (Gis Gelati-Bruciatori Ecoflam): 154 points
2. Rolf Sørensen (Ariostea): 131
3. Andy Hampsten (7-Eleven-Hoonved): 128

1989 Vincenzo Torriani, the grand old *patrono* of the Giro, was in failing health. Since 1975 he had been collaborating in running the Giro with Neapolitan lawyer Carmine Castellano, Castellano's assistance being limited at first to handling the logistics of southern Giro stages. Castellano moved to Milan in the 1980s and became more deeply involved in organizing the race. Although Torriani was credited as co-director though 1992, Castellano actually took over running the race in 1989. In the later years of Torriani's tenure, the Giro had opened up to become an important international race. Under Castellano, during the mid and late 1990s, the Giro would again become more of an Italian competition with fewer of the big international teams riding.

While Castellano was effectively in charge, Torriani hadn't gone home just yet. When he phoned Laurent Fignon to entice him to ride the 1989 Giro, he told Fignon that it was, "one of the toughest in history". The 1989 edition was indeed loaded with mountains, plus days of heavy roads and again was run without a rest day. World Road Champion Maurizio Fondriest said of the 1989 route, "With a course like this, Moser would never have won."

After winning the Tour for a second time in 1984, Fignon was plagued by injuries and went into a deep decline. In 1987 he began to recover and in 1988, beating Fondriest in a two-up sprint, he won Milan–San Remo. In 1989 he astonished the cycling world with a second consecutive Milan–San Remo victory. His squad, however, was a shadow of the powerful team that had supported him in the early 1980s. He and his director Cyrille Guimard now owned the team and Fignon wrote that Guimard had become penny-wise and pound-foolish in his management which was reflected in the reduced quality of the team and support staff.

Torriani pulled out his checkbook and was able to induce Fignon to return to the Giro, but the Frenchman had no trust in Torriani, calling him the "same old bandit".

Hampsten's 7-Eleven team also returned, but their real goal was the Tour in July. Looking at the 3,418-kilometer, 22-stage race, Hampsten told Fignon that this race would not be won by the strongest man in the peloton, but by the smartest.

After his abortive 1988 attempt to ride the Giro, LeMond returned with a new team, ADR, a squad made largely of Classics riders and generally unsuited to Grand Tours. LeMond's fitness for shorter races was tolerable: he came in fourth in the March two-day Critérium International. A three-week race would be an entirely different challenge.

After mass defections to other teams at the end of 1988 season, Alfa Lum found itself without riders. Maurizio Fondriest, for instance, moved from Alfa Lum to Del Tongo after winning the World Championship. In a perfect *deus ex machina,* a solution presented itself to the team management. The year before, the Soviet Union relaxed its ban on its riders turning pro. Alfa Lum pounced and signed up the cream of Russian cycling and instantly had a squad of fine riders. Alfa Lum's entry into the 1989 Giro represents a giant step in the mondialization of professional cycling.

With a Sicilian start followed by stages taking the peloton first to the Dolomites and then the Alps before heading to a finish in Florence, 1989's route left little of Italy unvisited.

After the three Sicilian stages, Contini led and his Malvor teammate Flavio Giupponi, fourth the year before, was sitting 15 seconds back, in third place. That third stage was a 32-kilometer team time trial and Fignon's weak Super U squad was seventh, a minute and a half slower than winner Ariostea. Hampsten's 7-Elevens were sent to the ground after a black cat picked a bad time to cross the road, making the team second to last, more than three minutes behind Ariostea.

The southern mainland stages, though hilly, produced no changes to the standings until the eighth stage which finished atop the Gran Sasso d'Italia. Marino Lejarreta, Erik Breukink and Colombian Luis Herrera, winner of the 1987 Vuelta, jetted off the front, gaining six seconds over the main body of contenders. Breukink was in pink by a single second over Acácio Da Silva.

The first individual time trial was at the Adriatic coastal town of Pesaro. Polish rider Lech Piasecki, a time trial specialist, won the 36.8-kilometer stage, but it was Breukink's second place that really mattered. Fignon created no fear in his competitors (but apparently a little in his director Cyrille Guimard who expected better) with his eighth place, a half minute slower than Breukink. Fignon pronounced himself satisfied with the effort as it was his best time trial since 1986. Roche looked good with a third place that was only 8 seconds slower than the Dutchman's.

After ten stages and with the Dolomites coming in just three days, the General Classification stood thus:

1. Erik Breukink
2. Stephen Roche @ 46 seconds
3. Laurent Fignon @ 1 minute 1 second
4. Piotr Ugrumov @ 1 minute 5 seconds
5. Flavio Giupponi @ 1 minute 23 seconds

Probably no one at the time was aware that history was being made, but the winner of the twelfth stage was 22-year-old neo-pro Mario Cipollini. That was the first stage win in a long and prolific career that would later see him try to break Alfredo Binda's record of 41 Giro stage wins.

Leaving Padua, stage thirteen was a rainy trip to the top of Tre Cime di Lavaredo. At twenty kilometers to go, Herrera blasted off. Fignon said it was an almost exact replay of Herrera's attack on l'Alpe d'Huez in the 1984 Tour de France and he got the same orders from Guimard, "Stay put!" Guimard surely feared Fignon's blowing up while trying to chase one of the best specialist climbers ever. Herrera rocketed up the steep mountain, leaving a grumbling Fignon exactly 1 minute back with Breukink a further 4 seconds behind Fignon. The result of Herrera's attack was Breukink's remaining in pink with Fignon second at 53 seconds.

The *tappone* arrived and what a queen stage it was, with five major passes: Giau, Santa Lucia, Marmolada, Pordoi and the Campolongo. The finish was in Corvara, at the bottom of a short but twisty descent from the summit of the Campolongo. It was a horrible day in the mountains with dense and dangerous fog, snow, rain and temperatures near freezing. Fignon, who normally rode poorly in cold, wet weather, consented to having his entire body massaged with an extremely hot embrocation. The hot liniment put him in misery until the stage started, but he said he barely noticed the cold once he got going. He did several probing attacks and finally went hell-bent for leather on the Campolongo, taking a few riders with him, including stage winner Giupponi.

Breukink lost six minutes after going weak from hunger while Herrera crashed on the Marmolada. Fignon was the *maglia rosa* with Giupponi second at 1 minute 50 seconds and a now-interested-in-the-Giro Hampsten third, 2 minutes 31 seconds behind the Frenchman.

The terrible weather kept coming. The sixteenth stage was to have both the Tonale and the Gavia passes, but amid cries from the Italian press that Torriani was favoring Fignon by running the stage despite the bad weather, the stage was cancelled. Fignon was actually in trouble with an old shoulder injury making climbing in the cold almost impossible. But given his history of not only favoring Italians, but specific Italians, the accusation that Torriani was working to help a Frenchman win the Giro seemed strange. Furthermore, he had already confided to others that he hoped Giupponi would win.

For the moment, Mother Nature was on Giupponi's side. The 10.7-kilometer timed hill climb up Monte Generoso, just over the border in Switzerland, was held under overcast skies. The day was cool enough to make riding up the mountain torture for Fignon. Herrera won the stage and all of Fignon's competitors did well. Hampsten was third, only 35 seconds slower than the Colombian rocket. Roche and Giupponi were another half-minute behind. Fignon was seventeenth, 1 minute 45 seconds off Herrera's pace.

Fignon was losing ground:
1. Laurent Fignon
2. Flavio Giupponi @ 1 minute 15 seconds
3. Andy Hampsten @ 1 minute 21 seconds
4. Urs Zimmermann @ 2 minutes 29 seconds
5. Franco Chioccioli @ 2 minutes 43 seconds

There were two hilly stages in Liguria and Tuscany and they might have spelled doom for Fignon, who was struggling. And then the worst possible thing for Giupponi happened, the weather turned warm and Fignon revived. Fignon mounted an attack on the Passo di Cento Croci, but had to slow because the lead motorbike wasn't moving fast enough. He led out the sprint out, won the stage, and took back 10 seconds.

Another five rated climbs awaited the riders in the penultimate stage, and this time Fignon came close to losing the race. He was marking Giupponi and while following him on a descent, crashed with Belgian Claude Criquielion. By this point Fignon's exhausted team was in tatters, leaving him without support when he needed it most. Fignon said Giupponi and Hampsten used the opportunity of the crash to

Fignon in pink, with Gianni Bugno

attack. Fignon had no choice but to straighten his handlebars and go after them, which he did, catching them after a ten-kilometer chase. Showing that there was no damage from the crash and chase, Fignon won an intermediate sprint, snaffling up five precious bonus seconds.

Gianni Bugno then took off and no one saw him until the end of the stage, but Fignon was third at the finish in Prato for another 3-second bonus. Going into the final stage, a 53.8-kilometer time trial finishing in Florence, Fignon had a 1 minute 31 second lead over Giupponi, who was waging a never-say-die battle down to the last stage. The last two stages were so hard, fifteen riders who thought they were going to make it to the end either retired or were eliminated.

Lech Piasecki won the time trial, but second place was a shock. It was Greg LeMond, more than a minute ahead of third-place Giupponi. He had been suffering like a dog almost the entire Giro, sometimes barely making it to the stage finish before the time cut-offs. Desperate and miserable, he called his wife, Kathy, in Belgium and worried that he might not be able to continue. She told him to tough it out and then flew down to Italy to give him support. LeMond continued to flog himself and towards the end he finally began to find some of his old form.

And Fignon? He came in fifth, 16 seconds slower than Giupponi, good enough to clinch the Giro. He was only the third Frenchman to win the Giro, after Anquetil and Hinault, and as of this writing no Frenchman has won it since.

Merckx thought that without his big time loss in the stage three team time trial, Hampsten could have been the 1989 winner. He certainly would have been in the fight.

Final 1989 Giro d'Italia General Classification:
1. Laurent Fignon (Super U): 93 hours 30 minutes 16 seconds
2. Flavio Giupponi (Malvor-Sidi) @ 1 minute 15 seconds
3. Andy Hampsten (7-Eleven) @ 2 minutes 46 seconds
4. Erik Breukink (Panasonic) @ 5 minutes 2 seconds
5. Franco Chioccioli (Del Tongo) @ 5 minutes 43 seconds

Climbers' Competition:
1. Luis Herrera (Café de Colombia): 70 points
2. Stefano Giuliani (Jolly Componibili): 38
3. Jure Pavlič (Carrera): 34

Points Competition:
1. Giovanni Fidanza (Chateau d'Ax-Salotti): 172 points
2. Laurent Fignon (Système U): 139
3. Erik Breukink (Panasonic): 128

Both LeMond and Fignon were back. Neither rider ever again found the extraordinary magic of the mid 1980s, but they were both so fabulously talented that even a diminished Fignon and LeMond were still better riders than anyone else.

After the Giro, while Fignon wanted to do nothing more than celebrate his Grand Tour comeback, a grim-faced Guimard insisted upon being the skunk at the picnic. Guimard was already planning their July Tour de France campaign and warned, "LeMond will be up there at the Tour."

Fignon was dumbfounded that LeMond, who had been nowhere for three weeks of the Giro, had ended up taking second in the final time trial. About Guimard's prophetic hand-wringing, Fignon wrote, "We all know what happened in July, 1989." Not only did LeMond win the Tour that July, he became World Champion, outsprinting one of those Alfa Lum Russians, Dimitri Konyshev.

1990 The 1990 edition started deep in the south, in Bari, and made a giant Z on the Italian map as it headed north. It worked its way to the western coast of Tuscany and then to Cuneo in Piedmont; then a nearly due eastward march all the way to Klagenfurt in Austria before the final week in the Dolomites and the Alps. It was a 20-stage race totaling 3,450 kilometers, just 32 kilometers longer than in 1989.

Who were the favorites? 1989 Tour winner and reigning World Road Champion LeMond came with his powerful new "Z" team. So far that spring, he hadn't notched any notable placings and had come to the Giro to train for the Tour.

And there was the winner of 1989 Dauphiné Libéré, Charly Mottet, who had just won the Tour of Romandie and was turning into one of France's finest riders.

Fignon had come into the start of the 1990 season as the number one world-ranked cyclist, but by the time the Giro rolled around, he was again struggling. After a lackluster Classics season he arrived at the Giro feeling his form was questionable.

Marco Giovannetti had just finished winning the Vuelta, but he would surely be too tired to contest the Giro, especially against Italy's newest strongman, Gianni Bugno.

Bugno had entered his time of grace. In the spring of 1990 he had already won Milan–San Remo and the Giro del Trentino. The first race required speed and power, the second, raced in the Dolomites, was a test of climbing ability. Bugno was a complete rider and Fignon tipped him as the favorite.

Bugno blistered the 13-kilometer prologue at a scorching 50.92 kilometers per hour. He had laid down the law and taken the *maglia rosa* at the first opportunity. It was not as if there were no competitors. Thierry Marie, a specialist who had a habit of winning Tour de France prologues, finished 3 seconds slower.

But the climbing? Could he climb with the Grand Tour men whose form was carefully cultivated to peak in May? Trying to take some of the pressure off, Bugno said he would just try to take each stage as it came, but he said he was reasonably sure his adventure in pink would soon be over.

He was saying one thing but planning another. Two days later Bugno laid to rest any questions about his abilities in the mountains when the Giro ascended Mount Vesuvius. Waiting until the road got steep, Bugno took off alone to chase down the day's earlier escapees, a group that included climber Eduardo Chozas. No one reacted to Bugno's bold move, and in a flash he was up the road with a good gap. He caught all but Chozas, but Chozas' 26-second lead was small enough to keep Bugno in pink. It was a surprising expenditure of energy so early in a Grand Tour. He was riding as if he knew how much better he was than the others.

Stage five, in Abruzzo, took the riders through a badly lit tunnel where several riders, including Fignon, crashed. Bugno and his team emerged from the tunnel unhurt and four minutes ahead of Fignon. Doing the honorable thing, Bugno's Chateaux d'Ax squad slowed things down until Fignon, suffering from a painful dislocated hip, could catch up.

Gert-Jan Theunisse had tested positive for high levels of testosterone in the Flèche Wallonne (this was not his first positive) and during the Giro, the reconfirmation of that test became known. At the start of stage six, the riders staged a strike, saying they would not ride if Theunisse were part of the peloton. The seemingly friendless Theunisse promised to ride quietly. And so he did, eventually finishing the Giro fifteenth, almost a half-hour down on the winner.

The Giro started in earnest with stage six, a northwest run from Fabriano in Umbria up to Vallombrosa, just east of Florence. The country is hilly and the final climb up to Vallombrosa is a twenty-kilometer ascent with sustained sections of twelve percent gradient.

Bugno kept the pressure on almost from the gun, shattering the peloton, and of the Giro contenders, only Mottet, Lejarreta, Chioccioli and Piotr Ugrumov could stay with him. After doing a huge amount of work, incredibly, Bugno out-sprinted Ugrumov for the stage win. Fignon lost 78 seconds while LeMond dropped a quarter of an hour.

Gianni Bugno takes the stage at Vallombrosa.

The General Classification now stood thus:
1. Gianni Bugno
2. Daniel Steiger @ 1 minute 12 seconds
3. Joachim Halupczok @ 1 minute 24 seconds
4. Marino Lejarreta @ 1 minute 25 seconds
5. Federico Echave @ 1 minute 33 seconds
6. Piotr Ugrumov @ 1 minute 40 seconds

The next day in the Apennines made history. When Vladimir Poulnikov crossed the finish line first at the end of stage eight, he became the first Russian (OK, until 1991, Soviet Union) rider to win a

Giro stage. His compatriot Dimitri Konyshev was second. Times were changing. The day's rainy weather proved too much for Fignon's hip and the Frenchman abandoned. LeMond, still not finding his form, lost a half-hour.

An estimated quarter-million fans lined the Piedmont road between Castello di Grinzane and Cuneo to watch Italy's hero demolish his opposition in the stage nine individual time trial. Bugno didn't win, headwinds came up late in the day when the top riders rode, but his second place to Luca Gelfi after 68 kilometers of solo riding was enough to further distance himself from the rest of the field and to send the *tifosi* into ecstasies of joy.

After a couple of days of climbing and a long time trial, Bugno didn't seem to have any weaknesses:

1. Gianni Bugno
2. Marco Giovannetti @ 4 minutes 8 seconds
3. Charly Mottet @ 4 minutes 9 seconds
4. Federico Echave @ 4 minutes 41 seconds
5. Joachim Halupczok @ 5 minutes 6 seconds

As the peloton made its way to its stage fifteen appointment with the Dolomites, Greg LeMond started showing signs that things weren't hopeless. He took a shot at an intermediate sprint, and then in stage fourteen, went off on a break that at one point gained twelve minutes. He was caught, but the legs were coming back. Too late for the Giro, but July and the Tour weren't far off.

The first day in the Dolomites had six major climbs: the Valparola, Gardena, Sella, Pordoi, Marmolada and then another trip up Pordoi. Charly Mottet provided all of the energy of the day, attacking on the Marmolada, unhappily taking along a watchful Bugno who easily matched the Frenchman's efforts. Then Bugno, in another display of power and confidence, insisted upon leading the pair to the crest of the pass. The two worked together on the Pordoi before Bugno gifted the Frenchman the stage win.

At this point Bugno seemed invulnerable. Halupczok, 1989's World Amateur Champion, had probably done more than his 22-year-old body could take, and abandoned his miracle Giro ride with an inflamed knee. That autumn heart problems forced the young Pole to retire from cycling. He died of a heart attack in 1994, which some blamed on his use of the new drug EPO (more about this later). This allegation has no proof, but in the early 1990s seemingly healthy young endurance athletes started dying in their sleep. After a bad crash, Urs Zimmermann also had to retire.

The second mountain stage, which included the Mortirolo ascent for the first time, changed nothing: the top riders finished together. Bugno was effortlessly leading the Giro with Mottet 4 minutes 13 seconds behind.

That left only the final 39-kilometer time trial, with its uphill finish on Sacro Monte in Varese. It was a wet, windy day. Bugno, who had started the day with both front and rear disc wheels, soon regretted the choice. When he flatted, a bike change let him rectify the equipment error. Bugno won the stage with Lejarreta second, 1 minute 20 seconds back. LeMond's ever improving form showed with his twelfth place, but nothing like his second place in the final time trial the year before.

As Mario Cipollini won the final stage, Bugno joined the elite club of riders who had won the Pink Jersey on the first stage and worn it all the way to the end. Only Costante Girardengo (1919), Alfredo Binda (1927), and Eddy Merckx (1973) had been able to wear the jersey from "sunrise to sunset". Critics said that Bugno had prevailed against a weak field with only Mottet able to provide real competition. The field may not have been as strong as in previous or future editions, but nevertheless, Bugno had simply crushed 198 of his fellow professional bicycle racers.

One of those greats called it quits. Giuseppe Saronni retired after his 45th place. He had a long list of impressive victories that included two Giri (1979, 1983) and a Rainbow Jersey (1982). He went on to be a successful team director, managing the Italian Lampre squad.

LeMond went from 105th in the Giro to 1990 Tour de France champion.

One of runner-up Mottet's soigneurs, Willy Voet, wrote that Mottet insisted on riding without dope. Given the startling frankness of Voet's memoir, one has to assume Voet's assertion was true. Voet wrote that during the rare times Mottet took corticosteroids for therapeutic purposes (while his competitors were using them to improve their performances) he "would breathe fire", showing that Mottet's scruples forced him to leave a lot on the table. Voet said that because of the rampant doping around him, Charly Mottet "simply did not have the career that he merited."

Final 1990 Giro d'Italia General Classification:
1. Gianni Bugno (Chateau d'Ax-Salotti): 91 hours 51 minutes 8 seconds
2. Charly Mottet (RMO) @ 6 minutes 33 seconds
3. Marco Giovannetti (SEUR) @ 9 minute 1 second
4. Vladimir Poulnikov (Alfa Lum) @ 12 minutes 19 seconds
5. Federico Echave (Clas) @ 12 minutes 25 seconds

Climbers' Competition:
1. Claudio Chiappucci (Carrera): 74 points
2. Maurizio Vandelli (Gis-Benotto): 56
3. Gianni Bugno (Chateau d'Ax-Salotti): 48

Points Competition:
1. Gianni Bugno (Chateau d'Ax-Salotti): 195 points
2. Phil Anderson (TVM): 176
3. Mario Cipollini (Del Tongo): 176

1991

With no podium placings so far in 1991, LeMond was again riding the Giro in training for the Tour and didn't look to be a factor. The man who had given LeMond fits in the 1990 Tour after gaining over ten minutes in a *fuga di bidone* (a successful break of innocent-looking riders that gains a large time gap) finally finishing second, did have a good spring. Claudio Chiappucci won Milan–San Remo and the Tour of the Basque Country. A poor time trialist, Chiappucci was a fearless aggressor who would attack when his opponents least expected it.

Franco Chioccioli had been knocking around for nearly a decade (he was Best Young Rider in the 1983 Giro) and perhaps if he had been given warm clothing at the top of the Gavia Pass, he might have won the 1988 Giro. Nicknamed "Coppino" ("Little Coppi"), as was Italo Zilioli, for his slender, lanky build and resemblance to the *campionissimo*, Chioccioli still ached to remedy his 1988 defeat. There was nothing in his 1991 win column so far.

The Giro started on Sardinia and after three stages on the island, Franco Chioccioli was the *maglia rosa* with Bugno and Chiappucci trailing at 5 and 11 seconds respectively. Since Chioccioli was one of those riders who always had at least one bad stage during a Giro, he wasn't expected to take the Pink Jersey all the way to Milan.

In fact he didn't take it to the finish line in Sorrento after the Giro transferred to the mainland. Frenchman Eric Boyer on LeMond's "Z" squad romped away from the field and there seemed to be no enthusiasm to catch him. Chioccioli, with the responsibility of the Pink Jersey, buckled down and did most of the work (according to his own recounting of the stage), keeping Boyer from running away with the race. Boyer got to take the *maglia rosa* after finishing a half-minute in front of the pack. Chioccioli was sitting in second place at 3 seconds but promised that the next day's race through Abruzzo, with three rated climbs, would see a different Franco Chioccioli.

As the word was spoken, the deed was done. Chioccioli and Marino Lejarreta broke away on the final climb of the day, Monte Godi, and maintained a 50-second gap over the Chiappucci and Boyer-led chasers all the way to the town of Scanno. Chioccioli had taken back the lead with Lejarreta (winner of the 1982 Vuelta and fifth in the 1990 Tour) second at 8 seconds. Boyer, Chiappucci and Bugno were trailing roughly a minute back.

The next day, with another three rated climbs, was ridden without any particular aggression until the last hill, bad weather and the difficult descents on wet roads having kept the riders plenty busy. Things broke up on the last ascent, but the climb to Castelfranco wasn't enough to pry apart Bugno, Chioccioli, Lejarreta and Chiappucci. Fignon and Boyer each lost a minute and LeMond struggled in more than two and a half minutes after stage winner Vladimir Poulnikov.

Before the stage ten 43-kilometer individual time trial in Langhirano, near Parma, the General Classification stood thus:

1. Franco Chioccioli
2. Marino Lejarreta @ 8 seconds
3. Claudio Chiappucci @ 57 seconds
4. Vladimir Poulnikov @ 59 seconds
5. Gianni Bugno @ 1 minute 3 seconds

In those 43 kilometers Bugno grabbed the Giro by the scruff of the neck and gave it a good shake. He won the stage, beating Chiappucci and Chioccioli by about a minute. The new General Classification:

1. Franco Chioccioli
2. Gianni Bugno @ 1 second
3. Marino Lejarreta @ 26 seconds
4. Claudio Chiappucci @ 56 seconds
5. Massimiliano Lelli @ 1 minute 18 seconds

People who knew about these things said that Bugno appeared to have the Giro nailed. From here it was just a matter of turning the cranks and waiting for the race's arrival in Milan. Bugno was bubbling with optimism, and referring to Chioccioli's miniscule lead he said, "This second is not a problem."

LeMond started to show a little sparkle when he and Maximilian Sciandri squeezed out a five-second gap as the race roared into the Riviera town of Savona. One couldn't help feeling he might be repeating 1989 and 1990, dragging himself around the Giro and finding form just in time to win the Tour.

Chioccioli definitely wasn't dragging around. The twelfth stage had a hilltop finish on Monte Viso, an Alpine ascent near the French border and the source of the Po, Italy's longest river. Lelli was the first to make it through the heavy fog to the finish with Jean-François Bernard with Chioccioli and Lejarreta just three seconds in arrears. Bugno was the surprise. No one expected him to lose two minutes in the first day in the Alps. He was supposed to inflict this kind of damage on the others.

The second Alpine day concluded with two ascents to Sestriere and the order of finish was Spanish climber Eduardo Chozas followed in by Chiappucci, Lejarreta and Chioccioli. Bugno lost another 43 seconds.

Heading off to the Dolomites, Chioccioli led Lejarreta by 26 seconds and Chiappucci by 1 minute 23 seconds. Bugno, two and a half minutes down, wasn't the dominating rider he was the year before.

Three days in the Dolomites started with at trip to Aprica via the Mortirolo and Santa Cristina. Chioccioli gave a master class in bicycle racing when he attacked on the Mortirolo and after reaching the crest alone, continued riding solo for 50 kilometers. He lost ground towards the end, but in Aprica he still was a half-minute ahead of Bernard and Boyer, and 46 and 48 seconds ahead of his two nemeses, Chiappucci and Lejarreta respectively. LeMond finally called it quits and abandoned.

The next day with the Tonale and Gardena didn't change things.

The last Dolomite day was the *tappone* with the Pinei, Nigra, Pordoi, Fedaia and then a second climb to finish at the top of the Pordoi. Chioccioli escaped on the second ascent of the Pordoi, the pass Coppi had used several times to clinch Giro victories. That fact wasn't lost on the history-conscious *tifosi*. Chioccioli may not have liked being called "Coppino" but he cemented the image of the *campionissimo* in their minds with his masterful attack on Coppi's climb that took another 38 seconds from Chiappucci.

The relentless Lejarreta crashed and with a time loss of over six minutes, his spirited pursuit of Coppino was over. Chioccioli's nearest competitor now was Chiappucci, almost three minutes down. It was too much for Fignon, who was not only struggling to reach the condition he had enjoyed a couple of years ago, he was in the midst of a complete breakdown in his relationship with Cyrille Guimard. He was among the day's seven abandons.

The final obstacle to the year's *fuoriclasse* (outstanding champion) rider was a 66-kilometer time trial at Casteggio, near Parma. Incredibly, the man of the mountains was also superb against the clock (though the day's course did have a climb). Chioccioli flattened everyone; his nearest challenger Bugno was almost a minute slower. After nearly a decade of trying (his first Giro ride was 1982 where he came in 25th), Franco Chioccioli had won the Giro d'Italia in commanding fashion. There was no doubt he was by far the strongest man in the race. One of his first requests after the final stage in Milan was for everyone to stop calling him "Coppino". That didn't happen.

Final 1991 Giro d'Italia General Classification:
1. Franco Chioccioli (Del Tongo-MG): 99 hours 35 minutes 43 seconds
2. Claudio Chiappucci (Carrera Jeans) @ 3 minutes 48 seconds
3. Massimiliano Lelli (Ariostea) @ 6 minutes 56 seconds
4. Gianni Bugno (Gatorade-Chateau d'Ax) @ 7 minutes 49 seconds
5. Marino Lejarreta (ONCE) @ 10 minutes 23 seconds

Climbers' Competition:
1. Iñaki Gastón (Clas-Cajastur): 75 points
2. Claudio Chiappucci (Carrera Jeans): 69
3. Franco Chioccioli (Del Tongo-MG): 57

Points Competition:
1. Claudio Chiappucci (Carrera Jeans): 283 points
2. Franco Chioccioli (Del Tongo-MG): 239
3. Mario Cipollini (Del Tongo-MG): 191

Chioccioli's win with a dominance that seemed to come out of nowhere wasn't without controversy. French racer Erwann Menthéour was among those who accused the 1991 Giro champion as well as future Giro winner Evgeni Berzin of using the new performance improving drug EPO.

In July Bugno and Chiappucci ran into a Spanish buzz-saw that splintered their Tour ambitions. Using the classic Anquetil strategy of defensive riding in the mountains combined with absolute mastery in the time trials, Miguel Induráin won the 1991 Tour with a quiet, seemingly effortless ride that left the fans speechless and his competitors helpless.

By any measure Bugno's 1991 season was still excellent: a fourth in the Giro (with three stage wins), second in the Tour, victory in the Clásica San Sebastián, and Italian and World Road Championships.

four

1992–1997

Foreigners Dominate and Cycling Enters its Most Troubled Time Ever

1992 Something strange was afoot. Some riders from a few teams, specifically Spanish and Italian squads, seemed to display an inexplicable superiority over other riders and teams that should have been on the same level. Greg LeMond said that in 1990 his "Z" team was among the most powerful in the world. Yet, in a remarkable turnabout, the same "Z" riders could not keep up with the best teams in 1991 Tour. A new drug had entered the pharmacopoeia of the competitive cyclist, EPO. Without EPO, it was nearly impossible for a racing cyclist of the 1990s to compete effectively, so great was EPO's performance improvement.

Hematocrit is the measure of the percentage of blood volume occupied by red blood cells, which the body uses to feed oxygen to the muscles. Normal men of European descent have a hematocrit in the low- to mid-40s. It declines slightly as a response to the effects of training. It does not increase during a stage race, as many racers accused of its use would assert over the next decade—it goes down. Exceptional people exceed these hematocrit values by a significant amount. Damiano Cunego, winner of the 2004 Giro, through a twist of genetic fate, is said to have a natural hematocrit of about 53.

To improve their performances, endurance athletes took to using synthetic EPO (erythopoietin), a drug mimicking the natural EPO the body makes to signal the body to produce red blood cells, thus raising their hematocrits. This is not without danger, because as the hematocrit rises, so does the blood's viscosity. By the early- to mid-1990s endurance athletes were dying in their sleep because their lower resting heart rates couldn't shove the red sludge through their blood vessels. In the early 1990s at least a dozen bicycle racers died in their sleep. Writer Jean-François Quinet put the number of dead athletes much higher, estimating that 80 riders (both amateurs and pros used the drug) perished as a consequence of EPO abuse.

I spoke to a mechanic who traveled with a top-flight Spanish pro team in the mid-1990s. What he saw frightened him. The racers slept with heart-rate monitors hooked up to alarms. If a sleeping rider's pulse fell below a certain rate, the alarm went off, the rider was awakened, given aspirin and a saline injection to thin the blood and put on a trainer to get his heart rate up and blood flowing. This was clearly dangerous stuff at the doses racers were using and everyone knew it, but it had a gigantic payoff to the talented and lucky user. As *La Gazzetta* put it, there was a change in the hierarchy of some teams: the doctor was now more important than the director.

Nearly all of the top riders of the 1990s had accusations of EPO use leveled at them. Some have confessed and more than a few have had health problems ever since.

❧

Miguel Induráin entered the Giro with the clear plan of riding conservatively, using it as training for the Tour. Fignon resigned himself to racing in the lesser capacity of road captain and advisor to Bugno's Gatorade squad. Fignon was entered with teammates Giovannetti, Alberto Volpi and rising hope Ivan Gotti. Bugno took a pass on the May race to concentrate on preparing for the Tour.

Chioccioli hoped to repeat his dominating 1991 performance and Chiappucci, nicknamed "The Devil", had followed up his second place in the Giro with third in the Tour, winning the climbers' prize along the way.

Prologue specialist Thierry Marie was first in the 8-kilometer opening individual time trial in Genoa, beating Induráin by 3 seconds. The

Spaniard's supposed low-key ambitions were betrayed when he voiced disappointment at not having taken the *maglia rosa* at the gun. That must have frightened the other competitors who were hoping the '91 Tour winner was just in Italy for a training ride and espresso.

Two stages later, the pretense was over as Chiappucci and Induráin, fighting for supremacy in the Giro's first stages, blasted over the Scopetone, a climb just outside Arezzo where the stage finished. Maximilian Sciandri won the stage, but in the havoc of the climb, Marie was dropped, making Induráin the Pink Jersey.

Professional racers ride close together, much closer than amateur racing cyclists or enthusiasts on club rides. Because of this, they are constantly on the alert for trouble. Fignon explained that crashes in the pro peloton can involve a large portion of the pack if they can't hear brakes being applied up ahead, and that is a common occurrence because the television helicopters like to fly low to get good pictures. The din of the rotors makes it impossible to hear what is going on and if a crash has occurred up ahead, the riders in the back can't hear the brakes and the sound of the crashing bikes, and keep pedaling at race speed right into the catastrophe. During this third stage Induráin was so bothered by the television helicopter that he rode over to the race director's car to complain about the danger.

The next day's 38-kilometer time trial was Induráin's. Of the competitors, the closest was Chiappucci, more than a minute slower. The form that had won the Tour the year before was present at the 1992 Giro.

Heading south, the race went through the Apennines over roads that weren't challenging enough for anyone to mount an assault on the Pink Jersey, that opportunity presenting itself in stage nine, with a finish at the top of the Terminillo. The first serious attack came from the Latvian rider Piotr Ugrumov. Then Roberto Conti shot up the road and got a good gap, which he managed to keep for a while. Meanwhile Induráin, a bigger rider (6'2", 176 pounds or 1.88 meters, 79.8 kilograms) who didn't change speed quickly on climbs, was getting his engine going. Finally, he came roaring up to Conti with Chiappucci, Hampsten, Giovannetti and Herrera hanging on to his wheel for dear life. Fignon couldn't stay with him, neither could Chioccioli, whose short time in the sun as the master rider was over. With a kilometer to go, the Spaniard was still pulling his train up the mountain. Herrera, no danger in the General Classification, took off for the finish, but Chiappucci had to let the Induráin group go and gave up 30 seconds.

After a transfer back to Tuscany, it took two stages to bring the Giro to Bassano del Grappa and the Dolomites. Stage twelve went over the Staulanza, Giau and Falzarego passes, and at this point Induráin saw no point in wasting energy in offensive climbing. When an attack went off, he would slowly climb up to the attacker's wheel. Chioccioli and Chiappucci (who seemed to have formed an alliance in an effort to destabilize the Spaniard) knew they had to gain time in the mountains because they were completely helpless in time trials against their powerful opponent. But with each acceleration, Induráin would calmly and easily close the gap with a pedaling cadence that was high for such a big man. Franco Vona won the stage with Induráin and Chiappucci together just three seconds behind.

The next day, with the Campolongo, Pordoi and Bondone ascents, it was more of the same. Induráin had things under control as few racers in cycling history ever have.

The third to last stage, with its four major rated climbs, was the last chance for Chiappucci and Chioccioli to take the Giro. Chiappucci was the first over almost all of the climbs and Chioccioli, displaying terrific form, hammered away. But Induráin was not to be dropped. Content to ride defensively, he continually marked his attackers. Chioccioli at least got a stage victory to show for his trouble while Induráin, Chiappucci and Lelli finished right with him in Verbania.

The three days in the Alps changed nothing. It was almost as if Induráin were deciding who would be allowed to win a stage: Giovannetti got the seventeenth, Udo Bölts won the next one and the unrelenting Chioccioli was victor in the nineteenth stage. Always, the *maglia rosa* was right next to any challengers to his supremacy.

The final stage was a 66-kilometer time trial into Milan. Of course Induráin won it, catching Chiappucci just meters before the finish. Induráin biographer Javier Gárcia Sánchez said that the gratuitous catch was intended to give Chiappucci a psychological blow for the upcoming Tour de France. If that had been his intention, it was a waste of energy; in the Tour Chiappucci was undaunted. His unsuccessful attempt to unseat Induráin with a brave and brilliant ride in the Tour's Sestriere stage has become the stuff of legends.

This was Laurent Fignon's final Giro ride. He finished 37th and went on to earn 23rd in the Tour, winning a single stage. He retired from racing the following year and in 2010 died after a brave fight against cancer.

Final 1992 Giro d'Italia General Classification:
1. Miguel Induráin (Banesto): 103 hours 36 minutes 8 seconds
2. Claudio Chiappucci (Carrera Jeans-Tassoni) @ 5 minutes 12 seconds
3. Franco Chioccioli (MG-Bianchi) @ 7 minutes 16 seconds
4. Marco Giovannetti (Gatorade-Chateau d'Ax) @ 8 minutes 1 second
5. Andy Hampsten (Motorola) @ 9 minutes 16 seconds

Climbers' Competition:
1. Claudio Chiappucci (Carrera Jeans-Tassoni): 76 points
2. Roberto Conti (Ariostea): 45
3. Miguel Induráin (Banesto): 35

Points Competition:
1. Mario Cipollini (MG-Bianchi): 236 points
2. Miguel Induráin (Banesto): 208
3. Maximilian Sciandri (Motorola): 177

1993 This Giro had a good helping of foreign teams: Telekom from Germany; Motorola from the U.S.; Kelme, a Spanish team mostly made up of Colombians; GAN from France; Festina, registered in Andorra but with riders from all over; Artiach and Banesto from Spain. They would be competing in what was regarded as one of the hillier Giri in recent history.

Bugno's 1992 had been creditable with a third in the Tour and a second consecutive World Championship, but the days when he could win almost at will seemed to have passed.

That ability was present in the returning Giro champion, Induráin, who had followed up his 1992 Giro win with a commanding Tour victory, putting him in the elite club of Giro/Tour winners Coppi, Merckx, Hinault and Roche. Induráin caught a lot of grief from his countrymen for taking a pass on the Vuelta to again ride the Giro. But at the time, the Giro was still ridden what might be called Italian style, with the riders going at a moderate tempo until the last hour, which was raced all out; perfect training for the Tour. Greg LeMond was also hoping the Giro might again bring him to top form.

The first day of racing was on the island of Elba, off the coast of Tuscany, where Napoleon had been sent for his first exile. It was a split-stage day with the first half an 85-kilometer road race to Portoferraio. Moreno Argentin left a small breakaway on the final climb and soloed in with a 34-second advantage on the field. What was most interesting about the stage was that once it was clear that Argentin's break was looking good, Induráin had his team start bringing it back. Induráin was already riding the Giro as if he were the leader.

The afternoon 9-kilometer time trial was won by Maurizio Fondriest with Induráin only two seconds slower.

The General Classification:
1. Moreno Argentin
2. Maurizio Fondriest @ 36 seconds
3. Miguel Induráin @ 38 seconds
4. Eddy Seigneur @ 41 seconds
5. Gianni Bugno @ 44 seconds

Upon landing in the Tuscan coastal city of Grosseto, the Giro headed southeast. By the end of the third stage with its uphill finish in the small town of Scanno, the race was due east of Rome. Argentin's Mecair team pulled a smart move. Rather than putting the team at the front to ride tempo all day to police the pack, Piotr Ugrumov was sent to join a break. The gambit was successful. Ugrumov jetted from the escape to a solo win. Induráin was forced to put his team to work controlling the break while Argentin's Mecair riders sat in and enjoyed the ride, not needing to chase down their own teammate. Ugrumov was now in second place.

As the race headed south for three days of racing in Sicily under a terrible baking sun, the top of the leaderboard didn't change. The race transferred to Montelibretti, near Rome, for a race to Fabriano in Le Marche. Again, no changes to the important standings nor any meaningful action.

That would end with the stage ten 28-kilometer individual time trial in Senigallia. Induráin simply smashed the other hopefuls, beating Argentin by a minute while Ugrumov lost 65 seconds. Bugno's performance was poor enough to effectively remove him from contention.

The Story of the Giro d'Italia

The General Classification stood thus:

1. Miguel Induráin
2. Moreno Argentin @ 22 seconds
3. Piotr Ugrumov @ 53 seconds
4. Maurizio Fondriest @ 54 seconds

The next day's stage went from the Adriatic coast to the hilltop town of Dozza, near Imola, and was ridden in a terrible downpour. A *fuga di bidone* was allowed to get a sizable gap; Fabiano Fontanelli led in the first of the scattered breaks 3 minutes 29 seconds ahead of the Induráin group. That led to a slightly reordered General Classification because some of the members of the break were not far down in time:

1. Bruno Leali
2. Miguel Induráin @ 6 seconds
3. Marco Giovannetti @ 13 seconds
4. Moreno Argentin @ 29 seconds
5. Piotr Ugrumov @ 1 minute 0 seconds

Leali and his Mercatone Uno team had their hands full defending the Pink Jersey. Stage twelve went to Asiago with a second-category climb in the way, and as soon as the racing started, so did the attacks, and they kept coming and coming. A small group did escape, but despite all of the day's action, the contenders finished together.

After the stage, Stephen Roche said that there were two races, one for the *maglia rosa*, which was already partly conceded to Induráin, and one for the first Italian, something that is usually true of any national tour with a dominant foreigner. Some observers thought Induráin looked less than his usually all-powerful self, but to this writer he looked the same, not bothering to waste a single watt and content to let Leali's Mercatone Uno squad do all the work of controlling the race.

Stage thirteen might not give him that luxury. It was the first Dolomite stage with two hard passes near the end of the day, the Passo di Eores and the Passo delle Erbe before arriving in Corvara. On the Eores a couple of small groups escaped and halfway up Andy Hampsten jumped, with Ugrumov and Massimiliano Lelli coming along for company. The three stayed together with Hampsten doing the lion's share of the work and Lelli doing none. Further back, seeing that Ugrumov was the virtual Pink Jersey, Mercatone Uno worked like dogs to minimize the gap. Throughout most of the stage Leali remained glued like a limpet to Induráin.

After the Erbe, the Hampsten trio still had over a minute. Induráin's Banesto riders threw their weight into the chase and then finally Induráin and Leali started working the front, there being no sense in toying with a threat like Ugrumov. As the break closed in on the finish at Corvara, Gianni Bugno jumped away from the chasers and bridged the gap to the lead trio. The pack caught the break just at the line allowing Argentin to win a second stage. Confounding the experts, Leali kept his lead for another day.

If Leali thought defending the lead in stage thirteen had been difficult, stage fourteen looked even more daunting. The day's racing served up several category one climbs, generally the hardest rating in the Giro: the Costalunga, two ascents of the Pordoi, the Marmolada and the Campolongo. Moreover, the day was brutally long at 245 kilometers.

Several riders, including Bugno—under intense pressure from the press to perform some sort of epic exploit—escaped before the Marmolada. On that almost interminable climb, the Spaniard looked for no help while setting such a hot pace that by the time his small group went over the top all the escapees had been reeled in and the few riders who remained with him looked to be holding on like grim death. Bugno had gone too deep for too long on the Marmolada and by the time he reached the crest he was pedaling squares with exhaustion written on his face.

On the second crossing of the Pordoi, Induráin had Lelli, Poulnikov, Chiappucci, Pavel Tonkov and Ugrumov with him. Thirty-two seconds back, Hampsten was in a small group with Fondriest, who was desperate to get back on terms with the leaders. Through the rain they chased, but at the top of the Pordoi the gap had grown from 32 seconds to over a minute. In trouble, Leali crested over four minutes after Induráin.

The Induráin group stayed away with Chiappucci winning the sprint after 7 hours 27 minutes of hard racing. Ugrumov was gapped at the end by 20 seconds and Induráin was back in pink:

1. Miguel Induráin
2. Piotr Ugrumov @ 49 seconds
3. Claudio Chiappucci @ 1 minute 18 seconds
4. Massimiliano Lelli @ 1 minute 38 seconds

The Giro headed out of the Dolomites and turned west. On the eighteenth stage, a young rider on Chiappucci's squad named Marco Pantani abandoned his first Giro.

There were no mighty Alpine stages scheduled, but stage nineteen was a 55-kilometer uphill time trial to Sestriere. This was one of the last two chances to upset Induráin and it was on his own turf, a race against the clock.

True to form, Induráin won the stage and extended his lead. Ugrumov, showing that he deserved second place in the General Classification, was second in the time trial.

Ugrumov wasn't giving up. The penultimate stage had a ten-kilometer climb to its hilltop finish at Oropa. Ugrumov attacked and attacked, trying to bludgeon the Spaniard into submission, and each time Induráin closed the gap. Induráin detested these constant accelerations and looked to be tiring. Finally Ugrumov let loose another bolt of speed and Induráin could not resist. He had cracked. As Induráin slowed, Chiappucci and several riders who had been dropped sped by. Ugrumov dug deep, trying to erase the 94-second gap that separated him from the Pink Jersey. But at the top, he fell short by 58 seconds.

That made two Giri in a row for the Spaniard.

Final 1993 Giro d'Italia General Classification:
1. Miguel Induráin (Banesto) 98 hours 9 minutes 44 seconds
2. Piotr Ugrumov (Mecair-Ballan) @ 58 seconds
3. Claudio Chiappucci (Carrera Jeans-Tassoni) @ 5 minutes 27 seconds
4. Massimiliano Lelli (Ariostea) @ 6 minutes 9 seconds
5. Pavel Tonkov (Lampre-Polti) @ 7 minutes 11 seconds

Climbers' Competition:
1. Claudio Chiappucci (Carrera Jeans-Tassoni): 42 points
2. Mariano Piccoli (Mercatone Uno-Medeghini): 40
3. Miguel Induráin (Banesto): 33

Points Competition:
1. Adriano Baffi (Mercatone Uno-Medeghini): 228 points
2. Maurizio Fondriest (Lampre-Polti): 187
3. Miguel Induráin (Banesto): 167

1994 Induráin came to the Giro with only twenty days of racing in his legs and no significant results. During the 1993 Tour he started to run out of gas as Tony Rominger cudgeled him day after day. The Swiss rider thought that if he hadn't given up time early in the Tour, Induráin wouldn't have had an early lead that allowed him to ride conservatively and negatively. Instead, he would have been forced to go on the offensive and that extra expenditure of energy might have cost him dearly and put the race in play. We'll never know. But it certainly looked like Induráin was taking the early 1994 season rather easy and was not going to repeat 1993 and get over-cooked attempting the Giro/Tour double.

Bugno had won nothing of note in 1993, but in the spring of 1994 he won one of the most prestigious of the Classics, the Tour of Flanders.

The Carrera team was always a problem for Induráin and this year he had to have an extra set of eyes. Not only did he have to worry about Claudio Chiappucci's constant and unexpected attacks, Carrera also had brilliant young climber Marco Pantani to torment the Spaniard.

As a teenager, Marco Pantani's climbing ability was already striking. Like Coppi, his parents were too poor to buy him a racing bike. But Italy is covered with a complex web of clubs and sponsors that help promising young riders get equipment and coaching, and this was true in Pantani's case when he joined the Fausto Coppi Sports Club. As he moved up the ranks of amateur racing, he made three attempts to win the Baby Giro. A fall ruined his first chance, but he still took third place. Inattention at a crucial moment in his second attempt led him to miss an important break, resulting in second place. But in 1992 he cemented his victory in the Girobio with a tour de force ride over three of the famous climbs that surround the Gruppo Sella massif: the Sella, Gardena and Campolongo passes. That August he signed a professional contract to race for Davide Boifava's Carrera team. Boifava had been in contact with Pantani for a while, watching him since 1990. Full of confidence, Pantani demanded bonus clauses in his pro contract for winning the Giro d'Italia and the Tour de France.

He may have felt sure of his cycling abilities, but during his short life he had already displayed some of the personality problems that would later spell so much trouble: a sense of insecurity that his Danish girlfriend would later say was rooted in a deep inferiority complex, as well as difficulty communicating and bonding in a normal way with friends, acquaintances and workmates.

From the last part of the 1992 season through the spring of 1993, Carrera raced Pantani hard, using him in short stage races as well as sending him to northern Europe for some of the Classics. He handled this trial by fire well, finishing nearly all of his races, and he showed the right stuff with a fifth in the Giro del Trentino. Then, insanely, Carrera tossed him into the Giro to help Chiappucci. It was all too much too soon and as we've seen, Pantani had to retire during stage eighteen with tendinitis, marking the end his 1993 season.

Gewiss had a formidable team. They were winning everything and the Giro was in their sights with Moreno Argentin, Piotr Ugrumov and the brilliant young Russian Evgeni Berzin, who had already won Liège–Bastogne–Liège that spring.

The Giro started with a split-stage day. In the morning the course was a loop out and back to Bologna. Endrio Leoni won the sprint, which was so fast the peloton splintered in the final kilometer.

More important was the afternoon seven-kilometer pan-flat individual time trial. Winner of the stage was a time trial specialist, Armand de las Cuevas. Berzin was second, only 2 seconds slower and Induráin was third at 5 seconds, while Bugno lost 14 seconds. De las Cuevas was the new leader with Berzin second and Induráin third.

During stage two the Giro traveled south along the Adriatic coast for an uphill grunt into the city of Osimo. Ugrumov took a flyer and was looking like a winner, but just as he started to fade, Argentin launched an attack that was nothing short of astonishing. He flew by his teammate and continued to distance himself from the field all the way to the line. Argentin was the year's third owner of the Pink Jersey.

Several times during the rolling stage three Bugno blasted away from the pack and was brought back. In the closing kilometers, with their steady climb into Loreto Aprutino, he escaped and managed to come across the line two seconds in front of the peloton. Good, but not good enough for pink. Argentin still held the lead with Bugno second at 7 seconds and Berzin third at 9.

The first of four hilltop finishes came in stage four in the south of Italy. The riders left the flat road after about 60 kilometers and spent the next 140 in the mountains to finish at Campitello Matese.

Oscar Pelliccioli went hunting for a stage win as the final hill began to rise. Others tried to get away, but when Berzin exploded out of what was left of the peloton it was over for everyone else. Beautiful is the only word for his form as he appeared to effortlessly stroke the pedals. He caught Pelliccioli near the top and out-sprinted him for the stage. Wladimir Belli was the first chaser across the line, coming in third; 47 seconds after Berzin was Marco Pantani. Argentin lost three minutes on the climb.

The General Classification stood thus:
1. Evgeni Berzin
2. Gianni Bugno @ 57 seconds
3. Wladimir Belli @ 58 seconds

The race headed north, up the Tyrrhenian side of the boot, without any particular effect upon the standings. Stage eight was a 44-kilometer individual time trial ending in the Tuscan town of Follonica. I don't

Berzin winning the stage eight time trial at Follonica.

think anyone could have predicted the outcome of this stage. Berzin destroyed the field. Induráin, unable to find his rhythm, could only manage fourth.

The stage results:
1. Evgeni Berzin
2. Armand de las Cuevas @ 1 minute 16 seconds
3. Gianni Bugno @ 1 minute 41 seconds
4. Miguel Induráin @ 2 minutes 34 seconds
5. Massimiliano Lelli @ 2 minutes 39 seconds

That yielded the following General Classification:
1. Evgeni Berzin
2. Armand de las Cuevas @ 2 minutes 16 seconds
3. Gianni Bugno @ 2 minutes 38 seconds
4. Miguel Induráin @ 3 minutes 39 seconds
5. Marco Giovannetti @ 4 minutes 20 seconds

A knife had been driven into the heart of the Induráin race strategy: gain significant time in the time trials and then match the climbers in the mountains. It was a coolly economic method, but one had to win the time trials to make it work. Induráin was aware of the danger of his situation and began scrapping for sprint time bonuses.

Bugno was riding as if he had limitless reserves. Strangely for a former Giro winner and a rider sitting in third, he assumed *gregario* duties for his Polti team, chasing down breaks and setting up sprints for Polti's speedster, Djamolidine Abdoujaparov. From the start of this year's Giro he had been careless about losing or gaining time. When he won stage three Bugno slowed well before the line, being vastly more interested in making sure he could do a two-arm crowd salute than in squeezing every possible second out of his break.

The Giro went into Austria and in stage fourteen, headed through the Dolomites to Merano, crossing four major passes on the way. It was on the final pass, the Giovo, that the real action occurred. A break had been away for many kilometers and on the Giovo it started to rain. Pascal Richard left the break as it began to disintegrate. Back in the *maglia rosa* group, Marco Pantani was finally given his freedom to seek a stage win, because his director knew that Chiappucci, also off the front, was not going to bring home the bacon in the 1994 Giro.

Pantani, then sitting in tenth place at 6 minutes 28 seconds, blasted off, catching and passing all of the breakaway riders but Richard, and on the dangerous wet descent, caught and passed him. Tiny Pantani was a fearsome descender, one of the best of his era. Bugno put his team to work chasing Pantani, who still had nearly 30 kilometers of solo riding to go. Pantani had no intention of letting the moment go to waste and took every chance, cutting every corner to stay ahead of his pursuers.

Pantani won the stage, 40 seconds ahead of the *maglia rosa* group led in by Bugno and Chiappucci. This perfectly executed ride was Pantani's first professional victory, moving him up to sixth place. That evening, hungry for more, Pantani badgered his director for more information about the next day's climbs.

That following day was harder still, with the north face of the Stelvio, the Mortirolo and the Santa Cristina. It was snowing at the top of the Stelvio and there was some discussion of cancelling the climb, but the organizers decided to take the chance. The riders went up between walls of snow lining the wet, sloppy road of the Stelvio. Franco Vona was first over, while the Classification men stayed together.

On the Mortirolo a small group of Berzin, Pantani and de las Cuevas formed behind Vona and a few other adventurers. And then Pantani was gone. Berzin tried to stay with him but soon realized the folly of his move.

Pantani flew by all the breakaway riders who had been in front of him and crested the Mortirolo alone. Further back, Induráin dropped the others including Berzin and went off in search of Pantani. At the bottom of the Mortirolo, Induráin, with Nelson Rodriguez on his wheel, caught Pantani, but only because Pantani was told by his director to wait for help. Still further back Bugno had lost several minutes and was going to lose his third place.

Pantani's ascent of the Mortirolo had been jaw-dropping. The previous speed record for the climb was Chioccioli's 15.595 kilometers per hour in the 1991 Giro, considered one of the great rides in Giro history. Pantani smashed the record, going 16.954 kilometers per hour. Italy was transfixed; more than six million Italian television viewers watched Pantani ride away from the world's finest living stage racer.

Induráin and Pantani formed a smooth-working duo with Rodriguez sitting on. As they went through Aprica for the first time, Berzin was two minutes back and Bugno over four. Next came the Santa Cristina ascent before the finish in Aprica.

On the Santa Cristina neither Induráin nor Rodriguez, both at the end of their tethers, could contain the surging Pantani. Off he went and soloed into Aprica almost three minutes ahead of Chiappucci, the first chaser. Induráin came in 3 minutes 30 seconds after Pantani with Berzin another half-minute later. Pantani had elevated himself to second place, revealing himself as the first pure climber in the peloton since Lucien van Impe and the best since Charly Gaul. Maybe the finest ever.

The new General Classification:
1. Evgeni Berzin
2. Marco Pantani @ 1 minute 18 seconds
3. Miguel Induráin @ 3 minutes 3 seconds
4. Gianni Bugno @ 4 minutes 8 seconds
5. Wladimir Belli @ 4 minutes 41 seconds

Stage eighteen was the scene of the final time trial, a 35-kilometer hill climb leaving from the Ligurian seacoast town of Chiavari. Berzin had recovered from his hard days in the Dolomites and earned a clear-cut stage win. Induráin had indeed come to the Giro under-trained and his second place seemed to indicate he was riding into condition.

Stage twenty was the first of two days in the Alps and it packed a wallop with the Agnello before crossing to France for a trip over the Izoard, Lautaret and a finish atop Les Deux Alpes.

A small group of non-contenders went away on the Agnello and then in a flash Pantani was up to and past the break with only Hernán Buenahora glomming onto his wheel. They were together as they went up and over the Izoard with the Pink Jersey group containing Induráin and Chiappucci following at 1 minute 51 seconds. Berzin got into a spot of trouble on the Izoard ascent, but teammate Moreno Argentin led him back up to the leaders. After descending the Izoard, Pantani, seeing that the Berzin group was closing in, sat up and let Buenahora go. Buenahora was caught by those six riders from the early break who had continued riding ahead of the peloton.

For a while Berzin had only Induráin and Pantani for company on the Deux Alpes climb. Induráin tried an acceleration, but it wasn't forceful enough to dislodge the Russian rider. In fact, Berzin answered with his own jump, which Induráin met, but Pantani was surprisingly gapped before slowly closing back up to the pair. After this the trio slowed and a few others joined them. Near the top, Poulnikov shot away from the break with Nelson Rodriguez and won the stage. Two minutes later Pantani led in Induráin and Berzin. Induráin was running out of Giro and Berzin and Pantani weren't looking any weaker for their three weeks of racing.

The General Classification was looking good for Berzin:
1. Evgeni Berzin
2. Marco Pantani @ 2 minutes 55 seconds
3. Miguel Induráin @ 3 minutes 23 seconds
4. Pavel Tonkov @ 11 minutes 16 seconds

There was still one more Alpine stage, number twenty-one, going from Les Deux Alpes to Sestriere. It took in the Lautaret, Montgenèvre and then did a loop that had the riders doing two ascents to Sestriere. It was a frigid day, with snow in Sestriere. The top riders stuck together and despite the harrowingly cold conditions, there was no change to the upper levels of the General Classification. There was now only the ride into Milan. Berzin had become the first Russian, in fact the first eastern bloc rider, to win a Grand Tour.

Final 1994 Giro d'Italia General Classification:
1. Evgeni Berzin (Gewiss-Ballan): 100 hours 41 minutes 21 seconds
2. Marco Pantani (Carrera Jeans-Tassoni) @ 2 minutes 51 seconds
3. Miguel Induráin (Banesto) @ 3 minutes 23 seconds
4. Pavel Tonkov (Lampre) @ 11 minutes 16 seconds
5. Claudio Chiappucci (Carrera Jeans-Tassoni) @ 11 minutes 58 seconds

Climbers' Competition:
1. Pascal Richard (GB-MG-Technogym): 78 points
2. Michele Coppolillo (Navigare-Blue Storm): 58
3. Marco Pantani (Carrera Jeans-Tassoni): 44

Points Competition:
1. Djamolidine Abdoujaparov (Polti): 202 points
2. Evgeni Berzin (Gewiss-Ballan): 182
3. Gianni Bugno (Polti): 148

Induráin's form was indeed improving. While he won no time trials in the Giro, it was a different case in the Tour. The Spaniard humiliated the field in the Tour's stage nine time trial. When the race hit the mountains, Induráin, who was regularly put on the ropes by the best climbers, soared with a newfound ability. He went on to take his fourth of five consecutive Tour wins.

Apparently he remembered the thrashing Pantani gave him on the Santa Cristina and during the Tour sought to avenge himself by working hard to specifically deny Pantani any stage wins, which caused the Italian, riding his first Tour, to complain bitterly. Pantani came in third, despite a bad crash that left him weeping with pain for much of the race. Italy was enchanted. Pantani's contract with Carrera was up at the end of 1994 and after looking at offers from other teams he signed for another two years with Boifava.

Berzin was part of one of the most successful teams of the decade, Gewiss-Ballan, which won the Giro as well as many important one-week and single day races. It is believed that the team was one of the first (but no one can really know for sure) to have a systematized doping program exploiting the performance benefits of EPO. The most extreme example of Gewiss-Ballan's dominance was the 1994 Flèche Wallonne. The team had already won Milan–San Remo, Tirreno–Adriatico and the Critérium International. In the Flèche Wallonne, three of the team's riders gapped the field, almost accidently, and rode a 70-kilometer team time trial to the finish. Moreno Argentin won, Giorgio Furlan was second and just a few seconds in arrears, coming in third, was Evgeni Berzin.

A test for synthetic EPO wasn't developed until 2000. Until an upper limit on a rider's hematocrit was established in 1997, doping with EPO was limited only by a rider's ambition and courage. Riders could use as much as they dared. Francesco Conconi, who is accused by CONI (Italian Olympic Committee) investigator Sandro Donati of introducing EPO to the pro peloton, had a brilliant assistant, Michele Ferrari, who was the Gewiss-Ballan team doctor. Ferrari famously said, "EPO is not dangerous, and that with regard to doping, anything that is not outlawed is consequently permitted."

Records of Gewiss-Ballan riders' hematocrits were uncovered by investigative journalists and they reveal what can only be presumed to be highly manipulated blood values. For example, the French sports newspaper *L'Équipe* said that in January of 1995 Berzin's hematocrit was 41.7 percent (quite normal) and in July, during racing season, it rose to 56.3 percent. I know of no explanation for this change that excludes exogenous substances. Gewiss-Ballan wasn't the only offender. The other teams couldn't let the ones with a "program" run away with everything. Soon many other squads either systematized doping within their teams (sometimes with the excuse that the riders were doping themselves with dangerous drugs and bringing it in-house under a doctor's care reduced doping's risk) or as they had for years, carefully turned a blind eye to their riders' actions.

1995

The starting field of 198 riders had some riders who were pretty good with a bike. Both Tony Rominger—already the Vuelta record holder with three wins (1992, '93 and '94) and owner of the World Hour Record—and Evgeni Berzin were in fine form. But Berzin couldn't expect undivided loyalty from his Gewiss team. Piotr Ugrumov was included in the team roster and the two had developed an intense dislike for each other. Missing was Induráin, who decided not to tire himself before the Tour.

Pantani was looking good, but on May 1, while on a training ride before leaving later that day to ride the Tour of Romandie, he was hit by a car. He had no broken bones, but he was beaten up badly enough that he had to miss the Giro. Pantani recovered in time to contest the Tour de France in July where he came in thirteenth, winning two stages and the Best Young Rider Jersey.

The first Giro stage was sited in Umbria, rolling out of Perugia and finishing in Terni. The pack came to Terni together and Mario Cipollini's Mercatone Uno team gave him a perfect leadout. He put several bike lengths between himself and second place Mario Manzoni, making the racer nicknamed the "Lion King" the year's first *maglia rosa*.

The men riding to own the Pink Jersey in Milan would be not be allowed to hide this year. The second stage was a 19-kilometer time trial from Foligno to Assisi, and being planted on top of a hill, the only way to Assisi was up. This was a stage for an all-rounder who could handle his bike, given the roads were slippery from rain.

Rominger destroyed the field with a superb winning ride and took the Giro lead for the first time in his career.

The General Classification at this point was thus:
1. Tony Rominger
2. Maurizio Fondriest @ 43 seconds
3. Rolf Sørensen @ 49 seconds
4. Francesco Casagrande @ 53 seconds
5. Evgeni Berzin @ 57 seconds

Stage four to Loreto in Le Marche featured four circuits over rolling roads, a route hard enough to keep the teams attentive to potential breaks by Classification contenders. Indeed, each lap's climb was raced aggressively with attacking riders gaining a few seconds only to be swept up by Rominger's *gregari*. On the final time up the hill, Berzin teammate Vladislav Bobrik jumped away. Rominger instantly had the Russian in his sights, swept by him and kept going for another stage win, distancing second-place Fondriest by four seconds.

The Story of the Giro d'Italia

The race headed south to the toe of the boot. Each day there were at least a few hills to chew away at the riders' reserves, stage seven being a good example with an uphill sprint after a day of rolling terrain. Rominger tried to repeat his stage four success, but Fondriest was tired of getting second and won the stage. Rominger remained the leader by 47 seconds over Fondriest.

The eighth stage had the potential to be game altering with its 18-kilometer climb to the finish at Monte Sirino. When he took the lead in stage two, Rominger had said that he didn't plan to keep the lead. But as the race developed it was looking like Rominger had no plans to cede the *maglia rosa* and his Mapei team was put at the front of the race day after day.

A small break escaped on Monte Sirino and Laudelino Cubino was first while Rominger led in the field only 4 seconds behind the last of the fugitives. The day had two serious casualties, Berzin and Fondriest, who both lost time.

The General Classification stood thus:
1. Tony Rominger
2. Francesco Casagrande @ 1 minute 17 seconds
3. Laudelino Cubino @ 1 minute 26 seconds
4. Piotr Ugrumov @ 1 minute 44 seconds
5. Evgeni Berzin @ 1 minute 52 seconds

Stage ten, a 42-kilometer individual time trial on an undulating course finishing in Maddaloni, just north of Naples, was another opportunity for the World Hour Record holder to tighten his grip on the race. Rominger rode a new carbon-fiber time trial bike that had been delivered just the day before. Yet, the bike's newness was no handicap: Rominger took 1 minute 24 seconds out of Berzin and Ugrumov, who finished within two-tenths of a second of each other. Rominger now had a 3-minute lead over Ugrumov and 3 minutes 8 seconds over third-place Berzin.

During the rest day that followed, the race transferred north to the coast of Tuscany. Stage eleven had a hilltop finish at Il Ciocco after a day of climbing in the Apuan Alps. On the road to Il Ciocco, Berzin tried to challenge Rominger, but the Swiss rider had no trouble marking the Russian. Ugrumov tried his hand and Rominger's answer was to go to the front. Though Rominger didn't look like he was going deep, only Berzin and Ugrumov were able to stay with him. They finished the stage together.

The Giro's final chapter opened in Trent with stage fourteen, the year's longest stage at 240 kilometers. There were four highly rated climbs with the finish atop the 2,004-meter-high Val Senales in the Dolomites.

At over twenty kilometers, the Senales ascent was long enough for the Gewiss drama to really play out. With about eight kilometers to go, Rominger was with Berzin, Ugrumov and Spanish rider Oliviero Rincon while a group with Chiappucci was a short distance behind them.

Rincon scooted away and Ugrumov decided to lead the Rominger trio. Crystallizing the split within the team, Ugrumov then attacked, taking Rominger with him, leaving teammate Berzin behind. Rominger and Ugrumov formed a working duo that temporarily distanced itself from Berzin, but as the road flattened out, Berzin clawed his way back. The trio slackened their speed slightly allowing the Chiappucci group to close up. There were now only two kilometers to go and no one was able to catch Rincon. At no time during the stage was Rominger ever in distress; he easily matched the efforts of his two Gewiss challengers and that was quite enough.

The General Classification stood thus:
1. Tony Rominger
2. Piotr Ugrumov @ 3 minutes 14 seconds
3. Evgeni Berzin @ 3 minutes 29 seconds
4. Francesco Casagrande @ 4 minutes 43 seconds
5. Claudio Chiappucci @ 5 minutes 25 seconds

Stage fifteen left Italy for Switzerland and a 185-kilometer day in the mountains ending with a climb to Lenzerheide/Valbella. Berzin wasn't giving up. On the Flüele pass, the day's penultimate ascent, Berzin attacked and bridged up to an earlier break. The stage was only about half over and Berzin had about a two-minute lead. Rominger didn't seem too concerned, putting his Mapei men to work controlling the gap.

Berzin was caught before the start of the final climb. He and Ugrumov kept trying to get away but Rominger had such deep reserves he was able to answer each attack. And that's how the stage ended with no change in the standings of the top three.

The year's final time trial was not designed for the big-gear boys, featuring an ascent of the 760-meter-high Gallo before the climb to Selvino Aviatico. Again, Rominger was supreme. Ugrumov faltered a bit and lost 24 seconds to Berzin, ceding second place to his rival.

The new General Classification:
1. Tony Rominger
2. Evgeni Berzin@ 5 minutes 8 seconds
3. Piotr Ugrumov @ 5 minutes 17 seconds
4. Claudio Chiappucci @ 9 minutes 35 seconds

It wasn't over as far as Ugrumov was concerned. Stage nineteen, going from Mondovì to Briançon in France offered no end of possibilities with its three major Alpine passes, the Sampeyre, the Agnello, and the Izoard.

Snowpack on the upper slopes of the Agnello from the previous day's snowfall avalanched onto the road a few kilometers from the summit, trapping some of the race caravan travelling ahead of the race. As a result, it was decided to end the stage just part way up the Agnello in Ponte Chianale where an intermediate sprint had been planned.

Since the announcement of the shortened stage came with only about an hour's worth of riding left in the now 130-kilometer stage, any plans for big moves on the final climb had to be forgotten. This might have been a gift to Rominger, who looked awful that day. No one was able to take advantage of his apparent *giornata no.*

The next day was another race in the Alps. Ugrumov went crazy trying to get away, but Berzin and Rincon stayed with him and no amount of attacking could drop them. They also refused to work with him to distance themselves from the Rominger group, being content to ride up to Ugrumov's wheel after each of his accelerations. The distaste the two Gewiss riders had for each other was starkly evident, the duo bickering their way to the line while Rominger led his group to the finish without any evident panic, feeling comfortable with a few seconds' time loss.

That evening the Gewiss director had a sit-down with his petulant racers, telling them that they should be attacking Rominger, not each other.

The second-to-last stage was not going to be easy with two ascents of the Cuvignone. It was another lousy day with the rain coming down in buckets. Berzin tried to escape on the second time up the Cuvignone, but had to surrender near the top. The descent was extremely technical and the riders were in no mood to take stupid chances on the slippery roads.

The final ascent of the day and the Giro was the 5.7-kilometer Salita di Montegrino Valtravaglia and Berzin used it to get away and stay away. He beat the Rominger group containing Ugrumov to the line by 25 seconds, thereby assuring himself of a secure second place.

Rominger's Giro win was as commanding and effortless as any Grand Tour victory. No one at any point had the ability to put him *in extremis*. He seized the lead at the first possible opportunity, the stage two time trial, and kept it the rest of the race. He was the third Swiss victor in Giro history, Koblet having won in 1950 and Clerici in 1954.

On the final podium Rominger and Berzin looked quite pleased with things but Ugrumov looked dour, probably replaying the race in his head and wondering where he could have taken 42 seconds out of his Russian nemesis.

Final 1995 Giro d'Italia General Classification:
1. Tony Rominger (Mapei-GB) 97 hours 39 minutes 50 seconds
2. Evgeni Berzin (Gewiss-Ballan) @ 4 minutes 13 seconds
3. Piotr Ugrumov (Gewiss-Ballan) @ 4 minutes 55 seconds
4. Claudio Chiappucci (Carrera Jeans) @ 9 minutes 23 seconds
5. Oliviero Rincon (ONCE) @ 10 minutes 3 seconds

Climbers' Competition:
1. Mariano Piccoli (Brescialat): 75 points
2. Nelson Rodriguez (ZG Mobili-Selle Italia): 45
3. Giuseppe Guerini (Navigare-Blue Storm): 43

Points Competition:
1. Tony Rominger (Mapei-GB): 205 points
2. Rolf Sørensen (Maglificio-MG): 153
3. Evgeni Berzin (Gewiss-Ballan): 148

That fall Pantani crashed again, this time it was a horrific, potentially career-ending racing accident. Fine-tuning his form before the 1995 Tour of Lombardy, he crashed into a car that had been allowed on the course of the late-season Milan–Turin Classic. As he was descending into Turin at high speed with two other riders they smashed into a Nissan 4x4 going the opposite direction. Pantani suffered, among other serious injuries, several broken bones in his left leg.

After a protracted and difficult recovery regimen, he was able to resume riding in March of 1996. In April, he signed to race the 1997 season with Luciano Pezzi's Mercatone Uno-sponsored team, which was to be built around him. Because this was a Pantani-centered squad, no sprinters were signed who might distract the team from its goal of delivering him to the finish first. By the end of 1996, still wearing his Carrera kit, Pantani was riding professional races in Spain. When Carrera pulled out of racing at the end of the year Mercatone Uno swept in and signed several more of the team's riders to be Pantani's *gregari*.

1996 To celebrate the centenary year of the modern Olympics, the Giro organizers unveiled an audacious start. The first three stages were to be in Greece, the first of which was a circuit around Athens.

All three Greek stages resulted in mass sprints. There were an unusual number of crashes but none of the serious Classification riders was hurt. When the race transferred to Ostuni in southernmost Italy Stefano Zanini was wearing the Pink Jersey. The Giro remained sprinters' property for several more days.

The widespread illegal use of EPO by professional racers had finally reached the ears of law enforcement. The Carabinieri are Italian federal police who are considered part of the military and have a branch called the NAS or *Nucleo Antisofisticazioni e Sanità* (usually rendered in English as the "Carabinieri Command for the Preservation of Health"). NAS was going to perform a big search of the teams when they arrived on the Italian mainland, but *La Gazzetta* got wind of the blitz and published details of the planned raid. With the element of surprise gone, it was called off.

Stage seven would smoke out the real Giro racers with its finish at the top of Monte Sirino, a ski station in southern Italy, southeast of Naples. Festina rider Pascal Hervé had captured the lead the day before. Since Hervé was a competent enough climber who might be able to keep the lead after the day's hard climb, his teammates killed themselves riding hard tempo and chased down all the attacks. On the ascent, the cream rose to the top. By the final kilometer, a small group was burning up the asphalt: Davide Rebellin, Pavel Tonkov, Ugrumov, Ivan Gotti and Stefano Faustini. The finish was perfect for Rebellin, a genius at winning uphill sprints. Hervé was unable to climb with the specialists and lost the lead. Bugno, the current Italian champion, lost over eleven minutes.

The General Classification was thus:
1. Davide Rebellin
2. Pavel Tonkov @ 4 seconds
3. Stefano Faustini @ 8 seconds
4. Leonardo Piepoli @ 16 seconds
5. Piotr Ugrumov @ 18 seconds

By stage ten they had reached Tuscany. So far, each of the last few stages had gone over a few climbs that might have affected the race's outcome, but they all came far from the finishes, allowing the peloton to regroup each time. Rebellin remained the leader.

Stage ten had the short, stiff Schignano di Vaiano before rolling into Prato. World Champion Abraham Olano stretched the peloton into a long thin line. Then it broke. Over the top, about ten riders stayed with the Spaniard, but on the eighteen-kilometer run-in to Prato, another ten joined them, meaning all the good riders remained together. Rodolfo Massi slipped away for the stage win, but the General Classification wasn't changed.

The first two weeks of the Giro hadn't been particularly challenging. The sprinters had lots of chances to look for glory but the legs of the Classification riders should have been relatively fresh at this point. Finally, stage thirteen was a stage worthy of a Grand Tour with the San Bernardo and Casotto coming before an assault on the climb to Pratonevoso.

Wap! Tonkov hit the field hard with a withering attack on the final ascent and only Ugrumov and Enrico Zaina could match his speed. Rebellin wisely didn't try to match the Russian's pace up the mountain and climbed at his own slightly slower speed.

Tonkov kept up the pressure, forcing Zaina to let go. Now it was down to Ugrumov and Tonkov with Tonkov doing all the work. Tonkov had enough stuff left to lead out the sprint and seriously gap Ugrumov and take the *maglia rosa*.

The Story of the Giro d'Italia

The General Classification was now thus:
1. Pavel Tonkov
2. Piotr Ugrumov @ 20 seconds
3. Enrico Zaina @ 38 seconds
4. Davide Rebellin @ 41 seconds
5. Ivan Gotti @ 1 minute 1 second

If the early stages hadn't been challenging, the Giro was making up for lost time. Stage fourteen crossed into the French Alps, sending the riders over the Maddalena (in French, Col de Larche), Vars, and Izoard before coming into Briançon. Yet, for all the difficulties that the stage presented, it didn't change the standings. Swiss rider Pascal Richard, not in contention, was allowed to escape on the Izoard while the heads of state marked each other and came in as a group.

From Briançon, the Giro went back to Italy and up to Switzerland and then across northern Italy to Vicenza. During these days of *piano* racing, non-threatening breaks were allowed to scamper off while the peloton took it easy. Stage nineteen was a challenging 62-kilometer time trial (I guess they all are to riders who are trying to win), going from Vicenza to Marostica with an ascent of the Rosina. Berzin won the stage with Olano one second slower. Tonkov rode well enough to keep his lead, barely.

After coming out from behind Induráin's shadow, Olano had been racing wonderfully well. In 1995 he was second in the Vuelta, became World Road Champion and was second in the World Time Trial Championship. Just before the Giro he had won the Tour of Romandie. If Tonkov were looking for someone to worry about, he need look no further.

After the time trial the General Classification stood thus:
1. Pavel Tonkov
2. Abraham Olano @ 1 second
3. Evgeni Berzin @ 14 seconds
4. Piotr Ugrumov @ 1 minute 58 seconds

The next stage gave Tonkov a chance to defend his microscopic lead in territory more suited to his talents. Going from Marostica, the twentieth stage crossed the Manghen, the Pordoi, the Marmolada and then around again to the top of the Pordoi. It was 220 kilometers of Dolomites that should have allowed the Russian to increase his lead.

It was Enrico Zaina who decided that the Marmolada was the place to hand out the big hurt. When he took the lead with Ugrumov, Tonkov and Olano on his wheel, Berzin had already been put to the sword. Olano looked to be suffering and finally he let go. Zaina had more where that came from and upped the pace, and then Ugrumov was dropped. Then Tonkov. Zaina was alone on the Marmolada.

Further back, Ivan Gotti was tearing up the road, passing rider after rider. This was racing at its best with each racer, knowing that the Giro was in play, going deep, deep into his reserves. Gotti was having a spectacular day and caught up to Tonkov. Then Ugrumov joined the pair.

Rather than respond to attacks, Olano climbed at his own pace and eventually caught Tonkov, who was by this time looking gassed. Zaina was up ahead followed by Gotti then Tonkov, Olano and Ugrumov. They all descended the Marmolada at speeds that must have required enormous courage.

As the second ascent of the Pordoi began, the Tonkov trio got another shock. Gianni Bugno, who was far down in the standings, caught them.

Zaina won the stage with Gotti 47 seconds back. Olano gapped Tonkov in the sprint for fourth place, taking the overall lead by .46 seconds, but called the same time in the standings.

The new General Classification:

1. Abraham Olano
2. Pavel Tonkov @ same time
3. Enrico Zaina @ 1 minute 41 seconds
4. Piotr Ugrumov @ 2 minutes 2 seconds
5. Davide Rebellin @ 3 minutes 39 seconds

There was still one stage left before the promenade into Milan, and with the margins razor thin, the five rated climbs in stage twenty-one would give the race the finality it needed. This was a long one, 250 kilometers covering the Mendola, Tonale, Gavia, Mortirolo and the relatively easy climb up to Aprica. The previous stage took a little over seven hours to complete and now the peloton faced a still harder day in the saddle.

The Mortirolo with its patches of twenty-percent gradient sorted things out. A single acceleration by Gotti dropped Olano from a small group of climbers: Ugrumov, Gotti, Tonkov and Zaina. This was it! The

Giro would go to one of these four. There was still a lot of Mortirolo left and the Aprica ascent was still waiting.

Gotti jumped again and took Tonkov with him. Gotti looked back hoping for some help but Tonkov was at his limit. Gotti stayed out of the saddle and beautifully danced up the hill with a horribly suffering Tonkov holding on for dear life. Gotti was leading him to the Promised Land, the land of Pink Jerseys.

A tired-looking Olano went over the crest of the Mortirolo 2 minutes 22 seconds behind Gotti and Tonkov. The pair increased their lead on the descent and climb to Aprica. Gotti bagged the stage, his first-ever professional win, without any resistance from Tonkov. Tonkov's booty from the day was more than enough, the 1996 Giro d'Italia. He became the second Russian to win the Giro.

Final 1996 Giro d'Italia General Classification:
1. Pavel Tonkov (Ceramiche Panaria-Vinavil): 105 hours 20 minutes 23 seconds
2. Enrico Zaina (Carrera-Longoni Sport) @ 2 minutes 43 seconds
3. Abraham Olano (Mapei-GB) @ 2 minutes 57 seconds
4. Piotr Ugrumov (Roslotto) @ 3 minutes 0 seconds
5. Ivan Gotti (Gewiss-Playbus) @ 3 minutes 36 seconds.

Climbers' Competition:
1. Mariano Piccoli (Brescialat): 69 points
2. Pavel Tonkov (Ceramiche Panaria-Vinavil): 37
3. Ivan Gotti (Gewiss-Playbus): 36

Points Competition:
1. Fabrizio Guidi (Scrigno-Blue Storm): 235 points
2. Giovanni Lombardi (Polti): 130
3. Enrico Zaina (Carrera-Longoni Sport): 120

1997

Not having a reliable test for EPO, the UCI set 50 percent as the ceiling for a rider's hematocrit. A finding of more than 50 percent was not to be considered a doping positive, because at the time there was no reliable way to detect synthetic EPO and therefore it couldn't be proven to be the cause of a high hematocrit. A rider found to be over the 50 percent threshold was declared unhealthy and immediately suspended for 15 days, which would, the line went, allow him to become well enough to resume racing. The ruling had a perverse effect. Any rider hoping to be competitive had to dope himself up to the 50 percent threshold. Conconi takes credit for suggesting this rule to the UCI, but he had actually advanced a 54 percent hematocrit as an appropriate upper level.

Fifty percent was settled on because it was thought riders would be less likely to die in their sleep. Looking back at this, it all seems crazy. At the Tour of Romandie, Chiappucci was snared by the limit when he was found with a 50.8 percent hematocrit. The two-week suspension kept him out of the Giro.

Pantani's spring program didn't shrink from hard racing and even took him to the brutal northern European Classics, where he did well enough, including a fifth in the Flèche Wallonne and good placings in other races. Pulling out of the Tour of Romandie, he complained that his form was still lagging and that he would never again be the rider he had been two years before. He said he had tried to race too much too soon after his accident and was circumspect about his own prospects.

The 1997 Giro looked like a climber's race. There were two time trials totaling 58 kilometers, the first one in stage three having a hard ascent at the end. Four stages with hilltop finishes, including a devastatingly difficult penultimate stage in the mountains, made it certain that a rouleur would not be triumphant in Milan. No prologue time trial was scheduled; the first stage would be sixteen laps up and down Venice's Lido beach.

Because the Giro organization had botched the sale of the television rights by demanding insanely high prices, large areas of Europe either didn't get the 1997 Giro at all or had to pay for it. Also, many riders with Tour ambitions decided to avoid tiring themselves in such a hard race. The result was a rather attenuated field with none of the world's top-ten rated riders planning to contest *la corsa rosa*. There was talk that the status of the Giro had fallen even below that of the Tour of Switzerland.

Even so, the race still had plenty of good riders. Tonkov had won the Tour of Romandie. Enrico Zaina, who earlier had been Chiappucci's *gregario*, was now free to race on his own account since Chiappucci was suspended. Frenchman Luc Leblanc was in good shape, having won the Giro del Trentino. The consensus was that if Pantani had returned to good form, the race would be between him and Tonkov.

Mario Cipollini won the first two stages. His leadout train lost control of the race in the final kilometers of the first stage, yet Cipollini bored through a nearly nonexistent hole next to the barriers and emerged the winner of the first Pink Jersey. The next day he led the sprint out from far back and no one could come around him.

Cipollini's days in pink had to come to an end, and with the uphill time trial in San Marino, they ended immediately: the course's eleven-percent gradient spelled certain doom for pure sprinters. Tonkov won the stage with Evgeni Berzin second, 21 seconds slower. Tonkov thought Berzin would have turned in a better time if he hadn't been over-geared in the first half of the course. Pantani did well enough, losing 1 minute 23 seconds. Tonkov was now the leader and Berzin was second, a single second behind.

So far the Giro had enjoyed lovely weather. In stage five, when the race arrived in Abruzzo with its hilltop finish at Terminillo, the rain came. The pack was all together for the start of the fifteen-kilometer, eight-percent grade and Tonkov had his team keep the pace warm during the first kilometers of the ascent. But soon Pantani's Mercatone Uno men decided the speed had to be increased and increase it they did. That effort had two surprising victims, Berzin (who got the hunger knock) and Ugrumov.

With about three kilometers to go the sun came out. Several riders attempted getaways, but Tonkov easily rode up to each attacking rider, including Pantani. His neutralizing efforts looked almost effortless, usually without his even getting out of the saddle.

After a final attack from Leblanc, Tonkov took the stage and further padded his lead. The General Classification stood thus:

1. Pavel Tonkov
2. Luc Leblanc @ 41 seconds
3. Ivan Gotti @ 1 minute 7 seconds
4. Roberto Petito @ same time
5. Marco Pantani @ 1 minute 31 seconds

Going southwest without any appreciable change to the standings, the Giro arrived on the Amalfi Road on the southern Italian coast. It was a *piano* day and while the peloton cruised down the Tyrrhenian coast, a group of non-contenders was allowed their day in the sun and finished fourteen minutes ahead of the disinterested pack. But the day profoundly affected the Giro's outcome in another way; thirty kilometers before the finish Pantani hit a cat while descending the Valico di Chiunzi. He didn't break any bones, but after getting badly bruised and losing twelve minutes, he abandoned.

After going all the way to the heel of Italy, the peloton spent its rest day transferring up to the Tuscan coast. The order of business when the Giro resumed was to boot four riders from the race, none of whom were in contention for the Overall, for excessive hematocrits.

Stage fourteen took the riders almost due north, sliding by the east side of Turin on the way to the Alps. It ended with a 2,100-meter-high sort-of mountaintop finish at Cervinia, on the Italian side of the Matterhorn. After they reached the summit, they had a two-kilometer downhill rush to the line.

On the penultimate climb, the San Pantaleon, things broke wide open. A small group of riders including Axel Merckx (Eddy Merckx's son) had been off the front for a while. Out of nowhere Ivan Gotti exploded from what was left of the peloton. Stefano Garzelli of Mercatone Uno was the only rider to mark the move. Gotti bridged up to the Merckx group with astonishing ease while Tonkov did nothing, keeping his attention on his *bête noire*, Leblanc.

Still Tonkov did nothing and Leblanc, not wanting to hand the Giro over to Gotti through inaction, led the chase. The Gotti group went over the Pantaleon 23 seconds ahead of the *maglia rosa*.

The Gotti group flew down the Pantaleon like madmen and by they time they got themselves organized on the way to Cervinia, they had enlarged their advantage to 64 seconds. Gotti, knowing the stakes involved, singlehandedly dragged his group up the hill.

With six kilometers to go the race had turned into an exciting pursuit. Up front Gotti was pounding away for all he was worth with Nicola Miceli hanging onto his wheel. One hundred seconds back, feeling the Giro slipping from his grasp, Tonkov had only Leonardo Piepoli for company while Leblanc, unable to maintain the white-hot pace, was nowhere to be seen. Tonkov had gambled and lost. Leblanc was not Tonkov's main challenger, it was Gotti.

Out of the saddle and digging deep, Gotti dropped Miceli and finished alone. Tonkov lost 1 minute 46 seconds. Leblanc had cracked badly, coming in 3 minutes 16 seconds after Gotti, who had profited hugely from Tonkov's tactical blunder. The new General Classification was thus:

1. Ivan Gotti
2. Pavel Tonkov @ 51 seconds
3. Luc Leblanc @ 3 minutes 2 seconds
4. Leonardo Piepoli @ 3 minutes 28 seconds

Gotti's lead shouldn't have been a surprise. He had been second in the 1990 Girobio, fifth in the 1995 Tour (including two days in yellow) and fifth in the 1996 Giro. Yet he had not been invited to the Giro presentation with the other contenders, a fact that was clearly on his mind when he spoke to the press after the stage, feeling he had been unjustly forgotten. They certainly knew about him now.

The Giro turned east for its appointment with what were intended to be the deciding stages: a 40-kilometer time trial followed by three days in the Dolomites.

Normally, since Tonkov was the superior time trialist, Gotti's lead might have been in danger. But just before the stage start the judges wouldn't let Tonkov ride his time trial bike because it had a projection over the rear wheel the officials deemed an illegal fairing. Tonkov switched to his back-up bike, one he didn't really like. The result? Tonkov was able to take back only fourteen seconds. The bike switch might actually have been a blessing because the hard-to-handle specialty time trial bikes proved to be lots of trouble on the technical, high-speed course. Both Alexandr Shefer (now lying in fourth place) and Leblanc were among those who crashed hard. Both riders abandoned.

At 5:30 in the morning, before the start of stage nineteen, NAS raided the hotel rooms of the MG-Technogym riders and found a large cache of dope. Among the finds were twenty boxes of anabolic steroids, three boxes of growth hormones and of course, EPO. At first team director Ferretti said the drugs were for his personal use, to help him improve his sexual performance. As we say out here in the Ozarks, that dog don't hunt. It was later admitted that the drugs were for the riders' use. The team left town that afternoon and the sponsors quit the sport at the end of the year.

Rain and six major climbs greeted the riders at the start of stage nineteen. Just listing what the peloton had to get over during its 222-kilometer Calvary is tiring: the Pinei, Sella, Pordoi, Campolongo, Furcia and the Riomolino with a final uphill grind to Falzes.

Tonkov, who crashed and remounted on the Campolongo, could not contain Gotti. On the Riomolino, Gotti, who had Leblanc teammate Giuseppe Guerini for company, had been hoping he would be able to work with and help Leblanc as a foil to Tonkov. With Leblanc now out, Guerini was given the go-ahead to work with Gotti and try to improve his own standing, then sixth place. Gotti was able to extend his lead by another 55 seconds.

The new General Classification shows it was a two-man race:
1. Ivan Gotti
2. Pavel Tonkov @ 1 minute 32 seconds
3. Giuseppe Guerini @ 6 minutes 0 seconds
4. Nicola Miceli @ 8 minutes 33 seconds

The stage nineteen seven-hour ordeal must have been enough. Even with stage twenty's finish at the top of the Tonale, Tonkov made a few half-half hearted attacks which Gotti, content to merely stay with Tonkov, easily handled. A group of non-contenders was allowed to come in ten minutes ahead of the *maglia rosa*. Now it was down to just one last mountain stage, with three hard passes, including the Mortirolo.

Gotti (front, in pink) and Tonkov (Mapei kit) duke it out.

Tired or not, Tonkov's Mapei team wasn't going down without a fight. They sent Gianni Bugno up ahead and then set a pace so hot that eventually nearly everyone was dropped. It was down to just Gotti and Tonkov as they caught Bugno on the Mortirolo.

The gradient rose to eighteen percent and on a switchback, a motorcycle fell over in front of Bugno. Now it was Gotti and Tonkov, the two best riders, riding side by side on the Mortirolo, one of the hardest ascents in cycling. Gotti tried several times to drop Tonkov, but the Russian stayed with him. It was thrilling duel. Finally Gotti took the front and it looked like Tonkov had thrown in the towel, but two kilometers from the summit there was a surprise. Wladimir Belli closed up to the two leaders and then led for the rest of the climb through a sea of fans lining the narrow road. The *tifosi* were sure an Italian was going to win the Giro and they weren't going to miss it.

Tonkov won the three-up sprint, but with only the final ride into Milan remaining, the Giro was Gotti's.

Final 1997 Giro d'Italia General Classification:
1. Ivan Gotti (Saeco): 102 hours 53 minutes 58 seconds
2. Pavel Tonkov (Mapei-GB) @ 1 minute 27 seconds
3. Giuseppe Guerini (Polti) @ 7 minutes 40 seconds
4. Nicola Miceli (Aki-Safi) @ 12 minutes 20 seconds
5. Serguei Gontchar (Aki-Safi) @ 12 minutes 44 seconds

Climbers' Competition:
1. José Jaime González (Kelme-Costa Blanca): 99 points
2. Mariano Piccoli (Brescialat): 35
3. Roberto Conti (Mercatone Uno): 28

Points Competition:
1. Mario Cipollini (Saeco): 202 points
2. Dimitri Konyshev (Roslotto-ZG Mobili): 146
3. Glenn Magnusson (Amore & Vita): 145

Pantani restarted his season at the Tour of Switzerland, which he abandoned. His Tour de France was a triumph for a man who was a shattered wreck little more than a year before. He came in third to Jan Ullrich, whom many thought would go on winning Grand Tours for a decade, and Richard Virenque, who soon would be at the center of cycling's greatest doping scandal. Pantani's Tour was particularly memorable because of his two spectacular mountain stage wins. By now Pantani had taken on the persona associated with his best years; he shaved his head and took to wearing a bandanna. He had become *Il Pirata*.

five

1998–2003

The Rise and Fall of Marco Pantani

1998 There seemed to be a consensus among a wide range of racers, managers and writers as to who was most likely to win the 1998 Giro. Alex Zülle, who had left the Spanish ONCE squad for the powerful Festina team, was the man to beat. He was an outstanding time trialist and the 80 kilometers of racing against the clock in the 1998 Giro certainly played to his strength. Gotti thought Zülle had a built-in four-minute advantage over the climbers that would have to be overcome in the high mountains. Easier said than done, because Zülle was also an excellent climber and capable Grand Tour rider, having won the 1996 and '97 Vueltas.

Others proposed the last two winners, Gotti and Tonkov. Only a couple of experts thought Marco Pantani could prevail on what was said to be a time trialist's parcours.

Zülle certainly lived up to expectations when he won the 7-kilometer prologue on a rainy day in Nice (the sixth time the Giro had started in a foreign country). The Swiss rider had the *maglia rosa* by 1 second over Serguei Gontchar.

The first stage returned the Giro to its home country with what was expected to be a sprint finish in Cuneo. Cipollini's lead-out train was late getting organized and two of his Saeco teammates went down as the peloton wound its way around the traffic circles. The loss of momentum was perfect for a clever and strong opportunist to try to slip away in the last kilometer. Mariano Piccoli's burglary in plain sight was perfectly executed. Piccoli got the stage while Zülle remained the leader.

Going from Cuneo to Imperia on the Italian Riviera with the Capo Berta ascent coming just five kilometers from the end, stage two's racing said this Giro was going to be a fight from the very beginning. Before the Capo Berta started to rise, Pantani sent his entire team to the front to bring up the pace. As the road rose, Paolo Bettini leaped out of the field with Pantani hot on his tail. Soon Michele Bartoli clawed his way to the duo. Bettini couldn't take his fellow escapees' supersonic speed and sat up, but Bartoli and Pantani screamed up the hill. Back in the pack, this was a four-alarm fire and the peloton strung itself out over the hill, desperate to retrieve the two gifted racers. Near the summit the catch was made and Zülle's lead was preserved.

The next day Zülle lost the Pink Jersey when he was caught behind a crash (not unusual for Zülle) near the finish, giving the Pink Jersey to Serguei Gontchar.

Again Bartoli and Pantani slapped the field around a bit. The last six kilometers of the fourth stage had a rugged sawtooth profile where Bartoli tried to get away. He was instantly marked by Pantani and Enrico Zaina. This trio could not be allowed any freedom and were painfully pulled back. Both Pantani and Bartoli were racing the Giro as if each day were a one-day Classic, not worrying about saving energy for later. After the big guns were caught, Nicola Miceli took advantage of that moment of relaxation that almost always occurs after breaks are caught and scooted off for the stage win. Bartoli, having a seemingly endless well of energy, took second, and with the attendant time bonus was 1 second short of becoming the Giro's leader.

Still headed south, the Giro had passed through Tuscany and was now rolling by Rome to the stage five finish in Frascati. At ten kilometers to go it looked like a typical Saeco lead-out-train finish with nearly all of Cipollini's team at the front, but by the final kilometer he had only one teammate left. It didn't matter. Cipollini led the sprint out himself, riding the final 200 meters on the brake levers with no one able to come around the powerful Tuscan. Bartoli had managed to gain some bonus seconds in the intermediate sprints and was now the Pink Jersey.

As the Giro rolled into Campania with its stage six finish at Lago Laceno, three rated climbs confronted the riders. Things were still together by the time they reached the final hill, the Valico Villagio-Laceno, with its short stretch of 21-percent gradient. When the peloton reached that steep part, Bartoli did a sharp attack that caught Pantani's attention. Pantani closed up to Bartoli and not being content with Bartoli's speed, ratcheted up the pace. Alert to the danger, Gotti and several others moved up to Pantani. He looked back and went still faster and then he was gone. Or was he? This day Pantani didn't appear to have his normal sharp climbing snap and first Bartoli went after him and was able to keep the small climber in sight. Then Luc Leblanc and finally Zülle were able to latch onto Bartoli.

Zülle lit the jets, gunning for and catching Pantani, but he wasn't content. He put in another dig and Pantani was able to stay with him for a few hundred meters, but Zülle was on fire. Even Pantani couldn't hold his wheel that day and he went over the crest of the hill eight seconds behind the Swiss superman. The final three kilometers were on flat road, happy hunting grounds for one of the world's foremost time trialists. Zülle extended his lead, won the stage and retook the *maglia rosa*. Bartoli, Leblanc and Pantani followed in 24 seconds later.

The General Classification now:
1. Alex Zülle
2. Michele Bartoli @ 13 seconds
3. Luc Leblanc @ 50 seconds
4. Pavel Tonkov @ 56 seconds
5. Paolo Savoldelli @ 57 seconds
6. Marco Pantani @ 1 minute 2 seconds

By the stage eight finish in Lecce, the 1998 Giro's southernmost point, the General Classification hadn't changed. The race turned north and headed for the Dolomites and the Alps. The route followed the Adriatic shoreline, making flat stages for the sprinters. Cipollini's win in Macerata in Le Marche was his 25th, tying Eddy Merckx's postwar Giro stage-win record. Although Bartoli had managed to take a few bonus seconds in sprints, there was still no change to the General Classification.

Stage eleven's climb to San Marino was the real start of the Giro. At the sign of the day's first gradient, José "Chepe" González decided to go for a long, lonesome ride. Andrea Noè initially spoiled his plans, but González was able to temporarily drop the Italian.

Back in the peloton, Pantani's Mercatone Uno team massed at the front. San Marino was Mercatone Uno's hometown, giving the team extra motivation for a stage win. As the road got ever steeper, Pantani attacked again and again. His relentless accelerations kept thinning the herd but there were tenacious contenders who were determined to stay with the Pirate. Up ahead, González had run out of gas. Noè, who was unhappy with the little Colombian's refusal to work with him, steamed right on by.

Tenacity wasn't enough. With a kilometer to go Pantani was able to get away from his followers and had Noè in his sights, but at the end of the stage still lacked 7 seconds to catch the fleeing Italian.

The General Classification:
1. Alex Zülle
2. Michele Bartoli @ 5 seconds
3. Luc Leblanc @ 50 seconds
4. Marco Pantani @ 51 seconds
5. Pavel Tonkov @ 52 seconds

The next stage, coming down from San Marino, was on a wet, sloppy day, perfect for letting a break of non-threatening riders get away. Laurent Roux, the best placed of the *fuga di bidone*, lifted himself into pink.

The Giro had departed from the warmth of southern Italy. Stage thirteen was cold and wet. To warm them a bit, the riders were to cross the 650-meter-high Passo dello Zovo, which crested a few kilometers before the finish. After two weeks of racing, Pantani's form had markedly improved and the new, improved Pirate bludgeoned the pack, landing blow after blow until they had to let him go. Zülle got up to him as did Bartoli, and at the top it was Pantani, Zülle and Tonkov.

On the descent Pantani flew down the wet roads fearlessly. On one curve he pushed his bike too hard and went sliding across the road, taking Zülle with him. In a flash they were both up, but not before a few riders had passed them. Zülle, a powerful but somewhat unskilled and crash-prone bike handler, almost went off the road at least one more time as did Tonkov. The Russian, not wanting to trade his skin for a few seconds, let Bartoli and several others go on ahead. At the bottom of the hill a group of four coalesced: Bartoli, Bettini, Giuseppe Guerini and Andrea Noè. Bartoli grabbed the stage win and the 12 precious bonus seconds. Pantani's group came in 16 seconds later and Zülle's was about another 6 seconds behind them. Noè was back in pink, Bartoli was second and Zülle had lost some valuable time to Pantani, who was turning out to be a relentlessly aggressive foe.

Now for the real mountains. Stage fourteen was a 165-kilometer trip to a finish atop Piancavallo, a nearly 1,300-meter-high, fifteen-kilometer long climb. Early on the ascent, the only one this stage, Bartoli took a long, out of the saddle, big-gear pull. That strung things out. He looked around for his teammate Andrea Noè and saw that Noè couldn't follow the pace, so he shut it down.

That didn't slow things down a bit, because just as Bartoli was looking around, he was swallowed up by Pantani's teammates, especially Stefano Garzelli, who initiated what looked like a ruinous pace. Zülle and Tonkov, knowing that Pantani was setting things up for a hammer blow, stayed glued to his wheel.

After each of his *gregari* had taken his last pull, Pantani took wing and only Tonkov, as usual with misery written all over his face, was able to hold his wheel. Soon even Tonkov had to let the Pirate go. Further back Zülle was now matching Pantani's speed. Noè, looking ghastly, was gone and Ivan Gotti, the previous year's winner, was quickly shown the back door.

Gotti said he had been unable to find any sort of competitive form this year and was completely out of contention after only a couple of kilometers of climbing.

Pantani was back! He won his first Giro stage in four years. Tonkov led in Zülle only 13 seconds later. Pantani wasn't in pink but he did get the green Climber's Jersey. Before the 40-kilometer individual time trial in Trieste, the General Classification stood thus:

1. Alex Zülle
2. Marco Pantani @ 22 seconds
3. Pavel Tonkov @ 40 seconds
4. Giuseppe Guerini @ 57 seconds
5. Andrea Noè @ 1 minute 5 seconds

Zülle answered a question that cyclists debated in the early 1970s. Do you push big gears or spin little gears? Zülle's time trial gave the answer. Spin big gears. On the long slightly downhill section followed by a flat road, he churned a gigantic 56 x 11, setting what was then a Giro time trial record of 53.77 kilometers per hour. At the halfway point he surged past Pantani, his 2-minute man. Zülle had now increased his lead to 2 minutes 2 seconds over Tonkov and Pantani was now in third at 3 minutes 48 seconds.

Stage seventeen, 215 kilometers going from Asiago to Selva Val Gardena, was *il tappone*. The riders had to cross the Duran, Staulanza, Marmolada and Sella (1998's *Cima Coppi*), all crammed into the final 100 kilometers. The contenders had taken it easy in stage sixteen, their legs sore from the time trial. Now there could be no relaxation, all knew that a hungry Pantani would be seeking the lead on these difficult passes in the high Dolomites.

The classification riders made it to the Marmolada together. It was Tonkov who threw down the gauntlet on the long and relentless ascent and it was Pantani who accepted the challenge. Guerini made it up to the duo but under this terrible pressure, Zülle folded.

Tonkov had brought a knife to a gunfight and had to let the pair go. Now it was just Pantani smoothly climbing in the saddle with Guerini stuck to his rear wheel. Bartoli, who had raced as if each stage were the last, was paying the price for his earlier efforts and was near the back of the peloton.

Pantani and Guerini went over the top of the Marmolada with Tonkov about a minute back. From then on Guerini and Pantani worked together, scorching the descent, and in the valley before the Passo Sella they picked up a few earlier breakaways. On the final climb, the pickups were dropped and the two riders continued to increase their advantage with every pedal stroke. Guerini was allowed the stage win and Pantani was the *maglia rosa*. Underlining his complete collapse, Bartoli failed to make the time cutoff and was eliminated.

The new General Classification:
1. Marco Pantani
2. Pavel Tonkov @ 30 seconds
3. Giuseppe Guerini @ 31 seconds
4. Alex Zülle @ 1 minute 1 second

There were still two more challenging mountain stages remaining as well as a 34-kilometer time trial on the penultimate stage. Could Pantani accrue a large enough lead to withstand another race against the clock?

Stage eighteen had three major rated climbs that were stacked up in the final 45 kilometers, including a hilltop finish at Alpe di Pampeago.

This certainly played to the Pirate's advantage. There were seven of the best left on the final climb. Pantani slowly, without any noticeable jump, upped the pace. Tonkov held on, but behind him the string broke. The two were gone and as the gradient went from fourteen percent to over twenty, Pantani was not looking nearly as formidable as he had earlier. Tonkov, sensing the weakness, led over the final kilometer and won the sprint. Zülle lost almost a minute, making his job of reclaiming the race in the time trial more difficult. Pantani still led Tonkov by 27 seconds and Zülle was still in fourth, but 2 minutes 8 seconds back.

The final mountain stage had two major ascents before a hilltop finish, this time at Plan di Montecampione. It was one mountain stage too

Pantani wins the stage in Montecampione.

many for Zülle, who suffered a *défaillance*. At the top of the Cadino, the penultimate climb, he was almost eight minutes behind the leaders.

If anyone thought Pantani was running out of gas in this third week, he had an answer. As his *gregario* Podenzana was killing himself keeping the speed high (successfully: most of the peloton was well back down the road) Pantani erupted out from behind his wheel with an astonishing acceleration. Just as astonishing, Tonkov was on him like stink on poo. With the time trial looming, Pantani needed more time and Tonkov was in no mood to give it to him.

With about fifteen kilometers to go, Pantani slowed a bit and asked Tonkov to pull through. "Nothing doing", seemed to be the reply. Further up the hill Pantani again motioned Tonkov to come through and this time he did. The two riders seemed to be almost perfectly matched. As the final three kilometers stiffened to over ten percent Pantani tried to get away again, his last chance to win the Giro. He'd already tossed aside his sunglasses and bandanna, now he removed the diamond stud from his nose, threw it away, and then rising out of the saddle, he lashed his bike with another brutal acceleration and this time Tonkov couldn't take it. Slowly the gap grew and Pantani, hands on the drops and out of the saddle, gave it full gas. The gradient increased to 23 percent and Pantani kept up the pressure. Tonkov looked at last to have been broken. He had been forced to dig too deep one time too many. At the line Pantani had gained 57 seconds. Zülle lost a half-hour.

Zülle's soigneur Willy Voet thought the Swiss racer's collapse was the needless result of incompetent doping. He wrote that Zülle had been brought along carefully with growth hormone and then a treatment of corticosteroids, and I assume also EPO, which his Festina team had become adept at using. Although Zülle was in superb condition for the start of the Giro, he saw how teammate Laurent Dufaux had overpowered the competition in the Tour of Romandie and asked for the same heavy dose of cortisone Dufaux had received. Voet was against it, thinking he had his Formula One engine perfectly tuned. So, according to Voet, Zülle turned to another soigneur on the team who injected him with "massive doses of corticosteroids". Voet said that the "cortico" devoured the muscle that had been so carefully built up and after about ten days of racing in which Zülle was the strongest rider in the Giro peloton, he started falling apart.

The new General Classification:
1. Marco Pantani
2. Pavel Tonkov @ 1 minute 28 seconds
3. Giuseppe Guerini @ 5 minutes 11 seconds

With the final 34-kilometer time trial left, it was a race between Tonkov and Pantani. In the stage fifteen time trial Tonkov, a fine time trialist, had beaten Pantani by 2 minutes 4 seconds, or about three seconds per kilometer. Those three seconds per kilometer were roughly the amount of time Tonkov would need to take from Pantani this day in order to be the Giro winner. On paper the race was a dead heat.

Before the race started it was announced that two riders had hematocrits over 50 percent: Nicola Miceli, who had been sitting in fifth and Pantani teammate Riccardo Forconi.

Tonkov's start was nearly perfect. If his stiff climbing style made one wince, his time trialing was perfection. Two minutes later Pantani roared out of the start house looking all aggression and taking crazy chances on the corners. The first time check was a shock. Pantani was ahead by two seconds.

The result was a stunner. Time trial specialist Serguei Gontchar won, but Pantani was third, only 30 seconds behind. Tonkov was fifth, 5 seconds slower than the remarkable Pirate.

Pantani had been getting stronger with every passing day and now was capable of taking on the big power men on their own turf. Pantani won the Giro by relentlessly applying pressure at every opportunity. It was a performance that can only be described as incredible, it being rare that a small man can summon up the absolute horsepower needed to drive his bike through the wind as fast as the bigger powerhouses.

Italy was insane with joy over a man they loved for his courage in adversity and his swashbuckling, fearless racing style. There was no Binda-Guerra, Coppi-Bartali or Moser-Saronni duel to divide Italy's loyalty, Pantani had the passionate love of the *tifosi* all to himself. This was a long-delayed fulfillment of the promise Pantani had shown when he won the Girobio in 1992.

Final 1998 Giro d'Italia General Classification:
1. Marco Pantani (Mercatone Uno-Bianchi): 98 hours 48 minutes 32 seconds
2. Pavel Tonkov (Mapei-Bricobi) @ 1 minute 33 seconds
3. Giuseppe Guerini (Polti) @ 6 minutes 51 seconds
4. Oskar Camenzind (Mapei-Bricobi) @ 12 minutes 16 seconds
5. Daniel Clavero (Vitalicio Seguros) @ 18 minutes 4 seconds

Climbers' Competition:
1. Marco Pantani (Mercatone Uno-Bianchi): 89 points
2. José Jaime González (Kelme-Costa Blanca): 62
3. Pavel Tonkov (Mapei-Bricobi): 49

Points Competition:
1. Mariano Piccoli (Brescialat-Liquigas): 194 points
2. Marco Pantani (Mercatone Uno-Bianchi): 158
3. Gian Matteo Fagnini (Saeco-Cannondale): 156

As soon as the Giro was over, Pantani started to talk of riding the Tour de France. The events of the 1998 Tour traumatized professional cycling for years. The story was told in detail in the second volume of our *The Story of the Tour de France*, but a summary is necessary to understand many of the events in later Giri.

Doping was and is a part of the sport and while you may not be able to dope a donkey into being a thoroughbred, with modern drugs you can make a damn fast donkey. As we proceed through the sordid story of the 1998 Tour and later the 2001 Giro, the actions of the riders to protect themselves and their doping speak volumes.

On his way to the start of the 1998 Tour in Dublin, Ireland, Festina (Zülle's team) soigneur Willy Voet was stopped by customs agents as he crossed from Belgium into France. Among the items found in Voet's car were 234 doses of EPO, testosterone, amphetamines and other drugs that could have only one purpose, to illegally improve the performance of the riders on the Festina team. Bruno Roussel, the team director, expressed his astonishment at the facts surrounding Voet's arrest.

Later, the police raided the Festina team warehouse and found still more drugs, including bottles labeled with specific riders' names. Roussel said he was mystified by these findings and promised to hire a lawyer to deal with all of the defamatory things that had been written and said about the team.

Still in police custody, Voet began to sing, claiming that he had been acting on instructions from the Festina team management. Roussel said he was "shocked" at these statements.

Roussel and Festina team doctor Eric Rijckaert were taken into custody. While all of this was going on, the Tour de France was entering its sixth stage and Tour boss Jean-Marie Leblanc said that so far, the actions of the Festina team had not constituted an infraction of Tour rules and the occurrences outside of the Tour were not the Tour's concern.

On July 15, one of the most important events in the fight against drugs in sport occurred. Roussel admitted that the Festina team had systematized its doping. His excuse was that since the riders were doping themselves, often with terribly dangerous substances like perfluorocarbon (Swiss rider Mauro Gianetti had nearly died during the 1998 Tour of Romandie after allegedly using the synthetic hemoglobin), it was safer to have the doping performed under the supervision of the team's staff. That was too much and the team was booted from the Tour.

Yet, almost as a metaphor of how the pros handled irrefutable facts regarding their doping, Festina team members Richard Virenque and Laurent Brochard called a news conference to assert their innocence and vowed to continue riding in the Tour. A day later they relented and the team, including Zülle, withdrew from the Tour.

The Tour's next act showed how completely everyone was willing to look the other way when they passed the train wreck of the Festina mess. Fifty-five riders were subjected to blood tests and none was found to have illegal substances in his system. The Tour then declared that this meant that the problem was confined to a few bad apples. What it really meant was that for decades the riders and their doctors had learned to dope so that drugs didn't show up in the tests. And, in 1998 there was no test for EPO or human growth hormone. The team doctors protested that the Festina affair was bringing disrepute upon other teams and their professions. The fans hated to see their beloved riders singled out and thought that Festina was getting unfair treatment.

Back in March, a car belonging to the TVM team had been found to contain a large supply of drugs. That case was reopened. A few days later Roussel accepted responsibility for the systematic doping within the Festina team.

On July 24, the day of Tour stage twelve, more Festina riders and staff were arrested and the first TVM arrest occurred.

So how did the riders handle this? They became indignant. They were furious that the Festina riders had, like any other arrestees, been forced to strip in a French jail and were fuming that so much attention was focused on the ever-widening doping scandal instead of the race. On July 29, stage seventeen, the riders staged a strike. They started the stage slowly and sat down by their bikes at the site of the first intermediate sprint, Pantani being one of the strike's leaders. After some talk with officials, they rode slowly to the finish with several TVM riders at the front holding hands, making the solidarity of the peloton clear.

There were more arrests. Several teams, including all four Spanish squads, were feeling the heat and quit the Tour. It was thought that the Festina scandal might just ruin the Tour. It didn't. It didn't ruin the Tour because Marco Pantani electrified the world with a fabulous performance that took a lot of the attention away from the doping scandal.

1997 Tour winner Jan Ullrich had allowed himself to become disgracefully deconditioned over the winter. With the arrival of the hard mountains in the later stages, Pantani put on a magnificent one-man show, ultimately beating Ullrich by 3 minutes 21 seconds and becoming the first Italian to win the Tour since Gimondi in 1965. He became the seventh man to do the Giro/Tour double, joining Coppi, Anquetil, Merckx, Hinault, Roche and Induráin. Pantani had gained renown and was one of the world's greatest sports celebrities.

Italy, no, the entire world went absolutely crazy over Pantani. On local club rides, cyclists would climb Pantani style, in the saddle, hands on the drops. Pantani now had fame and more money than he could spend.

1999

Starting in Agrigento in Sicily, the 1999 Giro route made its way north, mostly on the Adriatic side. When it hit Le Marche, the race headed west for a trip into the Alps, then east across Italy into the Dolomites for the final drama in the high mountains. The drama in the high Dolomites did decide the race, but we're getting ahead of ourselves.

The race was made for climbers. Or perhaps, a climber. The most popular sportsman in Italy, by a wide margin, was Marco Pantani and a second Giro win for the Pirate would send the *tifosi* into delirium. With five hilltop finishes and a large serving of mountains, it looked like Pantani's race to lose. His spring looked good with a win in the Vuelta a Murcia and a third place in the Giro del Trentino.

The problems uncovered by the Festina scandal remained unresolved and two riders with hematocrits over 50 percent were not allowed to start.

The first day's racing under the hot Sicilian sun was slow. Ivan Quaranta took the first stage with some smart sprinting, becoming the first Pink Jersey. Cipollini won the second stage and the lead, followed by Jeroen Blijlevens doing the same in the third stage.

After a trip up the instep of the Italian boot, the Giro hit its first hilltop finish in stage five. José "Chepe" González, Andrea Peron and Danilo Di Luca were able to escape early in the ascent of Monte Sirino. Zülle, back to racing after serving his suspension because of his part in the Festina affair, was driving the pack, trying to close the gap.

During the last five kilometers of the climb, Di Luca and González took turns attacking each other, really hard, resulting in Peron's dispatch. Close to the top González dropped Di Luca and took the stage win. Laurent Jalabert and Pantani, leading the first chase group, just made contact with Di Luca at the line. With the first hint of who was here to race, the General Classification had taken this shape:

1. Laurent Jalabert
2. Danilo Di Luca @ 7 seconds
3. Davide Rebellin @ 14 seconds
4. Paolo Savoldelli @ 16 seconds
5. Marco Pantani @ same time

In fact, Pantani was feeling super. Pantani and his team took advantage of the windy weather by making an attack that split the field so badly that half the peloton never regained contact. Excellent riders like Pascal Richard, Richard Virenque and Roberto Heras were caught napping and lost anywhere from two and a half to over seven minutes.

The next morning, the Italian Olympic Committee (CONI) sent technicians to make unannounced blood and urine tests on riders of three teams. As usual, the riders screamed bloody murder, complaining about "unhygienic" conditions. Perhaps the riders feared a competent authority performing the tests rather than the toothless UCI. Pantani led the usual call for a strike that was silenced by the team directors who said that CONI was within its rights. Further angering the rest of the peloton, the owner of the Mapei team said his team was happy to work with CONI. The other riders were so incensed they reduced Mapei team member Andrea Tafi, one of the finest riders of his time, to tears with their taunts and insults. Two of the riders tested in the CONI blitz were positive for dope. From inside their doping-culture bubble, the riders couldn't see how sick their attitude was.

Pantani, Jalabert, Cipollini, and Oscar Camenzind held a press conference and said that if the CONI intruded any further upon the testing regimen, which heretofore had been the responsibility of the UCI, they would stop racing. Camenzind tested positive for EPO in 2004 and retired after receiving a two-year suspension.

The stage eight ascent to a hilltop finish at Gran Sasso in Abruzzo was ridden in near freezing rain. Once on the climb, Pantani's team drove hard, catching all of the early breakaways. Not content with dropping Pink Jersey Jalabert and most of the rest of the peloton, Pantani put his hands on the drops and headed for the sky. He didn't jump hard. He just got out of the saddle and rode the peloton off his wheel. The last man on Pantani's wheel was Ivan Gotti, who looked perfectly miserable.

As he climbed, Pantani looked back at Gotti and yelled at him to pull through, but Gotti was suffering all the tortures of Hell just hanging on, and taking a pull with Pantani while he was in full flight was probably beyond any rider in the world. Finally Gotti did go to the front and the pair predictably slowed. Enough of that! Pantani shot away and, clearly not sparing the watts, put lots of time between himself and everyone else.

Pantani came in alone, and to the joy of his ecstatic fans, became the leader of the 1999 Giro d'Italia. Scattered behind him, anywhere from a half to a full minute, were the other Giro hopefuls: José Maria Jiménez, Gotti, Dario Frigo and Alex Zülle.

The General Classification stood thus:
1. Marco Pantani
2. José Maria Jiménez @ 38 seconds
3. Ivan Gotti @ 45 seconds
4. Dario Frigo @ 54 seconds
5. Laurent Jalabert @ 55 seconds

Jalabert, a former time trial world champion, won the 31-kilometer time trial at Ancona in Le Marche. Pantani also blistered the course, coming in third, only 55 seconds slower than the Frenchman. Jalabert took back the lead, being ahead of Pantani by one-tenth of a second.

This extraordinary time-trial ride of Pantani's began setting off bells and whistles among the more clear-eyed racing fans. Pantani, a light, small racer, weighed only 125 pounds (57 kilograms). His climbing was remarkable because his power relative to his weight was astonishing.

But to continue to believe this small man could naturally generate sufficient wattage to drive his bike fast enough in time trials to challenge the larger, heavier chrono specialists required a suspension of rational doubt.

The next day CONI officials showed up to perform more blood tests on riders. UCI boss Hein Verbruggen had earlier told the riders they didn't have to submit to the tests. Only riders from the Mapei team gave samples. Gotti, among others refused.

At Cesenatico, Pantani's hometown, the Giro finished stage eleven and started stage twelve. The only change to the standings was that Jalabert won an intermediate sprint and now had a four-second lead on Pantani.

The UCI performed blood tests and found nothing amiss. But *La Gazzetta* knew about the "surprise" tests in advance and published the names of teams who would be tested. The riders and their handlers knew how to reduce a rider's hematocrit in advance of a test. They would take saline solution injections along with aspirin and in no time the hematocrit was within the legal limit.

Stage thirteen came before the only rest day, taking the Giro over the Apennines to Rapallo on the Ligurian coast. Even though the roads were tough, there was no change to the top of the leader board. Jalabert hung on to his Pink Jersey by just four seconds, saying he knew he'd have to give up the lead when the Giro faced the first real day in the mountains.

Jalabert didn't have to wait long for the roads to rise. The first stage when the racing resumed was into the Piedmontese Alps. Paolo Savoldelli, soon to be nicknamed *Il Falco Bergamasco* ("The Falcon of Bergamo, his hometown), took off on the final climb, the Madonna del Coletto, and then used his breathtaking descending skills to carve a path ahead of everyone else to Borgo San Dalmazzo. Just behind him, the trio of Pantani, Daniel Clavero and Gotti arrived. Pantani was again the *maglia rosa*.

Pantani was looking like the boss of this Giro:
1. Marco Pantani
2. Paolo Savoldelli @ 53 seconds
3. Ivan Gotti @ 1 minute 21 seconds
4. Daniel Clavero @ 1 minute 22 seconds
5. Laurent Jalabert @ 1 minute 45 seconds

Set 'em up and I'll knock 'em down. That seemed to be Pantani's motto when he destroyed the peloton on the climb to Oropa, a 1,180-meter-high mountain west of Milan. Hoping for a stage win, Jalabert had gone early with Roberto Heras and Nicola Miceli. His fellow breakaways weren't going fast enough, so Jalabert dropped them. Eight kilometers from the summit, Pantani looked to have a jammed chain. He was an excellent mechanic and without any sign of panic, performed the repair himself.

While he was stopped, attacks started going off the front, the pace of the race at that point being white hot. Savoldelli tried to orchestrate a fair play slowdown rather than take advantage of Pantani's mechanical. Pantani's teammates waited for their leader and pulled him up to the peloton. Pantani relentlessly made his way through the scattered riders, even blowing by Roberto Heras, a fine climber. Now only Jalabert was away and with three kilometers to go, Pantani overtook him, winning the stage by 21 seconds.

The General Classification now:
1. Marco Pantani
2. Paolo Savoldelli @ 1 minute 54 seconds
3. Laurent Jalabert @ 2 minutes 10 seconds
4. Ivan Gotti @ 2 minutes 11 seconds
5. Daniel Clavero @ 2 minutes 12 seconds

There were four important stages left: the stage eighteen time trial followed by three high mountain stages in the Dolomites. Jalabert said he hoped to regain the lead in the time trial but felt he was really racing for second place because Pantani would take so much time out of him in the remaining mountain stages.

Jalabert couldn't do it. He was only able to pull 57 seconds out of the Pirate. Savoldelli, however, turned in a wonderful ride, coming in second to Gontchar and beating Jalabert by 24 seconds. That left Pantani the leader by 44 seconds over Savoldelli and 69 seconds over Jalabert. Tight race.

From here on there would be no good news for Jalabert. The next stage ended at the top of Alpe di Pampeago, eight kilometers of ten-percent gradient with a stretch that tilts to sixteen percent. On the penultimate climb, Passo Manghen, Pantani had his men turn the screws and at the crest of the Manghen there were only twelve left in the *maglia rosa* group. Savoldelli tried a suicide descent but couldn't get enough time to distance himself once the Pampeago ascent began. Midway up the Pampeago, Jalabert was dropped. Gotti looked awful while Gilberto Simoni looked cool and at the front, Stefano Garzelli was doing yeoman's work for the teammate on his wheel, Pantani.

About four kilometers from the summit, Heras attacked and drew Pantani. Pantani waited a few seconds before countering with a display of climbing power that was simply unbelievable, showing that no one could climb a mountain on a bike like he could. Gilberto Simoni was the first chaser in at 67 seconds, his ride confirming his promise as a coming talent in Grand Tour racing.

Pantani wins another stage wearing pink, at Madonna di Campiglio.

At this point Pantani was leading in the Points, Mountains and the General Classifications. After the Alpe di Pampeago stage the General Classification was thus:

1. Marco Pantani
2. Paolo Savoldelli @ 3 minutes 42 seconds
3. Ivan Gotti @ 4 minutes 53 seconds
4. Laurent Jalabert @ 5 minutes 24 seconds

Stage twenty was a hilltop finish at Madonna di Campiglio. Before the riders started the stage, fifteen of them were required to submit to blood tests. All were deemed clean and good, giving everyone a high degree of confidence that the Giro would not be facing any more doping troubles. It was on the final kilometers of that mountain that the real action occurred. With fifteen kilometers to go, Pantani came out of the peloton and exploded off the front. Again, the rest of the best cyclists in the world could only watch and limit their losses as best they could. The Pirate was well and truly gone. The first group came in as the day before, 67 seconds later. Pantani's performance in this Giro so far had been absolutely masterful.

The new General Classification:
1. Marco Pantani
2. Paolo Savoldelli @ 5 minutes 38 seconds
3. Ivan Gotti @ 6 minutes 12 seconds
4. Laurent Jalabert @ 6 minutes 39 seconds
5. Daniel Clavero @ 9 minutes 51 seconds

The next day's stage—number twenty one—promised only more of the same for a peloton riding under Pantani's tyranny. Leaving from Madonna di Campiglio, where stage twenty had ended, it was to be the *tappone* with the Tonale, Gavia, Mortirolo, Valico di Santa Cristina and a hilltop finish at Aprica. Surely Pantani, who had so far won four stages in the Giro, would again have his way with the other riders.

That morning in Madonna di Campiglio, Marco Pantani was awakened in his hotel room so that a blood test could be administered. His hematocrit of 52 percent resulted in his being ejected from the Giro. The effect of his *squalificato* was profound. The cycling world was stunned. Pantani partisans were sure that some sort of conspiracy was afoot to deny Italy's most popular sportsman a second Giro victory. It was said that this was a *giallo* (yellow, an Italian idiom meaning something with dark conspiratorial undertones) case. It hit cycling fans far harder than the 1998 Festina scandal because of Pantani's heroic image and the adoration the *tifosi* had for him. He had triumphed over what should have been a crippling accident and had stuck with and won the Tour de France in its deepest most troubling time. Distraught, the rest of the Mercatone Uno team packed and left the Giro as well.

Nearly all Italians expressed disbelief that Pantani would have taken any performance enhancing drugs. Almost to a man, racers lined up to express their support for the expelled rider and a belief in the cleanliness of his bloodstream. How many of them actually believed what they were saying is difficult to know, but I suspect damn few.

Pantani knew the night before that he was going to be subjected to a blood test in the morning. Like many pros of the era (two-thirds of the 1998 Festina squad owned battery-powered centrifuges so that they could "manage" their hematocrits) he had his own centrifuge and tested himself before going to sleep, satisfied with his 48.6 percent hematocrit. Riders who do not manipulate their blood have no need of a personal centrifuge.

Always trying to do damage to the drug testing programs, riders and managers cynically expressed criticism over the reliability of the hematocrit test. In fact Pantani's blood was tested twice and after it was shown to have a high hematocrit, three more tests were performed in the presence of Pantani's team doctor and team director Giuseppe Martinelli. Averaging the five tests gave a result of 53 percent. The rules, allowing for a margin of error, require that the average be reduced a point. Thus, Pantani's 52 percent.

The doctors who had performed the tests on Pantani's blood retested the samples when they returned to their hospital in Como. The Carabinieri later seized the samples and delivered them to yet another doctor for testing. The results remained unchanged. Later DNA tests were done to certify that the blood samples were indeed Pantani's. They were.

Pantani was distraught. When told the news he smashed out a window in his hotel room. He then quietly returned home. After a few days he held a short press conference where he forcefully asserted his complete innocence. He said that on his way home he had a blood test performed and the hematocrit reading was 48 percent, dreadfully high, but legal.

To me the entire affair has a sense of mystery about it. We've seen there were standard procedures teams used to lower a rider's hematocrit. The team knew Pantani was going to be tested in the morning. They even knew the time. Why wasn't his hematocrit brought down before the test? The team doctor spent much of the evening and early morning before the test at a disco, which Pantani's agent Manuela Ronchi thought strange given the importance of the coming stage. The test was administered a little after 7:30 in the morning, but the doctor, who so far has refused to discuss that day, didn't show up until after nine (although in one statement, he said he delivered Pantani to the testers but didn't stay while Pantani's blood was extracted because he went to get another rider, Marco Velo). It has been asserted that without medical assistance Pantani couldn't use the normal methods of achieving a short-term reduction in his hematocrit. Yet, on other teams, even the soigneurs knew how to put a bag of saline into a racer to get a temporary three-point reduction in a rider's hematocrit. Willy Voet wrote it was part of pro cycling's standard operating procedure and took about 20 minutes to do the job, which probably explains why Pantani was habitually late to his blood tests that require the rider to show up within ten minutes of being called. The conflicting accounts make it hard to understand exactly what happened that morning. But whether he didn't think he needed help to cheat the tests, based on his previous evening's hematocrit, or he just didn't have a technician available, he was a goner.

I've noted that Pantani's girlfriend has described him as having a severe inferiority complex and he was later clinically diagnosed with bipolar disorder. His actions from that day at the Madonna di Campiglio and the tragic events that fill the few years left to him can be explained by those insights. Falling from the extraordinary heights to which he had risen, the most adored sports personality in Italy, to doper hounded by the law, was a descent that his fragile ego was unable to handle while his manic-depressive tendencies made his impulsive tendencies all the worse.

The racers didn't threaten to strike this time. Many riders were tested that day and only Pantani's hematocrit was above the allowable level.

With Pantani booted, the next three places in the General Classification were close together in time, close enough that the queen stage would probably decide the winner. Savoldelli was now the leader, but he refused to wear the Pink Jersey.

After the Tonale and Gavia, the riders were together at the beginning of the Mortirolo. It was here, just as the gradient began to hurt, that Gotti made his move. Only Simoni and Heras were able to stay with him, Savoldelli and Jalabert chasing as best they could. Eventually the front trio formed a smooth working break and on the Mortirolo, Gotti didn't look back while he led the other two all the way to the top. The crowds who had wanted to see Pantani ice his Giro victory were huge. There was a banner that summed up the profound emotion of aspiration, joy and hope Pantani made Italian cycling fans feel, *"Pirata—farci sognare"* (Pirate, make us dream).

Savoldelli went over the top 3 minutes 3 seconds behind the leading trio. He went down the technical descent of the Mortirolo hell-bent on getting back on terms with the Gotti group. He caught a strong group of riders on the false flat leading to Aprica and finding their pace not to his liking, dropped them and continued his pursuit. Despite these efforts, he was never able to catch the leaders and finished 4 minutes 5 seconds back.

Heras won the stage and improved his overall position while Simoni was, for now, up to second in the General Classification and Gotti was the new leader and winner of the 1999 Giro d'Italia. Later in the day it was announced that the times had been recalculated and Savoldelli was in second place after all, a single second ahead of Simoni.

Gotti's victory was not embraced by the Italian public who felt their Marco was the true winner. As Gotti was putting on his new Pink Jersey in Aprica, whistles of derision from the crowd could be heard. Gotti was correct when he said that everyone knew and competed under the same rules, one of which was that racing with a high hematocrit was grounds for disqualification. Gotti said he was racing for second place before the Pirate was sent home because he knew "Pantani is the best and strongest rider in the world."

Final 1999 Giro d'Italia General Classification:
1. Ivan Gotti (Polti) 99 hours 55 minutes 56 seconds
2. Paolo Savoldelli (Saeco-Cannondale) @ 3 minutes 35 seconds
3. Gilberto Simoni (Ballan-Alessio) @ 3 minutes 36 seconds
4. Laurent Jalabert (ONCE-Deutsche Bank) @ 5 minutes 16 seconds
5. Roberto Heras (Kelme-Costa Blanca) @ 7 minutes 47 seconds

Climbers' Competition:
1. José Jaime González (Kelme-Costa Blanca): 61 points
2. Mariano Piccoli (Lampre-Daikin): 45
3. Paolo Bettini (Mapei-Quick Step): 44

Points Competition:
1. Laurent Jalabert (ONCE-Deutsche Bank): 175 points
2. Fabrizio Guidi (Polti): 170
3. Massimo Strazzer (Mobilvetta -Northwave): 126

Nothing was learned. A few days later four riders were kicked out of the Tour of Switzerland because they had high hematocrits.

2000
The Italian government passed a law making it a crime to dope in sports.

On May 5, eight days before the Giro was to begin, the great Gino Bartali passed away in his hometown of Florence. Over his career "Gino the Pious" had won the Giro three times, the climbers' competition seven times and the Tour de France twice. The man rightly nicknamed the "Man of Iron" was one of the greatest riders in the history of the sport.

The 83rd Giro seemed to have "climber" written all over it with 23,000 meters of elevation gain and three hilltop finishes.

Gotti wanted to erase the stigma of what some saw as his tainted 1999 win. This view was unfair: he had been the best rider to compete within the rules. Also entered were Tonkov, Simoni, Casagrande and Pantani's teammate Stefano Garzelli.

And what of Pantani? He took his disqualification harder than any other racer, ever. Convinced he was the victim of a conspiracy to defraud him of the 1999 Giro, he secluded himself in his house while an army of reporters and photographers camped outside. A few days after his expulsion Pantani began his descent into addiction and by June he was a regular user of cocaine. Meanwhile, symbolizing Italy's state of denial regarding Pantani, Italy's Prime Minister awarded Pantani the Collar for Sporting Merit.

During this time Pantani had stopped riding and the combination of poor condition, ruined mental state and cocaine use rendered a 1999 Tour attempt impossible. While his fellow riders and team manager were aware of his drug problems by early 2000, for years Pantani and his circle continued to hide his cocaine use from the team's sponsors and unbelievably, the team doctor.

A judicial investigation was launched into Pantani's disqualification and almost simultaneously the Turin prosecutor opened an inquiry into the weird blood values technicians found when Pantani crashed in 1995. When his broken body was brought to the hospital his hematocrit was over 60 percent and Pantani was therefore potentially guilty of the crime of "sporting fraud".

Meanwhile in Ferrara, an investigation into the good Doctors Conconi and Ferrari had yielded a gold mine of data after computers seized at Conconi's offices were made to spill their guts. The cream of Italian cycling was implicated in an extensive doping program, all documented with meticulous notes. Among the riders were Bugno, Chiappucci, Fondriest, Gotti, Ugrumov and Pantani. Information from the files was published in the daily *La Repubblica* in December and showed that Pantani's blood had been manipulated since at least 1996.

As in the 1998 Tour scandal, where Festina found its sales soaring as its team fell into disgrace, many of Pantani's sponsors found the publicity windfall helped business and were eager to use him to publicize their products.

In January of 2000 Pantani announced that the Giro and the Tour would be the centerpieces of his season. He spent part of the winter training in the Canary Islands. As the early season races drew nigh he postponed his racing start, feeling that things were not "tranquil".

Late in February Pantani entered and quickly retired from the Tour of Valencia. Ominously his doctor started talking about stress, saying Pantani's mental condition was far from ideal. By late March, Pantani was still postponing his racing restart. It later turned out that he was suffering cocaine relapses that kept setting back his training. On May 12, the day before the Giro's start, Pantani announced the he would indeed ride the Giro. Though he was titled the team captain, he would not actually be the team leader. "I am here to ride in support of my team. I am here to regain my form." Stefano Garzelli would be Mercatone Uno's protected Classification rider in a Giro Pantani had earlier said was "....tailor-made for Savoldelli, who in June got through the tests because his hematocrit was 49.9 percent and ended up finishing second behind Gotti."

Before the riders could race, they were all subjected to blood tests. One rider failed to pass, Evgeni Berzin. With too many red blood corpuscles, he wasn't allowed to start and his team, Mobilvetta, quickly sacked him.

The Catholic Church proclaimed 2000 a Jubilee year, so the Giro started with a 4.6-kilometer prologue bouncing over slippery cobbles starting at the Vatican and finishing in Rome.

Czech rider Jan Hruska won, beating Paolo Savoldelli by a fraction of a second. Cipollini was only a second back, putting himself within stage-win time bonus of the Pink Jersey. Pantani finished near the bottom of the standings, 40 seconds down.

Stage one was a short 125 kilometers south to Terracina. Cipollini gained enough time in an intermediate sprint to take the lead, but decided the final sprint was too dangerous and was content with the *maglia rosa* as Ivan Quaranta beat the other speedsters.

For their stage two journey into southern Italy, cold, rainy weather greeted the racers, which seemed to have cooled their racing ardor. A seven-man group with Cristian Moreni escaped and was never seen again. A few kilometers from the end in Maddaloni, Moreni jumped away from his breakaway companions on a small hill, beating the break to the finish line by 5 seconds and the peloton by another 25, moving the lead from Cipollini to Moreni.

Stage four, into Matera in the heel of the Italian boot, allowed Cipollini to claim his 30th stage. It wasn't pretty because there was a substantial hill in the day's route that should have left the Lion King gasping for air and unable to maintain contact with the peloton, but the television cameras told the dirty story. Cipollini got pushed up the hill by his *gregario* Mario Scirea while the judges pretended not to know about it. Furthermore, Cipollini *gregario* Giuseppe Calcaterra hit Freddy González in the head for attacking while Cipollini was being helped.

With its short climb to the finish line in Peschici on the Adriatic Coast, stage five offered a first real peek at who was ready to race. Matteo Tosatto took care of business early when he won an intermediate sprint and earned enough bonus time to make him the virtual leader.

Later, when the day's break took off, Tosatto's team didn't chase; they had no plans to waste energy defending his lead when they knew he couldn't take it to Milan. They were keeping their powder dry for their Classification man, Wladimir Belli. It turned out Fassa Bortolo could have their cake and eat it too when the peloton came together before the sprint, preserving Tosatto's lead.

The General Classification at this point:

1. Matteo Tosatto
2. Cristian Moreni @ 3 seconds
3. José Gutiérrez @ 14 seconds
4. Andrea Noè @ 25 seconds
5. Danilo Di Luca @ 31 seconds

The next couple of stages were ridden *piano*, but stage eight, raced over three ranked climbs, had some great, tongue-hanging, lung-searing racing. With about 50 kilometers to go, a small group containing Gutiérrez got clear and was joined by a trio containing Di Luca. The chase was on (I'm astonished that such a high quality group was allowed to get away) and after some hard-driving riding, the breakaway emerged in Prato 49 seconds ahead of the peloton, making Gutiérrez the new leader.

That was just a warm-up. The next day had a hilltop finish at Abetone, but before they did that ascent, the riders had to get over the San Pellegrino where the peloton came apart. The better riders each took a pull and the speed kept increasing. Pantani, not unexpectedly, was shelled. His ever-vigilant team surrounded him and did their duty, shepherding the out-of-form superstar to the finish.

Further up the hill Francesco Casagrande took his turn applying the pressure and only Danilo Di Luca could stay with him. Casagrande put the gas pedal down a little closer to the floor and still Di Luca clung to his wheel. Casagrande kept going harder and harder until finally Di Luca couldn't take it, letting Casagrande go. A chase group of the rest of the best formed: Simoni, Tonkov, Gotti, Frigo, Belli, Di Luca, Noè and Garzelli. Casagrande was spitting out watts as if the race would end tomorrow and held his lead to the end, beating the Garzelli-lead group by 1 minute 39 seconds. Casagrande was the *maglia rosa*. It was a gutsy move and an impressive display of authority.

The new General Classification stood thus:
1. Francesco Casagrande
2. Danilo Di Luca @ 51 seconds
3. Andrea Noè @ 1 minute 39 seconds
4. Stefano Garzelli @ same time
5. Dario Frigo @ 1 minute 40 seconds

It's always something at the Giro. The Association of Italian Cycling Teams began a mini-strike of sorts. The riders refused to talk to the press or attend the podium presentations. They were demanding RCS Sport give the teams a share of the television and merchandising license fees. RCS said this could be discussed after the Giro was over and the teams agreed. I don't think anything came of it.

Forty-two kilometers of time trialing was enough to tighten up the Giro before the first rest day. Casagrande lost time to all of his challengers, and after a week and a half, the race was virtually a tie among the top six places.

The General Classification:
1. Francesco Casagrande
2. Wladimir Belli @ 4 seconds
3. Pavel Tonkov @ 7 seconds
4. Danilo Di Luca @ 10 seconds
5. Jan Hruska @ 17 seconds
6. Stefano Garzelli @ 22 seconds

A sign that the high mountains had arrived was Mario Cipollini's withdrawal from the race. He did not start stage thirteen with the Falzarego, Marmolada and Sella ascents looming; abandoning must have seemed easier than having his team beat up all the climbers.

Part way up the Marmolada, after his *gregari* had done what they could to break the peloton, Casagrande snapped everyone's neck with a hard acceleration. That was it for Tonkov. Then from the small lead group, Di Luca, who had been riding well beyond anyone's expectations, came off. Casagrande and Garzelli hammered away at each other on the way up, spewing riders out the back.

Over the top, Simoni got a gap on the others with José Luis Rubiera able to catch him on the descent. Rubiera won the two-up sprint in Selva Val Gardena, followed by Garzelli and Casagrande 31 seconds later. Casagrande now had a 31-second lead over Garzelli.

Three more big ones, that's what faced the riders in stage fourteen: the Mendola, Tonale, and the south face of the Gavia followed by a monster-gear rip down into Bormio. Things broke up badly on the ice-cold ascent of the Gavia, but it was the descent that really decided things, as the more skilled and powerful riders passed those who would rather not go soaring off the dangerous road. The Gavia doesn't have many guardrails and there are times when the rider just has to gulp and hope his tires will hold.

A group of four coalesced: Casagrande, Belli, Eddy Mazzoleni and stage winner Simoni. Frigo, Gotti and Garzelli chased hard, but they ran out of stage before they ran out of gap.

The General Classification of this tight and exciting race stood thus:
1. Francesco Casagrande
2. Stefano Garzelli @ 33 seconds
3. Gilberto Simoni @ 57 seconds
4. Wladimir Belli @ 1 minute 5 seconds
5. Dario Frigo @ 1 minute 52 seconds

The race came out of the high mountains and raced to Liguria. During these mostly easier stages, there were no serious challenges to Casagrande's lead. But stage eighteen, heading north from Genoa, went right into the Piedmontese Alps with a hilltop finish at Pratonevoso. Di Luca, troubled with tendinitis, abandoned.

The Giro was wearing on Casagrande as well. He no longer rode with the same impregnable authority he had shown in the first stages. That and the closeness of the standings meant the stolid-faced Casagrande was probably in for some rough handling.

Midway up the final climb, a rejuvenated Tonkov was the first to cuff the *maglia rosa*. Simoni and Garzelli gave him a couple of kicks but Casagrande stuck around. Then Simoni attacked and when Garzelli closed up to him, he was without Casagrande. As the road flattened slightly, Casagrande dragged himself back up to the leaders. Garzelli, being a good sprinter, took the stage and the bonus seconds, putting him within 25 seconds of the lead. Simoni was still third, now at 53 seconds.

No rest. Stage nineteen had the 2000 *Cima Coppi*, the Colle dell'Agnello, followed by the Izoard and an uphill finish in Briançon. The best riders separated themselves from the peloton on the Agnello and managed to stay away on the descent. One rider managed to join the leaders and was he a surprise! It was Marco Pantani. In the third week he had found his legs.

As the Izoard started to bite, Simoni did a probe and found Tonkov didn't have what he had the day before. Then Pantani went hard to get up to Simoni but Garzelli couldn't hold his wheel. After the leaders came together, Pantani attacked again, marked by Simoni. Pantani relented and waited for Garzelli. Simoni kept banging away the entire way up the Izoard while Pantani did the job of bringing the others up to him. This entire distance *maglia rosa* Casagrande just watched without taking part in the fireworks, letting the others wear themselves out.

On the descent before the climb into Briançon, as the big dogs watched and marked each other, Paolo Lanfranchi, a gifted *gregario* of Tonkov's, took advantage of the slower pace to take a flyer. Further on Pantani gave chase. Too late. Lanfranchi won the stage; Pantani was an astonishing second and Simoni, Garzelli and Casagrande followed in at a minute. Garzelli said that he had hoped to conserve his energy as much as possible over this stage with the time trial coming the next day. Pantani had made sure everyone had worked hard.

The race was too close to call:
1. Francesco Casagrande
2. Stefano Garzelli @ 25 seconds
3. Gilberto Simoni @ 49 seconds
4. Pavel Tonkov @ 2 minutes 46 seconds
5. Hernán Buenahora @ 3 minutes 50 seconds

The penultimate stage was a 32-kilometer time trial going from Briançon up to Sestriere with the Montgenèvre mountain pass in between. Jan Hruska, who won the prologue, was also victorious in the

Garzelli (foreground, in pink) and Pantani enjoy a moment of cameraderie in stage twenty-one.

final time trial. Garzelli rode a perfect race, coming in third. And Casagrande? He looked awful, losing 1 minute 52 seconds to Garzelli and therefore, the Giro d'Italia, and he nearly lost second place to Simoni. Casagrande, ranked the number-one rider in the world, looked to have burned himself up trying to ride with Merckx-style authority. In his defense, he said he was suffering from sciatica and felt he could have won the Giro if he had not been suffering from the nerve problem.

Final 2000 Giro d'Italia General Classification:

1. Stefano Garzelli (Mercatone Uno-Albacom) 98 hours 30 minutes 14 seconds
2. Francesco Casagrande (Vini Caldirola-Sidermec) @ 1 minute 27 seconds
3. Gilberto Simoni (Lampre-Daikin) @ 1 minute 33 seconds
4. Andrea Noè (Mapei-Quick Step) @ 4 minutes 58 seconds
5. Pavel Tonkov (Mapei-Quick Step) @ 5 minutes 28 seconds

Climbers' Competition:

1. Francesco Casagrande (Vini Caldirola-Sidermec): 71 points
2. José Jaime González (Aguardiente Nectar-Selle Italia): 71
3. Stefano Garzelli (Mercatone Uno-Albacom): 47

Points Competition:

1. Dmitri Konyshev (Fassa Bortolo): 159 points
2. Fabrizio Guidi (Française des Jeux): 119
3. Ján Svorada (Lampre-Daikin): 116

Garzelli, a fourth year pro, had won the Giro in his fourth attempt. So far his career hadn't been spectacular, since he was primarily a *gregario*, but it did show the promise of what he could do. In 1997 he was ninth in the Giro, in 1998 he won the Tour of Switzerland and in 1999 he won the GP Miguel Induráin and was fourth in Milan–San Remo. His next challenge was to get a different nickname. During the Giro, to his chagrin, the press had begun calling him "the Little Pirate" (*il Piratino*).

With the Giro under his belt, Pantani had the beginnings of some of his old racing form and went on to enter the Tour de France, giving Lance Armstrong fits before retiring with stomach troubles. In December, as a result of the Turin hospital investigation, he was found guilty of sporting fraud and was given a suspended sentence which was later reversed because it was found that the law did not apply in Pantani's case. Meanwhile his cocaine use and the investigation into his ejection from the 1999 Giro continued.

Oh, and about that green Climber's Jersey Casagrande took home. On the last day González was leading in the Mountains classification. Then, after some complicated explanations, Casagrande was awarded the maximum possible points for the climb in the final time trial and with that, was given the Green Jersey. The Colombians of González's Aguardiente-Nectar team were outraged at the dubious calculations.

2001

In April a urine test for EPO was finally approved. So far the closest officials could come to dealing with EPO was the 50 percent hematocrit threshold, which tripped up Pantani in 1999 as well as teammate Riccardo Forconi in the penultimate stage of the 1998 Giro. CSC rider Bo Hamburger had the honor of being the first rider caught with the new test. The racers quickly learned that by taking daily micro-doses of EPO instead of a few large injections, they could lower the peak quantity of the drug in their systems below the detectable threshold and continue to evade the controls. Hence, few EPO positives occurred, allowing the officials and promoters to claim that the drug problem had been licked. Not by a long shot.

Meanwhile, another Pantani investigation was opened, this one in Florence, looking into Pantani's unusual blood values leading up to his participation in the 2000 Olympics. Pantani's EPO and other drug use were known by the Olympic team selectors, but it was papered over. The man was too valuable to be allowed to remain off his bike, doped or not.

At 3,364 kilometers, the 84th Giro presented more opportunities to the sprinters with eleven stages that were either flat or rolling. The total amount of climbing was lower and included just three hilltop finishes. Time trialing was also down, at 63 kilometers compared to 83 and 77 in the two previous Giri.

When the route was presented, both Felice Gimondi and Marco Pantani thought the route was particularly suited for Jan Ullrich, Gimondi going so far as to say the route might have been designed to entice the talented German *passista* (a rider who can turn a big gear over flat roads) to ride the Giro. Indeed, Ullrich and his Telekom team did enter, but he had again let his form lapse badly over the winter and was at the Giro solely for training.

Francesco Casagrande was the number one favorite, having just come off a win in the Giro del Trentino (Pantani was 29th). Next on the list was Dario Frigo, winner of Paris–Nice and the Tour of Romandie.

2000 winner Garzelli was sure that if he stayed with Mercatone Uno he would be reduced to being a *gregario* for Pantani again so he jumped to Mapei, which was probably the most powerful squad in cycling at the time. Simoni, third in the last two Giri, won a stage in the Tour of Romandie and was ready to race.

And of course, one must always include the unpredictable Marco Pantani. His team director, Giuseppe Martinelli, said that Pantani's last workouts showed sparks of real lightning. Alfredo Martini, the manager of the Italian National Team, also thought Pantani should be considered the favorite.

Celestino Vercelli, one of Pantani's sponsors and a friend, visited him two weeks before the Giro start and found him full of a desire to get even for the many past humiliations to which he had been subjected. Pantani said to him, "This is a very important test. I have the possibility to demonstrate to all, adversaries, critics, public, that Pantani 'is'. In the next Giro I will begin, maybe with suffering. But, I am sure that all my preparatory work will bear fruit—I will race against myself."

The first order of business was the 7.6-kilometer prologue held in the Abruzzo city of Pescara, on the Adriatic coast. Belgian Rik Verbrugghe thumped a gigantic 55 x 11 gear over the dead-flat course at a wind-aided 58.874 kilometers per hour, the fastest-ever Grand Tour individual time trial at the time. Not much slower at 8 seconds was Dario Frigo.

Stage one's trip over the wet, twisty roads of the Abruzzo saw several crashes, including one involving Casagrande, who broke his wrist. His Giro was over before it had really started. On the final climb of the day, a split in the field occurred and Garzelli and Savoldelli were caught out and both lost 37 seconds.

By stage three, the Giro had reached its southernmost point when it finished in Potenza in the Basilicata region. This is a wild and mountainous area and the day's challenging profile bore that out. When *maglia rosa* Verbrugghe crashed, Mercatone Uno had been hammering away at the front, making it difficult for Verbrugghe to regain the peloton. Showing slightly enlightened self-interest, Cipollini sent word up to the front that they should slow until the race leader had rejoined the field. The slower pace allowed the sprinters to stay with the peloton and Verbrugghe remained in pink.

Over to the coast, through Salerno and back into the hills for a hilltop finish at Montevergine di Mercogliano, the riders faced their first real test in stage four. Verbrugghe and Savoldelli were among the many other riders who couldn't keep their bikes upright on the wet streets. Verbrugghe's stage three fall had left him too sore and tired to follow the Classification riders as they raced up the hill while Savoldelli had a flat and couldn't get back on, costing him two and a half minutes.

The Montevergine's final selection was Di Luca, Simoni and Garzelli with Frigo chasing three seconds back. Di Luca took the stage and Frigo took the lead. Ullrich lost over eight minutes in that stage alone.

The General Classification stood thus:
1. Dario Frigo
2. Abraham Olano @ 12 seconds
3. Gilberto Simoni @ 13 seconds
4. Wladimir Belli @ 17 seconds

The next three stages headed north to Tuscany. They were typical Giro *piano* stages with their insanely fast final hour, all won in big sprint finishes and with no effect upon the Classification. The Giro's former style of riding at a more relaxed pace during a stage's first hours was not because the Italians were a bunch of lazy athletes. Professional cycling is a business and the *tifosi* have to wait by the side of the road, sometimes for hours, for their heroes to come whooshing by. The easier pace allowed the fans to get a good look at the riders while the sponsors were glad of the chance to allow the millions of roadside spectators to better inspect the riders' bikes and the logos on their jerseys.

Stage eight presented an interruption to the sprinters' show with a trip from the spa town of Montecatini Terme over the Apennines to Reggio Emilia on the Po River plain. The day's hilly roads almost shouted for a break to go, and one did get away, almost at the start of the stage. Early on there were fifteen escapees, but as the break went over one mountain after another, it spit out one rider after another. At the finish, the initiator of the break, Pietro Caucchioli, rolled in alone. Frigo and his Fassa Bortolo team lost control of the chase and a small group of dangerous riders slipped away in a hard-fought, big-gear downhill race for the line. José Azevedo was one of these adventurers and the day's plundering brought him to within 3 seconds of the lead.

The next day Cipollini got his second stage win of the year bringing his total to 32, passing Costante Girardengo's 30 and Learco Guerra's 31. Only Alfredo Binda, at 41, had more.

Gilberto Simoni was an alert, sharp racer. When Matteo Tosatto went for a stage win with three kilometers to go on a short hill in stage twelve, Simoni made sure he was part of the party. Tosatto won the stage but Simoni's third place was good for a little time bonus. Plus, the pack didn't cross the line in Montebelluna for another 10 crucial seconds. Now Frigo could really feel hot breath on his neck. Simoni, the real stage race deal, was only one second behind.

Into the Dolomites! Stage thirteen started with the Passo Rolle, followed by the Pordoi, the Marmolada and then a second trip up the Pordoi, where the stage ended. On the Marmolada several good riders saw their Giro chances fade. Simoni's Lampre *gregari* set a hot pace up the hill, tossing Garzelli, Di Luca, Pantani and Azevedo, among others. On the Pordoi it was just Simoni and Julio Pérez-Cuapio working together, making for a lean, mean climbing machine. Simoni was happy for the help and eased slightly to let Pérez-Cuapio take the stage. Frigo gave chase, but he was in Simoni's cherished mountains and had to concede 45 seconds and the lead.

Now the standings were thus:
1. Gilberto Simoni
2. Dario Frigo @ 48 seconds
3. Wladimir Belli @ 1 minute 27 seconds
4. Unai Osa @ 1 minute 52 seconds
5. Ivan Gotti @ 2 minutes 14 seconds

That evening the Financial Police searched the van of Ivan Gotti's parents, presumably looking for dope, but no contraband was found. The racers should have taken this as another warning shot over their bow.

Stage fourteen had two major ascents, Monte Bondone and the Santa Barbara followed by a seventeen-kilometer downhill roll to the finish in Arco. The pack had no real interest in racing until the slopes of the Santa Barbara were reached, allowing a rather large group of about 50 to begin the climb together. Simoni's Lampre team again thinned the herd, dropping most of the peloton after just a few kilometers.

Simoni had a fan club of particularly rabid *tifosi* who wore T-shirts proclaiming that they were "Simoni Hooligans". As the leading riders climbed up the Santa Barbara passing through the narrow defile of spectators, one of Simoni's Hooligans got too close to Wladimir Belli. Belli, feeling threatened, hit the fan squarely in the nose.

Simoni couldn't distance himself from Frigo, Belli, Buenahora and stage winner Carlos Contreras but the rest of the pack lost still more time.

That evening, after hearing from Belli's team director, the officials still didn't think much of Belli's smacking the fan's nose. Even though he was sitting in third place, Belli was ejected from the Giro.

Garzelli, suffering from bronchitis, lost gobs of time. His team, not seeing any chance of an immediate recovery, pulled him rather than race him into the ground.

Frigo was one of the best time trialists in the world, so when the stage fifteen time trial arrived, it was thought he would be able to crush Simoni and regain the lead, balancing the competition between the two, given the mountains to come. Frigo did win the 55.5-kilometer stage, but Simoni was riding in a state of grace and lost only 28 seconds, saving his lead. Frigo would have to find some magic if he were to dislodge Simoni in the remaining mountain stages.

Simoni and Frigo were forging a considerable lead on the others:

1. Gilberto Simoni
2. Dario Frigo @ 15 seconds
3. Abraham Olano @ 4 minutes 32 seconds
4. Unai Osa @ 5 minutes 22 seconds
5. Serguei Gontchar @ 6 minutes 10 seconds

June 5 was a rest day that was followed by stage seventeen, a figure-eight loop starting and ending in San Remo. Perhaps indicative of how the day would go, two well-known racers were positive for EPO: Pascal Hervé and Pantani *gregario* Riccardo Forconi (who, remember, had already been ejected from the 1998 Giro). The day's racing had no particular effect upon the standings. With stage eighteen being the last high-mountain stage, the riders were probably keeping their powder dry for what they knew were real fireworks to come.

The fireworks came to the Giro sooner than expected and not of the type the riders liked. At nine in the evening, 200 police descended upon race teams' hotels and performed a thorough search. Witnesses said they saw vials and bottles being tossed out of windows as the police began turning the hotel inside out. Giuseppe Di Grande of Tacconi

Sport tried to escape the search by climbing out of a hotel window, but was caught. The 2001 "San Remo blitz" was probably the biggest anti-dope operation cycling had ever seen.

Unlike the stage eight raid, which came up empty, this time NAS hit the mother lode. Vast quantities of doping products were found: EPO, steroids, testosterone, assorted stimulants, syringes. The cheating hadn't stopped or even slowed since the supposed cleanup of the sport after 1998.

So how did the sport react with the clear evidence of wrongdoing out in the open for all to see? Again, the racers, race directors and coaches circled the wagons and explained that they and the racers deserved dignity and respect.

The racers, represented by Pantani (an odd choice given his doping history) and Cipollini met with Giro boss Castellano while some team managers held a meeting to protest the raids and to see if the Giro should be cancelled. The head of the UCI, Hein Verbruggen, complained about previous drug raids, the severity of the Italian anti-doping drug laws and voiced support for the racers' decision to protest the sweep.

The San Remo police commander's comments on the racer's indignation at being rousted showed he had dealt with malefactors in the past: "In my experience, anyone who is searched reacts strongly and feels that they have been treated like a delinquent."

There were more meetings. The methods of the police were deplored. Prime Minister-to-be Berlusconi promised that such a raid would never happen again, in effect, telling the riders to go ahead, dope away.

Verbruggen chimed in again. When I first read his comment that with only six EPO positives out of 700 to 800 tests given, the EPO problem was largely solved, I didn't know whether to ascribe his words to ignorance, rascality or stupidity. In fact, Hein Verbruggen is neither ignorant nor stupid.

The Italian Federation decided to call a halt to races in Italy for five days starting with June 23, well after the Giro was over, in order to assess the situation in Italian cycling. It was an interesting, but empty gesture, given that no races were scheduled during that period.

First it was planned to shorten the upcoming stage, but then it was cancelled. The riders agreed to continue participating in the *Grand Guignol* after being threatened with severe penalties. The 2001 Giro, like the 1998 Tour, was almost destroyed by a doping scandal. Carmine

Castellano was saddened by racing's newest dishonor: "The Giro has lost an arm and I have lost a piece of my heart."

Mercatone Uno, disappointed by Pantani's indifferent performance, suggested that he depart the Giro, which he did, claiming a fever.

The racing restarted with stage nineteen, a sprinters' stage won by Cipollini. That evening there was more bad news. The police announced they had found doping products in Frigo's room and his team withdrew him from the race. Castellano expressed his sadness that Frigo, in particular, had been caught up in the business of drugs, saying that Frigo was supposed to be the new fresh face of racing. Frigo's team, Fassa Bortolo, had now suffered a double disaster with both of their Classification riders, Belli and Frigo, out of the Giro.

Simoni rides alone in the rain.

It is usually the intention of the Giro organization to design a given edition so that the final outcome remains in doubt until the last possible moment. They want the fans to keep turning on their televisions and radios and rushing to the newsstands. Stage twenty with its two ascents of the Mottarone was intended to settle the issue. If Frigo were still in the race, the final ownership of the Pink Jersey would indeed have been in doubt until the riders crossed the finish line in Arona. With a four-minute lead over new second place Olano, only misfortune (which seemed to be coming in large servings this year) could derail Simoni's ride to victory.

The dark, rainy weather seemed to mirror the mood of the Giro after Frigo's disgrace. There were still those who wondered, with this latest blow, if the riders would race aggressively. Even with the race in the bag, Simoni was not going to just phone in the last mountain stage. On the second trip up the Mottarone the pugnacious racer lit the jets and the rest were powerless to resist. Cresting the mountain with a 90-second lead, he big-geared it down the other side. Even Savoldelli, with his magnificent descending skills, was unable to close the gap. Simoni showed he was a worthy Giro winner, beating Savoldelli to the finish by 2 minutes 25 seconds.

Cipollini picked up his 34th stage win in Milan and Simoni finalized his victory in the most troubled Giro ever. With Frigo gone, no one else was close to riding on his level. He fulfilled the promise he had shown in 1993 when he won the Baby Giro and the Italian Amateur Road Championship.

Final 2001 Giro d'Italia General Classification:
1. Gilberto Simoni (Lampre-Daikin) 89 hours 2 minutes 58 seconds
2. Abraham Olano (ONCE-Eroski) @ 7 minutes 31 seconds
3. Unai Osa (iBanesto.com) @ 8 minutes 37 seconds
4. Serguei Gontchar (Liquigas-Pata) @ 9 minutes 25 seconds
5. José Azevedo (ONCE-Eroski) @ 9 minutes 44 seconds

Climbers' Competition:
1. Freddy González (Selle Italia-Pacific): 73 points
2. Gilberto Simoni (Lampre-Daikin): 42
3. Fortunato Baliani (Selle Italia-Pacific): 33

Points Competition:
1. Massimo Strazzer (Mobilvetta-Formaggi Trentini): 177 points
2. Danilo Hondo (Deutsche Telekom): 158
3. Mario Cipollini (Saeco): 136

2002

What a Giro! It wasn't the racing that concentrated everyone's attention so much as the other events that unfolded during this interesting three weeks. Gilberto Simoni said that the 2002 Giro would be unpredictable. Indeed it was.

Just before the Giro started, the Italian Cycling Federation suspended six riders for six months as a result of the 2001 San Remo blitz. Pantani's case, centering on a mysterious insulin hypodermic that was found in his hotel room in the San Remo raid, was postponed until after the Giro, allowing the troubled rider to continue racing. A recommendation came out of that same Federation meeting that Pantani, who was again relapsing badly into cocaine abuse, receive a four-year suspension.

The two most powerful Spanish teams, iBanesto and ONCE, decided not to ride the Giro because the race wouldn't be televised in Spain. It was said the Spanish broadcast rights cost €300,000 and like the previous year, the Spanish television stations took a pass.

The Giro started with a prologue time trial in Groningen, Netherlands and then raced four stages in Germany, Belgium, Luxembourg and France before transferring to Fossano, south of Turin. The northern start was to celebrate the adoption of the euro currency by many countries in the European Union.

There were three hilltop finishes, the first one being the end of that first Italian stage starting in Fossano. This looked like an ungainly stage race with lots of transfers to allow the Giro to leap from one region to another. Simoni was hoping for a Giro with more climbing and expressed his disappointment in the race's design.

Before the start of the Giro I asked several experts, including Felice Gimondi and Franco Bitossi, who they thought would win the Giro. All the lists had the same riders, Gilberto Simoni, Francesco Casagrande, Stefano Garzelli, and Dario Frigo. Everyone hoped that Pantani would be able to recover from his troubles and be competitive again and two days before the race began Mercatone Uno listed him as a starter.

Frigo was seeking redemption, having served his six-month suspension for possessing what appeared to be banned drugs in the 2001 Giro. It later turned out that the vials that were found in the 2001 San Remo sweep were filled with salt water. Frigo had been snookered by his drug dealer and served a sentence for what was turned out to be attempted doping.

Sprinter Mario Cipollini had his own motivations for this Giro. Reaching 41 stage wins to match Binda was unlikely in this edition but he had won at least four stages in a single year six times.

Prologue winner Juan Carlos Domínguez of Phonak was the first Pink Jersey. His win was not something that the Giro management expected, so there was no Phonak logo to put on the presentation Pink Jersey for the awards ceremony, mightily rankling the Phonak director. Nestled in among the day's top placers was Paolo Savoldelli at fourth, only 4 seconds behind. Pantani, sporting a mustache and soul patch, did well enough, coming in 163rd out of 198 riders, losing only 46 seconds.

Between an intermediate sprint and the stage one win, Cipollini accumulated enough bonus seconds to take the lead. Behind him, a crash had split the field and Garzelli and Simoni, two of the more astute and skilled stage racers in the business, were the only contenders in the front group. Riders in the second group losing 25 seconds and more included Pantani, Tonkov, Gotti, Casagrande and Tyler Hamilton.

Speaking of being an astute rider, Garzelli showed he had head and legs when stage two roared into Liège. The Côte de Saint-Nicolas came just eight kilometers before the end. Casagrande put in a massive big-gear attack on the four-kilometer, ten-percent hill and it was lights out for the sprinters. Garzelli still had teammate Cadel Evans with him, who led out Garzelli for the stage win while Hamilton and Casagrande finished with the same time. Garzelli took the *maglia rosa*.

At the end of the fourth and final northern European stage, Garzelli was still in pink and 36-year-old Cipollini had already snared two stage wins.

Halfway into the first Italian stage, a break rolled off that included Garzelli's teammate Paolo Bettini. When the peloton arrived at the Coletto del Moro, Casagrande and Garzelli set a red-hot pace that drew all the good Classification riders. Further up the road, Bettini waited for this elite group.

Crash-prone Hamilton fell while trying to get up to the leaders, a lightened freewheel body probably having failed. Pain seemed to mean nothing to Hamilton. So, banged up as he was, he chased and made contact with the powerful and fast moving break. Bettini gave the breakaways all the help he could before expiring on the final ascent to the line.

As the leaders got closer to the hilltop finish line at Limone Piemonte, the attacks kept coming. Garzelli timed it perfectly and whooshed by everyone, taking his second stage win. Pantani came in seven minutes later.

The General Classification stood thus:

1. Stefano Garzelli
2. Francesco Casagrande @ 43 seconds
3. Gilberto Simoni @ 1 minute 0 seconds
4. Santiago Pérez @ 1 minute 3 seconds
5. Wladimir Belli @ 1 minute 6 seconds

On May 18, before the start of stage six, Stefano Garzelli's "A" urine sample, taken after his stage two win in Liège, tested positive for a diuretic called Probenecid. At the time, a positive test was called "non-negative" until a test of the second, or "B" sample confirmed the presence of the banned substance.

Probenecid was an old drug that had been easily detectable for over a decade. In the 1980s Probenecid was used to mask steroids, which are probably (we can never really know) no longer the choice of cheats. A diuretic can also raise a rider's hematocrit and an elevated hematocrit was a fast ticket home, making it less likely a racer would intentionally take the drug.

Garzelli was adamant about his use of the drug, "I would be a complete *testa di cazzo* [dickhead] to take something like this that could ruin my life, my family and my career. I had never heard of this drug or taken this drug. Even so, I did not want to continue, but the team has convinced me."

There were other drug problems. Roberto Sgambelluri (Mercatone Uno) was positive for a new version of EPO called NESP. Three Panaria riders were also caught using EPO: Faat Zakirov, Nicola Chesini (who was arrested for drug dealing), and Filippo Perfetto. Domenico Romano, a rider for the small Landbouwkrediet squad, heard that the police were looking for him in regards to drug trafficking and simply vanished.

At the time of Garzelli's positive I thought something was weird and I still do. It was confirmed that most of the riders in Garzelli's Mapei squad had to stop to urinate several times during stage two and Bettini and Garzelli said they had to stop several times to urinate in the first hour. I think someone spiked the team's food. By this point the reader should know that I am no fan of cheaters and have little patience for racers who claim to be innocent when the mass spectrograph finds them out, but sometimes things just don't add up and this is one of them.

Garzelli was allowed to continue racing pending the test of his "B" sample. Remembering the pain and humiliation of Madonna di Campiglio, Pantani said that Garzelli should not have been allowed to continue racing after his "A" sample positive. Garzelli shot back that he had every right under the rules to be in the race.

Stage six took the Giro out of Piedmont and on to the Ligurian coast, finishing in Varazze. A nine-rider *fuga di bidone* carved out a five-minute lead, letting an unlikely German rider who had begun his racing career under the old East German regime become the new overall leader. Jens Heppner of the Telekom squad now had a 3 minute 33 second lead over Garzelli.

Cipollini's stage nine win brought his total to 37. Heppner was still in pink and Garzelli was out of the Giro, the "B" sample confirming the presence of Probenecid in his system. Garzelli's exit gave Heppner a larger time cushion because the new second place was Yaroslav Popovych, 3 minutes 50 seconds behind.

Before the start of stage ten, it was announced that Simoni had tested positive for cocaine in an out-of-competition test performed before the start of the Giro del Trentino. Because the sample wasn't taken while Simoni was riding the Giro, his continuation in the race was not immediately endangered. Insisting he was innocent, Simoni speculated that a dentist's anesthetic might have triggered the positive.

The race was now at its southernmost point, Campania, for stage ten. Robbie McEwen won a stage whose uphill finish was too much for Lion King Cipollini.

Moving north into the Matese Mountains, southeast of Rome, the Giro got its first chance to test the riders' climbing legs with a hilltop finish at Campitello Matese. The leaders were together for the final rush up the mountain and with three kilometers to go, the ever-aggressive Simoni took off with Casagrande barely holding his wheel. Simoni won the stage, perhaps erasing some of the misery of the previous day's doping mess. Heppner kept his lead and Pantani remained in the race. He was with a large group that lost over eight minutes but was ahead of the autobus that lost fourteen.

The bright, good feeling Simoni enjoyed after his stage win was dashed the next day. Upon returning to his hotel after winning the Campitello

Matese sprint, three policemen were waiting for him, wanting to learn more about his cocaine positive. After this, pressure on Simoni's Saeco team grew to pull him. The next day Saeco did just that and now the last two Giro winners were watching the race on television.

After stage twelve was won by a break of five non-contenders the General Classification was thus:

1. Jens Heppner
2. Francesco Casagrande @ 2 minutes 58 seconds
3. Paolo Savoldelli @ 3 minutes 43 seconds
4. Pietro Caucchioli @ same time
5. Fernando Escartin @ 3 minutes 46 seconds

Stage thirteen with its arduous profile and hilltop finish changed the race, but in a way that wouldn't be completely apparent for a few days. Julio Pérez-Cuapio had the wings of an angel as he soared to the top of the San Giacomo climb for his second-ever Giro stage win. Behind him Casagrande wasn't feeling well and moreover was feeling grumpy because he was being marked so carefully by the others. The surprise was Australian Cadel Evans, who was the last rider to hold on to Pérez-Cuapio's wheel. Evans came in second, four seconds ahead of a charging Dario Frigo, making him fifth in the Overall, 2 minutes 39 seconds behind the still pink-clad Heppner.

Next was a hilly and technical individual time trial in Le Marche. So far Tyler Hamilton had accumulated three crashes. That collection didn't seem to hold him back when he soundly thrashed the rest of the field, leaping from eleventh place in the General Classification to third. Meanwhile Francesco Casagrande looked to have peaked too early. He had commanding form at the Giro del Trentino and again seemed to be running out of gas at the Giro. Tough-guy Heppner remained the leader.

With a rest day before the Dolomites, this was the General Classification:

1. Jens Heppner
2. Cadel Evans @ 48 seconds
3. Tyler Hamilton @ 1 minute 6 seconds
4. Francesco Casagrande @ 1 minute 7 seconds
5. Dario Frigo @ 1 minute 11 seconds

Francesco Casagrande kept inventing new ways to lose the Giro. In stage fifteen he ran Colombian rider John Freddy García into the barriers while sprinting for King of the Mountains points. He got nothing more for his nasty riding than a ticket home. Now three of the Giro's top riders were out. Cipollini won a rain-soaked sprint for number 38.

I'm sure Cipollini was not looking forward to the next stage, but he stuck it out. Stage sixteen, *il tappone*, had four major passes to negotiate: Staulanza, Marmolada, Pordoi (the *Cima Coppi*) and the Campolongo.

Pérez-Cuapio, who still posed no threat to the Classification riders, made a gutsy move on the Marmolada and managed to stay away over all three of the remaining major passes, riding in alone to Corvara in Badia where the champagne was waiting for him. Back in the peloton the contenders arrived at the base of the Pordoi together. Pietro Caucchioli executed his grand move to take the lead with a well-timed attack and then made contact with a teammate who had been off the front. But, his teammate had been away for too long and had no more gas in the tank; Caucchioli was on his own. Meanwhile, Paolo Savoldelli set the road on fire descending the Pordoi and passed Caucchioli. He came within 53 seconds of Pérez-Cuapio at the end with Frigo finishing two seconds later. Pantani, suffering from bronchitis, abandoned at the feed zone.

As expected, the first day in the Dolomites cost Heppner his lead. And who was the leader now? Ex-mountain biker Cadel Evans, who had been brought to the Giro to help Garzelli. Here was the new General Classification:

1. Cadel Evans
2. Dario Frigo @ 16 seconds
3. Tyler Hamilton @ 18 seconds
4. Aitor González @ 24 seconds
5. Pietro Caucchioli @ 32 seconds
6. Paolo Savoldelli @ 48 seconds

The Financial Police, finding that raiding cyclists' hotel rooms was an easy way to catch malefactors, went hunting again, conducting ultimately fruitless searches of teams that had raised their suspicions: Mercatone Uno, Mapei, Panaria and Saeco.

No one could have predicted the twists and turns of this Giro. Stage seventeen, the final day in the high mountains, supplied enough surprises for an entire three-week race. The Dolomites weren't letting the racers leave without enduring a serious caning in the form of the Gardena, Sella, Santa Barbara, Bordala and Folgaria climbs.

Pérez-Cuapio thought he was on a roll and took off again, this time on the Santa Barbara. Pavel Tonkov instantly gained his wheel and the pair soon had a two-minute lead. This was where Pérez-Cuapio discovered that he wasn't Superman. After three weeks of aggressive racing behind him and about ten kilometers to go before the stage's end, his legs exploded. Tonkov said "Adios" and motored up the Passo Coe for the stage win in Folgaria while Pérez-Cuapio lost more than ten minutes.

The same Passo Coe that put paid to Pérez-Cuapio's stage win ambitions cracked the Giro wide open when the *maglia rosa* group hit it. First Dario Frigo started turning squares. In an instant he went from second place in the Giro and looking like a possible overall winner to a man who could barely turn the pedals. Then, wham! Giro leader Cadel Evans hit the wall. In those last few kilometers he lost seventeen minutes. Evans, climbing on pure determination, crossed the line in a daze and kept riding right past his waiting soigneur.

Savoldelli, sensing that the moment had arrived, jumped away with Hamilton on his wheel. And now Hamilton couldn't maintain the pace and had to let *Il Falco* go. Two minutes after Tonkov, Savoldelli crossed the finish line and claimed the Pink Jersey. Hamilton lost almost two minutes to Savoldelli in those final kilometers.

The new overall standings:
1. Paolo Savoldelli
2. Pietro Caucchioli @ 55 seconds
3. Tyler Hamilton @ 1 minute 28 seconds
4. Juan Manuel Gárate @ 1 minute 39 seconds
5. Pavel Tonkov @ 3 minutes 8 seconds

Before the final time trial, the sprinters had another drag race, this time in Brescia. Cipollini made it five for this Giro and 39 for his career.

At 44.3 kilometers and with lots of curves and always slightly uphill, the final time trial required a good all-around bike rider. If Hamilton were to take the Giro lead, he would have to gain about two seconds per kilometer on The Falcon, a tall order given that Savoldelli was looking stronger with every passing day and Hamilton had shown real fatigue in stage seventeen.

Two time trial specialists took the first two places, Aitor Gonzáles and Serguei Gontchar. But Savoldelli, the rider who looked so young the

Italians nicknamed him "Babyface", came in third. Hamilton, usually good against the clock, lost 13 seconds and the Giro was Savoldelli's.

The final rush into Milan was Cipollini's, making six stage wins for the year and bringing his total to 40, still one shy of the great Binda.

Savoldelli, who had suffered from back problems for a couple of years, wasn't on the likely-winner lists. Yet his second place in 1999 with almost no team support should have been a warning that this man was not to be ignored. Savoldelli was a complete rider; his descending skills were legendary, but his climbing and time-trialing were also world-class.

La Gazzetta lamented the inglorious doping-caused departure of six riders along with the race's other troubles, and forgetting other, more troubled editions, called it the most unfortunate edition in its history.

Final 2002 Giro d'Italia General Classification:
1. Paolo Savoldelli (Index-Alexia) 89 hours 22 minutes 42 seconds
2. Tyler Hamilton (CSC-Tiscali) @ 1 minute 41 seconds
3. Pietro Caucchioli (Alessio) @ 2 minutes 12 seconds
4. Juan Manuel Gárate (Lampre-Daikin) @ 3 minutes 14 seconds
5. Pavel Tonkov (Lampre-Daikin) @ 5 minutes 34 seconds

Climbers' Competition:
1. Julio Pérez-Cuapio (Ceramiche Panaria-Fiordo): 69 points
2. José Joaquim Castelblanco (Colombia-Selle Italia): 33
3. Pavel Tonkov (Lampre-Daikin): 25

Points Competition:
1. Mario Cipollini (Acqua & Sapone-Cantina Tollo): 184 points
2. Massimo Strazzer (Phonak): 166
3. Aitor González (Kelme-Costa Blanca): 106

Pantani was handed a penalty of 3,000 Swiss francs and an eight-month racing suspension over the insulin syringe found during the 2001 San Remo raid. This was just the sporting penalty; a criminal investigation regarding the syringe continued. Pictures of Pantani in 2002 show the effects of the stress, the cocaine and the performance-enhancing drugs that had been pumped into his veins to keep him racing during the three years since his *squalificato*. He had aged visibly.

2003

The 86th Giro departed slightly from previous editions by scheduling the first five stages in the southernmost regions of the peninsula. The 17,300 meters of total elevation gained weren't great by Giro standards, but with five hilltop finishes the climbers had plenty of chances to assert their superiority.

Simoni was exonerated from the cocaine doping charges. His explanation that a present of candy from Peru triggered the positive was accepted. He was back to racing and raring to go. His form was excellent, with victories in both the Giro del Trentino and the Giro dell'Appennino.

Garzelli served a suspension after his Probenecid positive and stopped riding for five months. He started racing in April. He must have been doing something right because he took the first stage of the Trentino tune-up and finished second overall to Simoni.

Neither of the two unexpected heroes of the 2002 Giro, Savoldelli and Evans, entered. They had both signed with the German Telekom outfit and were focusing their efforts on getting ready for the Tour de France.

After being disqualified from the Gent–Wevelgem race in April for throwing a water bottle at an official, Cipollini, now the World Road Champion, had decided to stop racing for a while. He entered this Giro to capture those two stage wins he needed to surpass Binda.

Again, Pantani was going to give the Giro another shot. After serving his eight-month suspension, he had been training diligently in Spain. Everyone wanted a piece of Pantani: sponsors, race promoters and prosecutors. Although he was in adequate physical condition, the real truth was heartbreaking. He was by this time a cocaine-addicted, paranoid, bipolar mental basket-case who was in no state to withstand the stresses of high-level professional racing.

And again, no Spanish teams entered.

Cipollini, showing the effects of his time off the bike, was denied his heart's desire when young Alessandro Petacchi out-sprinted him in Lecce, earning both his first-ever Giro stage win and 2003's first Pink Jersey.

If there were questions about Garzelli's ability to be competitive in a major stage race given his recent return to racing after his suspension, he stopped a lot of tongues when he easily took the stage three uphill sprint ahead of Casagrande and Petacchi. The heavy roads were expected to shell all the sprinters but Petacchi wasn't giving up his Pink Jersey without a fight and got to spend another night with his *maglia rosa* while Garzelli moved into second place.

The warm sun of Sicily seemed to slow the riders. The first three hours of stage five were ridden at the easy pace of 29 kilometers per hour, but there is never anything easy about the final hour of a Giro stage, which is normally blitzed at just slightly faster than the speed of sound. Petacchi finished off the southern stages with another stage win, again denying Cipollini one of the two stages he wanted so badly, allowing Petacchi to take his lead back to the mainland.

After five stages the General Classification was thus:
1. Alessandro Petacchi
2. Stefano Garzelli @ 49 seconds
3. Francesco Casagrande @ 59 seconds
4. Franco Pellizotti @ 1 minute 4 seconds
5. Gilberto Simoni @ same time

The transfer to the mainland brought the race to Maddaloni, just north of Naples. From here the race would point almost directly to Northern Italy and the high mountains. After being outsmarted in the sprints by Petacchi, Cipollini was refreshingly frank about his lack of recent success, taking the blame and ruing that he was getting on in years.

So far the climbers hadn't been able to strut their stuff, but the Terminillo ascent at the end of stage seven should solve that problem. As the peloton started the climb, Garzelli had his teammates up the pace. Almost immediately Frigo, Vuelta winner Aitor González, Pantani and Casagrande were dropped. Further up, Simoni had his remaining *gregari* lighten the field a bit more. Then it was down to Garzelli and Simoni. Simoni tested Garzelli with several accelerations. This jumping and pausing slowed their pace and allowed Andrea Noè to join them, making the stage finish a three-up sprint. Under these conditions Garzelli was almost unbeatable. Exactly one year after he won at Limone Piemonte, Garzelli had won the year's first crucial stage and taken the overall lead.

The real contenders were now in the open:
1. Stefano Garzelli
2. Gilberto Simoni @ 31 seconds
3. Andrea Noè @ 44 seconds
4. Marius Sabaliauskas @ 1 minute 28 seconds
5. Franco Pellizotti @ 1 minute 36 seconds

He had to get one eventually, and in Arezzo Cipollini finally won his stage and equaled Alfredo Binda's 41 Giro stage wins.

NAS continued its program of making sure that the riders kept their dope out of their hotel rooms by searching the rooms of the Formaggi Pinzolo team. They came up empty-handed.

The next morning Cipollini got the unwelcome news that his Domina Vacanze team (as well as Pantani's Mercatone Uno squad) was not invited to the Tour de France. With the emotion of that rejection fueling his ride, Cipollini made it two stage wins in a row, making him the absolute Giro stage win record holder at 42.

Starting in Montecatini, west of Florence and going northeast over the Apennines into Emilia-Romagna for a finish in Faenza, stage ten's rugged profile promised a hard day in the saddle.

A break of sixteen riders, mostly good journeymen, took off on the day's first climb, the Croce di Calenzano while Garzelli's boys worked to keep them from disappearing too far into the distance. When the break hit the penultimate climb, Monte Casale, Simoni's teammate Leonardo Bertagnolli escaped. Shortly thereafter the peloton arrived on the Casale and Simoni got out of the saddle and just rode away, quickly gaining 30 seconds. Strangely, this move seemed to generate no interest on Garzelli's part.

Up ahead, Bertagnolli was waiting for Simoni and on the final climb, Simoni made contact with him and two of the other breakaways, Norwegian road champion Kurt-Asle Arvesen and Paolo Tiralongo. Now it was a smooth-working team of four good riders gutting themselves to stay away from a chase group that expected the *maglia rosa* to do almost all of the work. The result? Arvesen won the stage and Simoni's third place in the stage was good for an eight-second time bonus. When Garzelli came in 25 seconds later, he was no longer the Giro's leader. Simoni's tactical exploit had made him the Pink Jersey by two seconds.

The new General Classification:
1. Gilberto Simoni
2. Stefano Garzelli @ 2 seconds
3. Andrea Noè @ 56 seconds
4. Franco Pellizotti @ 1 minute 38 seconds
5. Pavel Tonkov @ 1 minute 52 seconds

Cipollini's Giro went from joyous triumph to painful misery. The next day's stage took the Giro to the start of the high mountains, a pan-flat run to San Donà di Piave held on a rain-soaked day.

Looking for stage win number 43, Cipollini's lead-out train was churning giant gears as Isaac Galvez tried to pass up the inside of a hard left hand corner. The wet, oily streets didn't hold his tires and he slid into Cipollini, taking them both across the street and into the barriers. After an evening's visit to the hospital, Cipollini withdrew from the Giro. Later Cipollini said this crash effectively ended his career.

Simoni had been complaining that so far the climbs had been inadequate. The steeper the road, the greater his advantage. With the Fuessa, Sella Valcalda and a new-to-the-Giro hilltop finish at Monte Zoncolan, stage twelve would advantage the hell out of him. Marco Pantani mounted a 28 on the rear of his bike while Simoni had prepared a spare machine with a triple crankset to handle the Zoncolan's final kilometer of 22 percent gradient.

A small group arrived at the Zoncolan climb together. Local rider Marzio Bruseghin had tried his luck with a gutsy earlier escape and still had a small gap. Riding tempo at the front was…Mercatone Uno! Pantani was feeling good and asked his teammates to keep the pace high and breakaways in sight.

It wasn't until the Zoncolan pitch became a wall that Simoni made his move. When he jumped away the others could only work to limit their losses. Garzelli kept him to within 34 seconds, but Simoni was the rider of the day. Pantani was looking like third place, until Casagrande and Yaroslav Popovych crawled by him on the near vertical hillside. That was still good enough for fifth place, ahead of Pérez-Cuapio.

Simoni now had a 44-second lead on Garzelli and Pantani had pulled himself up to ninth place at 5 minutes 56 seconds.

Stage fourteen was another climber's fest. After crossing three major passes, the contending riders found themselves together at the foot of Alpe di Pampeago, nine kilometers of 9.6-percent gradient. At about halfway up, Simoni tested the climbing legs of the others and then eased to let things come together. Popovych tried his luck and then it was over when Simoni did a smashing counter-attack and sped by everyone. Garzelli's response to Simoni's explosive accelerations had been consistent. He didn't get rattled and rode as if he knew that he had to do the climbs at his own pace and not try to match a specialist on his own turf. This time Simoni's stage win cost Garzelli 35 seconds. Pantani was not as brilliant as he was in stage twelve, but still finished a credible twelfth, two minutes behind Simoni.

Garzelli was expected to close the gap to Simoni in the stage fifteen 42.5-kilometer individual time trial. The route followed the Adige River south to Bolzano and should have presented a rider with Garzelli's sterling time trial skills a golden opportunity, but the lack of competition in Garzelli's legs was beginning to show. Instead of gaining time, he lost more ground to Simoni who seemed to be getting better with every passing day. That left the General Classification thus:

1. Gilberto Simoni
2. Stefano Garzelli @ 1 minute 58 seconds
3. Yaroslav Popovych @ 4 minutes 5 seconds
4. Andrea Noè @ 5 minutes 16 seconds
5. Raimondas Rumsas @ 6 minutes 11 seconds

After all this intense racing there were still the Alpine stages to ride. Arguably the year's *tappone*, stage eighteen had four major passes including the Esichie/Fauniera—the 2003 *Cima Coppi*—and ended with a hilltop finish at Valle Varaita. Following the Esichie, Simoni reduced the field on the Sampeyre with a red-hot blast up the mountain. Over the top of the Sampeyre as snow began to fall, Simoni managed to drop Garzelli, having only Popovych, Frigo and Georg Totschnig for company as they rode in the wheeltracks of the lead cars. Popovych bombed the descent and arrived at the bottom ahead of the trio. At the start of the final climb, with Simoni on his wheel, Frigo caught and dumped Popovych. After doing most of the work he out-sprinted Simoni for the stage win.

Garzelli was having a rough time of it. He and Pantani crashed while descending the wet roads of the Sampeyre. Garzelli was up in a flash, but Pantani looked hurt. He eventually got back on his bike and finished the stage. Garzelli saved his second place, but only just, his crash more or less sealing the Giro for Simoni. The difficulties this stage presented are hard to overstate—both the Esichie and the Sampeyre descents are demanding under good conditions, let alone with rain or snow. Thirty-five riders failed to make the time cutoff and were eliminated from the race.

The standings:
1. Gilberto Simoni
2. Stefano Garzelli @ 7 minutes 8 seconds
3. Yaroslav Popovych @ 7 minutes 19 seconds
4. Andrea Noè @ 9 minutes 19 seconds
5. Georg Totschnig @ 9 minutes 29 seconds

There was one mountain stage left, a trip due north just west of Milan and into the Alps with a hilltop finish on the Cascata del Toce. During the last kilometers of the final ascent, Garzelli was dropped from the group of climbers that remained: Simoni, Pellizotti, Frigo, Pantani and Belli. Now a sight occurred that warmed the hearts of the *tifosi*. Out of the saddle, in his trademark style with his hands on the drops, Pantani took off. A Pantani attack on a mountain road is taken lightly only by the foolhardy. Simoni immediately went after him. Pantani went again, and again Simoni closed the gap. Now Pellizotti jumped and Simoni made the decisive counter-attack. No one could go with the soaring *maglia rosa* and Simoni won his third stage while Garzelli kept his second place over Popovych by two seconds. Pantani's fans were thrilled, it seemed almost like 1998 again.

That left only the final time trial. Simoni's lead was impregnable but Garzelli's two-second lead over Popovych was tissue paper. Garzelli defended his place and extended his lead by three more seconds.

There can be no doubt that the best rider won the race. Simoni said that unlike 2001 when he was scrambling for seconds at every opportunity, this victory was the result of several set pieces that had been planned well in advance.

Final 2003 Giro d'Italia General Classification:
1. Gilberto Simoni (Saeco) 89 hours 32 minutes 9 seconds
2. Stefano Garzelli (Vini Caldirola-So.Di) @ 7 minutes 6 seconds
3. Yaroslav Popovych (Landbouwkrediet-Colnago) @ 7 minutes 11 seconds
4. Andrea Noè (Alessio) @ 9 minutes 24 seconds
14. Marco Pantani (Mercatone Uno-Scanavino) @ 26 minutes 15 seconds

Climbers' Competition:
1. Freddy González (Colombia-Selle Italia): 100 points
2. Gilberto Simoni (Saeco): 78
3. Constantino Zaballa (Kelme-Costa Blanca): 65

Points Competition:
1. Gilberto Simoni (Saeco): 154 points
2. Stefano Garzelli (Vini Caldirola-So.Di): 154 (although Garzelli was tied on points Simoni won more stages)
3. Jan Svorada (Lampre): 137

❧

In the final days of the Giro, as he was beginning to find his form, Pantani started wondering about riding the Tour and testing his abilities against Armstrong. Mercatone Uno had been built around him and almost entirely depended upon him for victories and was thus low in the team standings and could not get an invitation to the Tour. Inquiries were made on Pantani's behalf to see if he might be allowed to ride the Tour on Jan Ullrich's Bianchi team. Initially Bianchi said no because the team already had two classification riders and there was no room for him. An attempt was made to find a place for Pantani on Garzelli's Vini Caldirola squad.

Both Bianchi and Vini Caldirola eventually said they would accept the 1998 Tour winner in their ranks. The UCI and the Tour organization also agreed to it. But then, as the negotiations dragged on, Pantani hung up his bike and decided that as a former winner he should not be riding as some sort of special guest. The troubled rider effectively said no to the Tour. As this play was going on, Pantani again descended into a round of cocaine abuse.

With difficulty he was talked into checking into an Italian clinic for treatment of addiction. When the media found he was at the clinic, he left and released a letter to his fans saying that in his present state he was unable to race and would return to the sport when he had overcome his troubles. Meanwhile, the inquiry into his disqualification from the 1999 Giro finally came to a conclusion. Although there was clear evidence showing he was doped, he was found to be innocent of any crime against then-existing Italian law. The 2003 Giro was Pantani's last race. In February of 2004 he was found in a hotel in Rimini, dead of a cocaine overdose.

❧

On November 23, 2003, Judge Franca Oliva acquitted Francesco Conconi of the doping charges that had been pending against him for so long. The ruling said that if sporting fraud were not a crime at the time of the offense, which it wasn't, Conconi could not be guilty of a crime of sporting fraud. Moreover, there was no specific evidence proving Conconi had been personally involved with helping riders break any drug laws.

In late March of 2004, Oliva issued a 44-page report on the lengthy Conconi investigation and prosecution. While Conconi and his assistants weren't legally guilty of a crime, Oliva stated unequivocally that they were morally guilty of helping athletes dope. The report was damning in its list of Conconi clients who had exhibited highly volatile hematocrit values. Hematologists hired by the Italian government said these highly variable blood values could be assumed to show EPO use. Among the riders the report said had used EPO were Giro/Tour/World Champion Stephen Roche, Marco Pantani, Claudio Chiappucci, Evgeni Berzin, Ivan Gotti, Gianni Bugno and Piotr Ugrumov. This was a Who's Who of cycling in the 1990s and showed how deeply the fangs of organized doping had sunk into professional cycling.

Drugs change the sport. We like athletic competitions to be a test of an athlete's physical gifts honed through endless hours of training and well as his mental toughness and tactical skills. But bodies respond differently to drugs and some athletes, who would otherwise have to fight as one of many near equals, become magnificent champions when doped. Witness Bjarne Riis' sudden and almost effortless rise from domestique to winner of the Tour de France. Pantani was one such (un)lucky man. He had been the amateur Giro champion (there is reason now to believe even that victory may have been purchased with dope) and hence was a man with amazing physical gifts. With the addition of cutting edge drugs, in 1998 and 1999 he was the finest rider on Earth.

Was he a bad guy? Was he a hero? I think he was neither. He may have been either delusional or dishonest about his own doping, but the idea that he alone was caught and humiliated when the rest of the peloton was also obviously drugged seems to be the basis of his paranoid feelings of conspiracy. I think it was Poulidor who felt that drug testing was inherently unfair because so many could evade drug controls. Most racers understand the devil's deal of professional competition and drugs, but Pantani's mental instabilities made tragic the consequences of being caught. One could make a strong argument that he was, above all, a tool of an unbelievably corrupt sport that saw him as a fabulous money machine.

He was pulled apart by competing interests. When he should have been given time to recover and find peace as his psychologists had counseled, others—some of whom honestly believed it would be the best way for him do deal with his mental problems—urged him to keep racing. He was too valuable to be cloistered in a clinic recovering.

All over northern Italy prosecutors harassed him. Pier Bergonzi of *La Gazzetta dello Sport* said there were at least seven investigations into Marco Pantani opened by various police and judicial bodies. Yes, he had misbehaved, but so had much of the professional peloton. Pantani, being Italy's most famous sportsman, was singled out for celebrity justice. One wonders, if Pantani's handlers had been more honest about the poor state of his mental health, would he have so unrelentingly targeted by law enforcement.

The *tifosi* now understand all about who Pantani was and what he did, yet they still adore him. For all his flaws, for a couple of years he was extraordinary and he did make them dream.

six

2004–2011

Angelo Zomegnan Takes Over and the Giro Thrives

2004 The 2004 Giro was one of the most interesting in modern history because of the fascinating interplay between its two main protagonists.

Compared to the two previous editions, from a sporting point of view the 2004 Giro was more like other recent editions. Instead of about 80 kilometers of time trialing, the 2004 Giro had only 59, split into a 6.9-kilometer prologue and the stage thirteen 52-kilometer individual time trial at Trieste. The three hilltop finishes were in line with regular Giro design.

Simoni's spring racing results didn't give any sign that he was going to be particularly competitive. But just before the Giro, he pulled a rabbit out of his hat by taking third in the Giro del Trentino. His team director said that Simoni's build-up was intended to be slow because Simoni planned to ride both the Giro and the Tour. He was to be the team's undisputed Classification leader and the Saeco team would ride completely at Simoni's service.

All of the other fine riders entered were thought to be nothing more than podium contenders: Giuliano Figueras, Wladimir Belli, Yaroslav Popovych and Franco Pellizotti. One of Simoni's teammates, 22-year-old

Damiano Cunego, was considered a somewhat remote possibility for a top three placing. That was badly underestimating the man who was victorious (over Simoni) in the Giro del Trentino while winning two stages. The young man had shown a mastery of the art of bicycle racing far beyond his years.

The prologue was run through old Genoa over a highly technical course, which Australian Bradley McGee won, snagging the year's first Pink Jersey. Neither Garzelli nor Simoni embarrassed themselves, finishing within 11 seconds of each other, both relieved to have finished their rides safely and without major time loss. The surprise was that Simoni was the faster of the two. Moreover, Simoni's *gregario* Cunego was able to beat Garzelli by a second.

From Genoa, the Giro headed south down the western side of the peninsula. In stage two, Simoni's Saeco squad showed their confidence in Cunego's all-around talents. Near the crest of the final hill they had Cunego take a hard pull to break up the peloton. Then, in the 21-kilometer descent to the finish they continued to keep the speed high, preventing a regrouping, although all the favorites were in the front group.

For the sprint Saeco formed a train that led Cunego out for a surprising win, considering that speedy Bradley McGee was right in the sprinter's scrum. With the time bonus for second place, McGee regained the lead he had lost in the first stage. Cunego was now in fourth place, well ahead of Simoni and Garzelli. Simoni pronounced himself well pleased with the result and glad that Popovych, who had also joined the sprint mix, had been denied any bonus time.

Stage three, the first hilltop finish of the year, took the riders through the mountain terrain north of Lucca and Pistoia and past the Saeco espresso machine factory. On the day's final climb, to the Corno alle Scale ski station, the Saeco squad hit the front hard, some of them in the big ring. With two kilometers to go the best riders were still together, so Saeco's Eddy Mazzoleni took the pace up another notch and then Cunego exploded off the front. Then Simoni sped past Cunego for the solo stage win and the Pink Jersey. Cunego was caught by the chasers, but even after working all day as a *gregario*, he out-sprinted them for second place. It was early days, but so far Saeco was demonstrating complete control of the race. Garzelli lost 34 seconds, putting him slightly more than a minute behind Simoni.

The Story of the Giro d'Italia

The General Classification stood thus:
1. Gilberto Simoni
2. Damiano Cunego @ 13 seconds
3. Yaroslav Popovych @ 21 seconds
4. Franco Pellizotti @ 29 seconds
5. Gerhard Trampusch @ 41 seconds

The next three stages were taken over by the sprinters as the Giro wound its way south through Tuscany, Umbria and Lazio. Alessandro Petacchi won two more stages, bringing his total so far for the year to three. Robbie McEwen took stage five, sandwiching himself between the extraordinary Italian's victories. Through these high-speed flatter stages Simoni kept the *maglia rosa*.

Stage seven was the year's second hilltop finish, at the Montevergine di Mercogliano, sited a bit east of Naples. While Saeco kept the speed high and did all it could to discourage attacks, no one was deterred in the slightest. A third of the way up the climb Simoni tried to get away, but Garzelli was having none of that. Giuliano Figueras launched himself up the road three times, but each time Cunego marked him. With less than two kilometers to go Simoni went again and again Garzelli was on his wheel. After a short pause, Simoni moved to the front and just rode hard. With a half-kilometer to go, out from behind Simoni, Cunego blasted away and took the stage win, the twenty-second time bonus and the *maglia rosa*.

Simoni said that he couldn't get away with all the other riders watching his wheel. That made a nice excuse, but Cunego didn't win because the others weren't policing him. He won because he simply went faster than anyone else could. He was winning hard stages with an ease reminiscent of the young Greg LeMond. Cunego voiced hope he would keep the lead for another week, before the Giro hit the high mountains, while Simoni expressed pleasure that a teammate was keeping the Pink Jersey warm for him, allowing him to race without the pressure of defending the lead.

The new General Classification:
1. Damiano Cunego
2. Gilberto Simoni @ 10 seconds
3. Franco Pellizotti @ 28 seconds
4. Yaroslav Popovych @ 31 seconds
5. Giuliano Figueras @ 52 seconds

The next day Petacchi showed how talented he was when he won stage eight, meaning that so far he had won half the year's stages. Robbie McEwen tried to get up to Petacchi for the sprint by getting a madison-type hand sling from a teammate. He was caught by the judges and relegated.

As the Giro finished its ride across the arch of the Italian boot, American sprinter Fred Rodriguez caught Petacchi and his Fassa Bortolo team napping by jumping early and taking stage nine, taking the first Giro road stage win by an American since Andy Hampsten in 1988.

With the first rest day came a long transfer from the southernmost part of Italy up to Le Marche. Some observers noted the similarities between the Saeco of 2004 and the 1986 La Vie Claire team with young Greg LeMond and the aging master, Bernard Hinault; yet the two showed no signs of strain between them during the day-off press conference. Simoni said he was grateful Cunego had assumed the weight of the Pink Jersey. Cunego in turn, was humble and appreciative of the guidance Simoni gave him and said that some day in the future he would also like to win the Giro.

Stage eleven, finishing in Cesena, showed that while Saeco may be the strongest team in the race, their power and endurance did have limits. A capable break went off the front after about 65 kilometers and with 45 kilometers to go, on the Passo delle Siepi, neo-pro Emanuele Sella took off.

Back in the peloton, it dawned on the Saeco team that the little Sella, who was showing a heretofore-unrevealed ability, was the virtual *maglia rosa*, forcing the red-suited Saecos to try to put an end to this nonsense. Soon the chase group was down to fifteen, with Cunego and Simoni the only Saeco riders left, the others having been burnt up in the pursuit. Unafraid to help their own cause, the team leaders did yeoman's work and kept Sella's lead manageable. Even though the speed over the stage's rolling terrain was fearsome (over 48 kilometers per hour at the 133-kilometer point), Sella managed to stay away and take the solo win. Cunego kept the Pink Jersey but the Saeco team was showing wear and tear with more than a week of racing left.

All nine Fassa Bortolo riders lined up to head for the stage nine finish in Treviso and let loose "Ale-Jet" Petacchi for another stage victory. The other sprinters had figured out that the only chance for a win was to be on Petacchi's wheel in the final kilometer and as the Giro progressed, they grew more desperate, each stage exhibiting ever more furious and dangerous fights for his wheel. No matter how hard they tried, no one seemed to be able to get past the speedy Italian when his sprint machine was working perfectly. Stage twelve was no exception. So far Petacchi was still victorious in half the year's stages.

Stage thirteen was the Giro's race against the clock. It was a difficult course, technical and with a climb that had a short patch of fourteen-percent gradient. To make the ride even more challenging, before the main contenders hit the road a light rain began to fall. The racers nonetheless still used their tricky-handling but faster time trial bikes. Simoni crashed and Garzelli, who had taken off like a rocket, had to change machines because of a broken derailleur. He never regained his rhythm and lost a half-minute. Mister Big-Gear himself, Serguei Gontchar, won the stage, but his Ukrainian compatriot Popovych got the big prize, his third place being good enough for pink.

That made for a rearranged General Classification:
1. Yaroslav Popovych
2. Serguei Gontchar @ 3 seconds
3. Bradley McGee @ 1 minute 2 seconds
4. Gilberto Simoni @ 1 minute 27 seconds
5. Franco Pellizotti @ 1 minute 32 seconds
6. Damiano Cunego @ 1 minute 48 seconds

Stage fourteen went due south through the Istrian peninsula to Pola where Petacchi made history by winning seven stages in a single Giro, equaling the postwar record of de Vlaeminck, Maertens and Saronni. Popovych stayed in pink.

Seven weren't enough. In the last stage before the high mountains, the Fassa Bortolo team did another perfect lead-out into San Vendemiano. Now Petacchi joined the truly great. With eight stage wins in the 2004 Giro, he joined Binda (1923) and Girardengo (1929), extraordinary company. Binda's 1927 absolute record of twelve stage wins (out of a possible fifteen that year) still looked to be safe, perhaps forever.

Stage sixteen, *il tappone*, was of surpassing difficulty with four major climbs: Forcella Staulanza, Passo di Valparola, Passo Furcia and the Terento, totaling 46 kilometers of climbing.

By the time the Valparola had been crossed, Saeco had three good riders in various escapes that were ahead of the *maglia rosa* group. On the Furcia, Simoni stretched his legs and found Garzelli was having another bad day, and Popovych's weak Landbouwkrediet team had already left him isolated. When the group got near the top of the Furcia, Cunego went like a bullet. Popovych had to make a choice, stay with Simoni, the team leader, or try to go with Cunego, who might be trying to get him to waste his energy by chasing a *gregario's* attacks. There were no good choices. Popovych decided to stick with Simoni as Cunego disappeared.

Martinelli told the scattered Saeco riders up the road to wait for Cunego, which they did, and soon there were four of them working together. By the final climb Cunego had dropped everyone and soloed in for his third stage win along with the overall lead. Saeco's execution of a tactically perfect stage brought admiration from competitors and spectators alike.

The General Classification at this point:
    1. Damiano Cunego
    2. Serguei Gontchar @ 1 minute 14 seconds
    3. Yaroslav Popovych @ 2 minutes 22 seconds
    4. Gilberto Simoni @ 2 minutes 38 seconds
    5. Giuliano Figueras @ 3 minutes 31 seconds

The evening before the second rest day, NAS executed another blitz on targeted Giro riders' hotel rooms as part of an Italy-wide raid and came up empty.

In the rest day interviews Simoni talked through clenched teeth when discussing Cunego's Pink Jersey. Both Saeco riders explained that a pact had been made. While each would be free to ride his own race, neither would attack the other. Simoni said that he wanted to win this Giro with or without Cunego, but wasn't sure how that eventuality could be brought about. The knowledge that Cunego had been given (or had taken) too much rope in the last stage seemed to weigh heavily upon Simoni who was already talking about the Tour and taking on Armstrong.

Stage seventeen, with its single major climb, the Passo della Mendola before an uphill drag to Fondo Sarnonico was an unusual day of racing. Cunego had bike problems early in the stage and was given the wrong bike. Even more strangely, the *maglia rosa* had to chase back to the peloton largely on his own. It was a while before a couple of Saeco riders dropped back to help. Cunego continued to have mechanical problems and had to change bikes at least one more time.

By far the weirdest event of all was Pavel Tonkov's behavior. Halfway through the stage Alessandro Bertolini escaped with Oscar Pozzi. Late in the stage, on the Mendola, Tonkov bridged up to the now solo Bertolini. With a few kilometers to go Tonkov dropped Bertolini and soloed in to the finish. It would have been fine win, except he saluted the crowd with a vulgar gesture as he crossed the line. Tonkov had suffered through several bad years and this was his first big win in some time. He showed his pent-up anger that was caused, in part, by teams that had had either folded midseason (Mercury) or had failed to pay him. Cunego took his difficult day in stride. It's easy to be nice when wearing pink.

There were still two hard days before the promenade into Milan. Stage eighteen featured the Tonale, the south face of the Gavia (the 2004 *Cima Coppi*) and a hilltop finish at the Bormio 2000 ski station.

Garzelli had no intention of giving up. On the Gavia he attacked and got a sizable gap. By the time he crested, riding by snow banks that lined the road, he was about two minutes ahead of the Cunego group, which contained all of the other contenders. Saeco labored to bring Garzelli back. Even though he had picked up some riders from earlier breakaways, Garzelli was forced to do all the work down in the valley, and into a headwind at that. At the start of the climb to Bormio 2000, Garzelli was caught. A couple of kilometers later Simoni made his big move to take the lead, but it was an attack without real bite. Sella, Gontchar, Cunego, Pérez-Cuapio and Dario David Cioni clawed their way up to Simoni. It was a nervous group of five that approached the sprint. Cunego seemed to be looking around for Simoni to give him a lead out but Simoni was out of suds and couldn't answer the call. Finally Cunego just kicked it and easily won the sprint, making four stage wins for Cunego, now nicknamed "The Little Prince of Verona".

Simoni didn't handle the loss well. After the stage, while Cunego was basking in his glory, surrounded by photographers and writers, Simoni went by on his way to the hotel and called him a bastard. Cunego didn't have dinner until after Simoni had left the dining room. In Simoni's mind, Cunego had betrayed him by riding too hard in the final kilometers, weakening the older rider who was desperate for the stage win. Simoni felt Cunego then jumped too fast in the sprint rather than giving a Simoni a proper lead out.

The new General Classification was thus:

1. Damiano Cunego
2. Serguei Gontchar @ 1 minute 31 seconds
3. Gilberto Simoni @ 3 minutes 7 seconds
4. Yaroslav Popovych @ 3 minutes 23 seconds
5. Dario David Cioni @ 4 minutes 44 seconds

Stage nineteen, the Giro's penultimate day, was to be just as hard as the last few days in the mountains with the Mortirolo, Vivione and Presolana passes, totaling about 40 kilometers of climbing. The split between Simoni and Cunego was certainly no secret. *La Gazzetta Dello Sport's* headline for stage nineteen: "*Simoni-Cunego: Il Grande Freddo*" (literally, "The Big Cold").

Garzelli still had no thought about laying down his arms, even though he was five and a half minutes behind Cunego. Garzelli attacked hard on the Mortirolo, taking with him Simoni and Tadej Valjavec. This trio, picking up and dropping earlier breakaways, forged ahead resolutely.

Cunego was down to only one teammate, but that teammate was Eddy Mazzoleni, an experienced *gregario di lusso*. Mazzoleni advised his young charge to remain calm. As the pursuit rolled up and down the mountains, the Garzelli/Simoni group was never able to enlarge the two-minute lead they had over the Cunego group when they crested the Mortirolo.

On the final kilometers of the Presolana, it was down to just Simoni and Garzelli with the Cunego group containing Gontchar and Tonkov about a minute back. Garzelli took the well-earned stage victory. Since the duo had only managed to carve out a 52-second lead over Cunego, the young man stayed in pink and Gontchar kept second place, but only by 3 seconds. Simoni's attempt to undercut Cunego had failed. The 2004 Giro was Cunego's, Simoni acknowledging that he had not brought the same form to the 2004 Giro that had won him two earlier editions.

That left only the final run-in to Milan. Fassa Bortolo gave another class on lead-out trains and Petacchi scored in the final stage, giving him nine stage wins.

Simoni hugged Cunego on the final podium and said nice things about the new young star. But before the Giro was even over, Simoni was already talking about getting out of his Saeco contract.

Final 2004 Giro d'Italia General Classification:
1. Damiano Cunego (Saeco): 88 hours 40 minutes 43 seconds
2. Serguei Gontchar (De Nardi) @ 2 minutes 2 seconds
3. Gilberto Simoni (Saeco) @ 2 minutes 5 seconds
4. Dario David Cioni (Fassa Bortolo) @ 4 minutes 36 seconds
5. Yaroslav Popovych (Landbouwkrediet-Colnago) @ 5 minutes 5 seconds

Climbers' Competition:
1. Fabian Wegmann (Gerolsteiner): 56 points
2. Damiano Cunego (Saeco): 54
3. Gilberto Simoni (Saeco): 36

Points Competition:
1. Alessandro Petacchi (Fassa Bortolo): 250 points
2. Damiano Cunego (Saeco): 153
3. Olaf Pollack (Gerolsteiner): 148

Cunego had an incredible 2004. He not only won the Giro with four stage wins, he took the Giro del Trentino, Tour of Lombardy (masterfully), Giro dell'Appennino and raced the Vuelta and the Japan Cup. Plus he traveled to the U.S. for a bicycle trade show. This was an insane schedule for a rider 22 years old and he paid dearly for it. He never again had a season like this.

The 2004 Giro had no doping positives. That does not mean that the riders were clean. It means simply that the testers were unable to find any objective, verifiable evidence that a rider was competing in the Giro with banned substances in his system. NAS certainly believed that that the riders were up to no good. So in early June they executed another giant raid and this time came up with lots of bad stuff. NAS was targeting riders who were known to have had an association with Dr. Carlo Santuccione, one of several doctors who have had a poisonous effect upon Italian racing for many years. In his 1994 doping investigation, Sandro Donati listed him as being particularly influential in assisting cyclists who wanted to dope.

Santuccione's phone had been tapped and hidden microphones had been placed to record his conversations. They revealed that Santuccione was both advising several riders how to dope and also prescribing drugs to athletes. By late June the fallout from the raid was extensive. Fifteen bicycle racers were among those whom the police net had ensnared. Among those implicated were three Saeco riders: Eddy Mazzoleni, Danilo Di Luca and Alessandro Spezialetti. This was happening just days before the Tour de France was to start.

Saeco was combative regarding bringing the implicated riders to the big race. Mazzoleni was suspended but Saeco Manager Claudio Corti argued that Lance Armstrong was also accused of using drugs and he was starting the Tour. Under these circumstances Corti said he saw no reason against using his other accused racers.

This whole scandal was given a name, "Oil for Drugs". The name's origins are impossible to pin down now, but it appears to be a take-off from the "Oil for Food" program that was designed to allow Iraq to sell oil for humanitarian purposes.

In late June the Tour organization announced that no rider under investigation or involved in legal procedures involving doping could ride the Tour. Di Luca, up to his chin in both was excluded from the 2004 Tour.

The Italian judicial system can proceed at a glacial pace and the Oil for Drugs scandal took years to resolve; only in October of 2004 did the trial for the defendants of the 2001 NAS blitz begin.

In the fall of 2004 RCS Sport reorganized the management of the Giro. Angelo Zomegnan, a senior editor at *La Gazzetta dello Sport*, succeeded Carmine Castellano, who had directed the Giro since 1989. Zomegnan's new official title was "Director of Sporting Events".

2005 Professional racing was given a profound re-organization with the institution of the Pro Tour. UCI boss Hein Verbruggen rammed through his vision of how the sport should be run. The twenty best teams were given a "Pro Tour" license good for four years. The most important races, which included the Grand Tours and the Classics, were given Pro Tour status. All Pro Tour teams would have to compete in all races that were on the Pro Tour calendar. The purpose of this reorganization was to give stability to the teams and a high quality peloton to all the major races. Not happy with what they saw as a bald UCI power grab, the promoters of the Grand Tours pushed back, finding many of the Pro Tour rules encroaching on their ability to run their races as they saw fit. While negotiations between the UCI and the Grand Tour organizers dragged on, both sides agreed to disagree and proceeded to run the season under a flag of truce. The result for the Giro was that all 20 Pro Tour teams had an automatic invitation to ride and the Giro organization could give one team a wild card invitation.

Over the winter Saeco and Lampre merged their squads into a new Lampre-Caffita team. The new super team signed both Cunego and Simoni and brought in Giuliano Figueras. Team boss Claudio Corti said that Simoni was the sole team leader for the 2005 Giro. Months later Simoni was still complaining about the 2004 stage eighteen sprint at the Bormio 2000 ski station, claiming again that Cunego had reneged on a promise to help him.

Cunego took it all in stride, denying that there had been a deal and announced his own goal of defending his Giro championship, yet he also said that Simoni was the team leader. Both riders showed admirable form coming into the Giro. Cunego, planning to ride both the Giro and the Tour, rode well in the Tour of Romandie, winning a stage and coming in second overall. Simoni won the Giro dell'Appennino.

Cunego thought the Giro would be harder this year because the Pro Tour brought more top teams to the race, improving the quality of the field. Perhaps this was what the Giro needed to help it finally make the leap from an important regional race to becoming a real competitor to the Tour.

Other potential challengers included Savoldelli, Garzelli, Di Luca and Ivan Basso. Savoldelli moved to T-Mobile in 2002 and suffered through two years of crashes and sickness. Now riding for the Discovery Channel squad, he was fit, confident and ready to put the bad years behind him. Still, Discovery team boss Johan Bruyneel didn't send a strong support squad to help Savoldelli. He wasn't about to use up his best riders on the Giro when he needed them to help Armstrong win a seventh Tour. Savoldelli would largely be on his own.

Ivan Basso, on Bjarne Riis' CSC team, said that he was going for the Giro/Tour double but had no notable success so far in 2005. Garzelli and Di Luca were teammates on the Liquigas team with Garzelli being the designated leader. Di Luca was enjoying a year of grace, having already won Tour of the Basque Country, Amstel Gold and the Flèche Wallonne, and he was the current leader in the Pro Tour standings.

The Giro was still going through a financial rough patch. Again, RCS Sport had not been able get the expected price for the Giro's television rights. Because of this financial shortfall the prize money was reduced by fifteen percent and the Giro tried to avoid paying the UCI mandated €60,000 per team start money. This, while the Tour was swimming in cash and had almost doubled its prize money over the previous half-decade.

Despite the Giro's troubles, the start list had riders from 29 countries and was probably the most international ever. Of the 197 starters, 145 were foreign.

The 2005 route was rather straightforward. Starting at the tip of the Italian toe with a short prologue, the route headed up the boot, mostly keeping to the western side of the peninsula until it reached Tuscany. Then it scooted over to the eastern side and up into the Dolomites. The penultimate stage was planned to be a big and possibly decisive show with an ascent on the unpaved road up the Finestre, a diabolically steep mountain. The 2005 Giro wasn't designed to be a complete free-for-all for the climbers. A second time trial was restored so that the total distance against the clock was 73.65 kilometers, enough to give the race some balance.

The prologue, a pan-flat 1.15-kilometer time trial along the shore of Reggio Calabria, was the second-shortest stage in Grand Tour history (the shortest was the 1986 Giro's prologue). Track rider Brett Lancaster won, but sitting in fourth, with the same time as Alessandro Petacchi and only 1 second slower than Lancaster was Savoldelli.

The first stage had a short, hard uphill finish, a perfect place for the racer nicknamed *Il Grillo* (The Cricket) to launch a decisive attack and leave the fastest men in the world behind. This victory gave Paolo Bettini, the reigning Olympic Road Race Champion, two things he had never had before: a Giro stage victory and the *maglia rosa*.

Stage two should have been the place for Petacchi to start where he had left off the year before. With four kilometers of straight road leading to the finish line, the Fassa Bortolo train was expected to lead Petacchi to the first of several stage wins. Not this time. Several speedy racers created a traffic jam, boxing Petacchi in and allowing Robbie McEwen to take the stage and the Pink Jersey.

The next day Di Luca won stage three by millimeters from a 50-man group, the 20-second time bonus putting him a hair's breadth from the lead.

The General Classification was thus:
1. Paolo Bettini
2. Danilo Di Luca @ 9 seconds
3. Damiano Cunego @ 17 seconds
4. Stefano Garzelli @ 23 seconds
5. Paolo Savoldelli @ 26 seconds

The Giro went north and stage five brought it to Abruzzo, Di Luca's home region. At 223 kilometers and with plenty of hills, it was the year's longest stage. Bettini had been relegated the day before for irregular sprinting and was so angry he threatened to withdraw from the Giro. Since he was in pink, no one took his bluff seriously. In stage five he got in a good break of non-threatening riders that was caught in the final kilometers. That allowed Di Luca to take a clean win and regain the lead by three seconds over Bettini.

The next day was again expected to be perfect for Petacchi. This time the Fassa Bortolo train crashed just before the line and McEwen, a skilled opportunist, won. So far, no stage wins for Petacchi. Cunego's prediction had been correct. Making the Giro a Pro Tour race improved the quality of the field so that Fassa Bortolo could not dominate the sprints the way it had in the past.

Through Tuscany they raced, and race hard they did. After only a few kilometers into stage seven, a large, well-organized group broke away, eventually gaining thirteen minutes from an indifferent peloton. Finally, the team directors figured out that this could turn out to be a dangerous *fuga di bidone* and the chase began. There were two climbs in the final quarter of the stage. The first one, the San Baronto, let Spanish rider Koldo Gil escape the break as it was losing steam. On the second, the short but stiff Salita di Sammommè, an unsuccessful attack by José Rujano was answered by an acceleration from Simoni that broke the string. Garzelli and Basso couldn't take the speed and a new group with Simoni, Cunego and Savoldelli headed down the hill in the rain, hell-bent to make sure the dropped riders stayed dropped. Gil took the stage and only 20 seconds later Cunego won the field sprint.

The year's first extended individual time trial was held over the hills west of Florence. American rider David Zabriskie was told to go all out so that his CSC teammate Ivan Basso would have good time splits to follow. Basso couldn't maintain stage winner Zabriskie's pace, but he came close, coming in second, moving him up to second place.

The reordered General Classification:

1. Danilo Di Luca
2. Ivan Basso @ 9 seconds
3. Paolo Savoldelli @ 35 seconds
4. Damiano Cunego @ 1 minute 15 seconds
5. Dario David Cioni @ 1 minute 27 seconds

Finally Petacchi got one. After a flawless lead out from what was by now a team under a lot of pressure, the man who the year before had won flat Giro stages at will took the victory in Ravenna.

The first stage after the rest day took the race to Rossano Veneto for another McEwen victory and another NAS raid. Even though nothing was turned up, the riders threatened the race organization with a strike. There was no strike.

The race made a short transfer to Marostica, where the eleventh stage started, the stage that Simoni said marked the beginning of the real Giro.

The General Classification was still tight with barely more than two minutes separating the top ten riders. Stage eleven featured four ascents, the last of which was a hilltop finish at Zoldo Alto (the Dolomiti Stars ski station).

The action began on the thirteen-kilometer Passo Duran, the penultimate climb. Early on Lampre started going unpleasantly fast. As the peloton was being shattered by his team's efforts, Simoni made a hard dig and few riders could hold his wheel. Neither Cunego (who seemed to be riding with legs of wood) nor Garzelli could follow him. Survivors of Simoni's move kept the pace hot, wanting to make sure the two former Giro winners were well and truly gone.

And then Basso gave a hard acceleration of his own, taking Simoni, Savoldelli, Di Luca and José Rujano along for company as he raced for the mountain's summit. As Basso kept pouring it on, only Simoni could match his speed. Near the top the other three rejoined Basso and Simoni.

On the challenging descent Savoldelli took off. As the final ascent began, first Basso and then Simoni made it up to *Il Falco*. Basso didn't want to take the others with him, and just hammered away, eventually dropping Simoni. Basso was unconcerned about winning the stage, he was doing all he could to gain time on the dropped riders. Strangely, he seemed to be riding as if Savoldelli weren't a threat. Savoldelli was able to hang on to Basso and beat him in the sprint while Simoni and Di Luca came in 21 and 61 seconds later. Basso was now the *maglia rosa* while Cunego's and Garzelli's Classification hopes were in tatters.

The General Classification was now thus:

1. Ivan Basso
2. Paolo Savoldelli @ 18 seconds
3. Danilo Di Luca @ 1 minute 4 seconds
4. Gilberto Simoni @ 2 minutes 27 seconds
16. Damiano Cunego @ 7 minutes 20 seconds
17. Stefano Garzelli @ 7 minutes 40 seconds

Stage thirteen was the queen stage, making the riders go over five major passes: Costalunga, Sella, Gardena, Erbe and Pontives. Starting in Mezzocorona, it went up the Brenner Pass and then headed east for the Gruppo Sella. Garzelli didn't start, having decided that the effect of a crash in stage seven left him too injured to race.

In the first kilometers a break of a few good riders that eventually grew to twenty went away and stayed away, although it would be whittled to a final eight as the mountains took their toll, with Colombian Ivan Parra finishing alone. Admirable though this was, it wasn't the real race. None of the breakaway riders were contention for the Overall, although Juan Manuel Gárate, who came in second that day, should not have been ignored. Back in the peloton, Basso's CSC team rode a hard tempo to keep the break from getting out of hand.

The action started on the narrow ascent of the Passo delle Erbe, where the peloton started to fall apart and Cunego and Simoni escaped. Basso's *gregari* did the chasing for their team leader; Di Luca, and Savoldelli were glad for the shelter and help. The *maglia rosa* group caught the fleeing Lampre boys, setting things up for the drama of the final climb. Given the short distance from the crest of the Pontives to the finish line in Ortisei, it was almost a hilltop finish.

Midway up the climb, the always aggressive Simoni exploded off the front with Savoldelli for company. Basso had shown no aggression the whole day and hadn't marked any of the major attacks. This time, he couldn't go with what was obviously the day's, and perhaps the Giro's pivotal move. Savoldelli was having another superb day and left Simoni seven seconds behind. The race lead changed hands as Basso, suffering from stomach problems, lost almost a minute. Savoldelli was the Giro's leader.

Stage fourteen had 50 kilometers of climbing, including the south face of the Stelvio sandwiched between the Frassineto and the Foscagno climbs. This was the ninth time the Giro had ascended the Stelvio since it was introduced in 1953.

Stage thirteen winner Ivan Parra got into a breakaway and the peloton never saw him again. Back with the Pink Jersey group, Ivan Basso was still being tortured with gut trouble and after the Frassineto, CSC gregario Giovanni Lombardi asked Savoldelli to slow things down because Basso had to stop.

Basso lost contact with the leaders half way up the Stelvio and from that point, suffered what he called his own "Calvary" and lost over 40 minutes. The entire CSC team went to Basso's aid and led him up the snow-covered mountain.

Savoldelli was again completely isolated with no teammates to help him chase or even bring him food and water. Di Luca gave Savoldelli some of his own supplies.

There was a final short climb of the Passo d'Eira before a short descent into the finish city of Livigno. Simoni, ever active, attacked and Savoldelli, suffering from cramps, had to let him and Di Luca go, costing him 28 seconds. Savoldelli was still the leader, but his lead over Di Luca was only 25 seconds.

So far this had been a superb race with almost no *piano* riding.

That *piano* day did come with stage sixteen, the first stage after the second rest day, the riders were facing both the second time trial and the Alps and were in no mood to exhaust themselves.

Stage seventeen with its hilltop finish at Limone Piemonte was exactly the sort of stage they were saving themselves for. Basso had recovered and was looking good, and on the flatter road between the final climbs he escaped with teammate Frank Schleck. No longer posing a Classification threat, he was allowed to ride away. Basso, with Schleck's generous help, caught all of the earlier breakaways and soloed in for a redemptive win.

Further back, Simoni and José Rujano left Savoldelli behind on the final climb and stung him for 42 seconds. Going into the time trial, the General Classification looked like this:

1. Paolo Savoldelli
2. Gilberto Simoni @ 58 seconds
3. José Rujano @ 1 minute 24 seconds
4. Danilo Di Luca @ 1 minute 36 seconds

The Turin 34-kilometer time trial gave Savoldelli some breathing room. While Basso won the stage, Savoldelli, coming in fourth, did better than any of the other Classification riders, even beating time trial specialist Serguei Gontchar.

That left the penultimate stage with its climbing challenge, the never before used Colle delle Finestre, placed between two ascents to Sestriere. This stage was one of the greatest bike races ever. This day the riders threw caution to the wind and rode until they could barely turn the pedals.

The first ascent to Sestriere was done at high speed, but the contenders were still together at the top and were still grouped as they began the Finestre. The Finestre is not only long and steep, the final 8 kilometers

On the Colle delle Finestre, Savoldelli is in the center group, chasing.

are what the Italians call *strade bianche*, or white, unpaved roads. In the Giro, normally the hardest climbs are called Category One. Because of the Finestre's staggering difficulty, it was labeled *categoria speciale*.

Rujano's teammate Rafael Iliano attacked as the Finestre started to bite and it was over for all but twelve riders with both Basso and

Savoldelli missing this train. The pace up the Finestre was so hard that even before the unpaved portion was reached it was down to just three: Rujano, Di Luca and Simoni. Simoni had said that he would do everything he could to win the Giro on this stage and he was certainly fulfilling his promise. About two minutes behind this trio was Savoldelli who was again without teammates.

On the descent Savoldelli caught several riders who had dropped him. While the Simoni group remained well clear, Savoldelli was still ahead of the shattered remnants of what might be called the peloton.

Early on the second ascent to Sestriere, which at about five percent is not nearly as stiff as the Finestre, Di Luca couldn't stay with Simoni and Rujano. Cramps made each pedal stroke a misery. A few kilometers later Simoni also cramped and had to watch Rujano slowly ride away from him and win the stage.

Not one to give up, Savoldelli was able to close in on the trio and at the end he was 1 minute 29 seconds behind Simoni and therefore the winner of the 2005 Giro.

Savoldelli rode about as perfect a race as could be imagined. He was with a team that did him almost no good while a determined and well-supported Gilberto Simoni hammered him day after day.

In interviews after the Giro, Savoldelli said that he had ridden Giri with less support in the past, noting that in 2002 his Index-Alexia team seemed more devoted to sprinter Ivan Quaranta and when he came in second in 1999, his Saeco team was first and foremost Cipollini's lead-out train.

Final 2005 Giro d'Italia General Classification:
1. Paolo Savoldelli (Discovery Channel): 91 hours 25 minutes 51 seconds
2. Gilberto Simoni (Lampre-Caffita) @ 28 seconds
3. José Rujano (Colombia-Selle Italia) @ 45 seconds
4. Danilo Di Luca (Liquigas-Bianchi) @ 2 minutes 42 seconds
5. Juan Manuel Gárate (Saunier Duval-Prodir) @ 3 minutes 11 seconds

Climbers' Competition:
1. José Rujano (Selle Italia-Colombia): 143 points
2. Ivan Parra (Selle Italia-Colombia): 57
3. Gilberto Simoni (Lampre-Caffita): 45

Points Competition:
1. Paolo Bettini (Quick Step-Innergetic): 162 points
2. Alessandro Petacchi (Fassa Bortolo): 154
3. Danilo Di Luca (Liquigas-Bianchi): 136

2006

The 2006 route featured five hilltop finishes, making it a climbers' race. Starting outside of Italy for the eighth time, the riders would spend four stages in the Walloon section of Belgium, home to hundreds of thousands of Belgians of Italian descent whose forefathers had migrated to the area to work Belgium's coal mines. After a transfer to Italy for the first team time trial since 1989, the Giro would work its way down the Adriatic coast as far south as northern Puglia before another transfer north to Tuscany. At stage thirteen, the final week of hard stages that were intended to decide the race's outcome would begin with the ascent of the Colle San Carlo in Piedmont.

To keep the drama building, the last-but-one stage had 4,000 meters of vertical ascension that included the Gavia Pass. Originally the final day was to have a split stage with a time trial up the Ghisallo followed by the race into downtown Milan. UCI rules forbade Grand Tours' having split stages and after some fussing on the part of the Giro organization, just the usual promenade into Milan was scheduled.

This looked to be a Giro that would be beyond Savoldelli and his tactic of minimizing losses on the ascents and making up time on the descents and time trials. The two favorites were Basso and Di Luca, with Basso's climbing abilities making him the stronger entry. Basso, who took second in the 2005 Tour, had been the only rider to consistently stay with Lance Armstrong in the Tour's toughest climbs. He announced that he was again planning on attempting the Giro/Tour double, so confident was he of both his own abilities and those of his team (CSC was probably the strongest squad entered).

Savoldelli abandoned the Tour of Romandie with stomach problems, but showed no sign of weakness as the Giro began with the stage one individual time trial that went through the industrial city of Seraing. Savoldelli's power and outstanding bike handling skills left Basso, Di Luca and Cunego about 20 seconds behind as he took the first Pink Jersey of the year.

Savoldelli had to yield his lead to Stefan Schumacher when the German gapped the field on the uphill finish in stage three, winning the stage, the time bonus and the Pink Jersey.

When the four crash-filled Belgian stages finished with all of the Classification contenders still uninjured, the Giro transferred to Italy for the team time trial, and the General Classification stood thus:

1. Stefan Schumacher
2. Paolo Savoldelli @ 13 seconds
3. Davide Rebellin @ 23 seconds
4. José Gutiérrez @ 29 seconds
5. José Luis Rubiera @ 31 seconds

The flat stage five 35-kilometer team time trial went from Piacenza to Cremona and the riders were awarded their actual time trial times. The result of the ever-improving Giro field was a new record speed of 56.86 kilometers per hour. Basso's CSC team won the stage. T-Mobile, with chrono specialists Jan Ullrich, Michael Rogers and Serguei Gontchar, was only one second slower, giving the overall lead to Gontchar.

Stage seven, 236 kilometers, was the year's longest stage. But it was more than just long: it was over the hilly roads of Le Marche. The riders would be going either up or down the entire stage. Belgian Rik Verbrugghe escaped from a break in the closing kilometers and took a solo win in Saltara. On the steep ascent to the line Savoldelli jumped away for second place and the twelve-second time bonus, good enough to put him within 6 seconds of Gontchar. Di Luca, not looking good and unable to stay with the leaders as they raced up to the finish, lost 16 seconds.

So far, with the exception of Di Luca's small time loss, the Giro contenders were all relatively close together in time and none had yet shown what he could do. Stage eight clarified the situation. Starting with a flat run down the Adriatic coast it turned into the hills for a hilltop finish at Maielletta, a 27-kilometer ascent with a section of ten-percent gradient. With about eight kilometers to go Gontchar was dropped. A kilometer further up the hill Savoldelli had to let go. Then Di Luca was dropped.

With a little over four kilometers to the summit Cunego made his move. Only Basso could hold the Little Prince's wheel. Then Basso jumped and was gone for good. Cunego lost 30 seconds, Simoni

75 seconds, Di Luca 92, and Savoldelli 2 minutes 20 seconds. Gontchar came in 14 seconds after Savoldelli, making it unlikely he would regain the lead.

The General Classification:
1. Ivan Basso
2. José Gutiérrez @ 1 minute 34 seconds
3. Damiano Cunego @ 1 minute 48 seconds
4. Paolo Savoldelli @ 2 minutes 35 seconds
5. Serguei Gontchar @ 2 minutes 43 seconds

The next two stages that continued down the Adriatic coast didn't change the standings. And with that came the first rest day and a transfer north to Tuscany for the stage eleven 50-kilometer individual time trial. Starting in Pontedera it headed west along the Arno River to the historic center of Pisa followed by a straight shot back to the finish.

And who should win the stage? Jan Ullrich! The same man who a few days before had been unceremoniously shelled on the Maieletta and had lost over sixteen minutes on that stage alone, crushed the crème of the cycling world with a fabulous ride. Basso could only come within 28 seconds of the talented German who was now looking pretty good for the Tour. The others? There was no good news for them. Savoldelli lost about 50 seconds to Basso and Simoni almost four minutes. Cunego was caught and passed by Basso, losing more than five minutes.

With the high mountains still several days away, Basso looked to be completely in charge with second place José Gutiérrez already 2 minutes 48 seconds behind.

Stage thirteen took the riders into the Piedmontese Alps. In the first kilometers, with CSC battering away at the front and spending watts as if this were the Giro's final day, the peloton was quickly whittled down to fifteen riders. The effects of the high speeds on the steep mountain were dramatic. Savoldelli then Cunego and Di Luca were dropped. As the road reared up to its full fifteen percent, Basso made his move and only Simoni's *gregario* Leonardo Piepoli, who had already received permission from his team to go for a stage win, held his wheel.

The weather had gone from warm sun to near freezing rain as Basso and Piepoli crested the Colle San Carlo together. Piepoli took off like a fiend, fearlessly racing down the dangerous, wet and twisty roads for his victory. Basso, an indifferent descender, took his time and came into La Thuile 44 seconds later. Simoni and Gutiérrez, who chased aggressively, finished 35 seconds after Basso.

The General Classification gaps had grown:
1. Ivan Basso
2. José Gutiérrez @ 3 minutes 27 seconds
3. Paolo Savoldelli @ 5 minutes 30 seconds
4. Wladimir Belli @ 7 minutes 35 seconds
5. Gilberto Simoni @ 8 minutes 0 seconds

Basso and Piepoli had put on a jaw-dropping performance. Michele Ferrari calculated Basso's average rate of vertical ascent (called VAM by sports physiologists) on the Colle San Carlo to be about 2,000 meters per hour. Any VAM over 1,800 should cause at least a raised eyebrow. The San Carlo is steep and a racer's rate of ascent gets higher on steeper climbs, but 2,000 is a big number and it had some wondering where the ability to perform like this had come from.

Rujano climbed off his bike a few kilometers from the finish line, complaining that he didn't feel good. It later turned out to be a ploy for more money from his team. After his wonderful performance in the 2005 Giro, Rujano had demanded a sharply increased salary and the freedom to move to a new, richer and more powerful team, which had been previously granted if he would merely finish the 2006 Giro with his old team. Rujano, who was riding for savvy team manager Gianni Savio, would never again rise to the heights that he did in 2005. Years later Rujano voiced regret over this episode and rejoined Savio.

Normally men like Simoni and Cunego are licking their chops at the prospect of racing in the high mountains and seizing control of the race. Not this year. Basso had broken them and no one was speaking of taking the race from a rider who seemed to grow stronger every day. Journalists were beginning to compare Basso to Lance Armstrong in both his dominating style and the high pedaling cadence he employed in the mountains.

Stage sixteen finished at the top of Monte Bondone. At the stage's start, Basso's CSC team rode moderate tempo at the front of the peloton, letting non-contenders test their legs in escape attempts. As the pack started the climb, CSC increased the intensity of their efforts, leaving a trail of dropped riders. Halfway up Piepoli smashed the peloton with a hard attack. Instantly only ten were left and none of them were

Savoldelli, Di Luca or Cunego. Simoni, still with some fight left in him, thought there were still too many left and had Piepoli bash the *maglia rosa* group again. Now it was six.

For a third time Piepoli went, this time with the intention of launching Simoni. Simoni went but Basso, the only rider with the horsepower to stay with Simoni, was vigilant and made staying with the two-time Giro winner look like child's play. And then Basso was gone. By the finish, the gap to Simoni had grown to 86 seconds. Basso had ridden some of the best riders in the world off his wheel with unbelievable ease.

The General Classification:
1. Ivan Basso
2. José Gutiérrez @ 5 minutes 24 seconds
3. Paolo Savoldelli @ 9 minutes 17 seconds
4. Gilberto Simoni @ 9 minutes 34 seconds

While the racers were turning themselves inside out on Monte Bondone, far away in Spain an arrest was occurring that would have far-ranging consequences for professional cycling. Manolo Saiz, director of the Spanish Liberty Seguros team, was arrested with a briefcase full of cash and bags of blood, a combination that's hard for any cycling team director to explain away. We'll come back to Señor Saiz and his friends later.

Stage seventeen was planned to be a showpiece stage. After the previous year's success using the unpaved Finestre, the 2006 edition included a hilltop finish at the Plan de Corones with its final unpaved section of 24 percent gradient.

Fans and riders had been anticipating this stage for months but when morning came they were greeted with reports of snow falling on the Dolomite mountaintops. The riders staged a short strike, delaying the day's start until the management agreed to shorten the stage. The planned crossing of the technical and narrow Passo delle Erbe, probably dangerous in bad weather, was eliminated. As the weather worsened, the finish was moved five kilometers down the mountain to the crest of the Passo di Furcia, removing the dirt road and its super-steep slope. Not all the riders were pleased with the compassionate alteration of the route. Knowing that Basso descended poorly, some thought the possibly muddy and dangerous conditions were ideal for putting it to the unstoppable Pink Jersey.

On the final ascent Pérez-Cuapio was feeling good and subjected the small leading group to repeated attacks. This was perfect for Piepoli who again had the freedom to ride for a stage win. He spun up the road in the final kilometers, taking Basso with him. Near the end Piepoli again jumped and left Basso to ride away from the others in the freezing, miserable weather.

The peloton was whipped, and it showed in the way they rode stage nineteen, *il tappone*, that had some the Dolomites best-known climbs: the Staulanza, Marmolada, Pordoi and a hilltop finish at the top of the San Pellegrino.

Early on, a break with Di Luca, Gárate, Jens Voigt, and Emanuele Sella, among others, was allowed to roll off the front. Normally this would be considered an intolerable combination of talent that would be run down. That didn't happen. A listless chase ensued while the mountains slowly ground most of the escaping riders into dust. Gárate and Voigt survived, and coming to the finish Voigt, ever the gentleman, waved his breakaway companion off and wished him well in his approaching stage victory. Voigt said that since he had not contributed to the break he had no business trying to win the stage. Simoni and Basso extricated themselves from the peloton on the final ascent and finished together. The others dribbled in, conceding still more time to the invincible Basso.

Barring misfortune, the standings showed Basso had the race in the bag:

1. Ivan Basso
2. José Gutiérrez @ 6 minutes 7 seconds
3. Gilberto Simoni @ 10 minutes 34 seconds
4. Paolo Savoldelli @ 12 minutes 59 seconds
5. Damiano Cunego @ 15 minutes 13 seconds

No, it wasn't over yet, after all. The penultimate stage still held the Tonale, the south face of the Gavia, the Mortirolo and a finishing climb to the city of Aprica. Basso had the Classification contenders with him as the Mortirolo began to have its expected effect upon the riders.

First Simoni accelerated and then Basso attacked and emerged with Simoni on his wheel. The two joined forces and together went past the new Marco Pantani memorial on their way to the summit. On the descent of the Mortirolo, Basso was again cautious. Simoni, by far the better descender, said Basso had asked him to stay with him on the descent, which he did. They began the final climb to Aprica together. As they got closer to the finish Basso started winding it up and it became too much for Simoni. Basso came in alone holding a picture of his newborn son, whom he had not yet seen. Simoni followed, 77 seconds behind. Gutiérrez and Cunego finished about three minutes behind Basso. The rest of the riders had been humiliated. Savoldelli and Piepoli, the next best, were over six minutes behind Basso.

Simoni was livid. He said that when Basso asked him to stay with him on the descent of the Mortirolo, he assumed Basso would let him take the stage win and felt betrayed. It turns out that when Basso had gone back to the team car and explained the situation to his director, Bjarne Riis, Riis told Basso to win the prestigious stage and that Simoni had already won lots of stages. Furthermore, winning the stage would mean valuable prize money for Basso's *gregari*.

Simoni had more to say. He had never seen anyone as strong Basso was that day, likening Basso's performance to that of an extraterrestrial, a blunt hint at doping.

On the final day, the still enraged Simoni had one more arrow in his polemical quiver. He accused Basso of trying to buy the stage win from him on the climb to Aprica, an accusation he later withdrew.

And that was the 2006 Giro. At no point did Basso show the slightest weakness and also at no point did he waste any energy. It was superb performance put on by an athlete displaying extraordinary strength. Basso and Riis immediately set about planning their assault on the Tour de France. At this point, if Basso could hold his form, he looked to be a near sure thing to win the Tour.

Final 2006 Giro d'Italia General Classification:
1. Ivan Basso (CSC) 91 hours 33 minutes 36 seconds
2. José Gutiérrez (Phonak) @ 9 minutes 18 seconds
3. Gilberto Simoni (Saunier Duval-Prodir) @ 11 minutes 59 seconds
4. Damiano Cunego (Lampre-Fondital) @ 18 minutes 16 seconds
5. Paolo Savoldelli (Discovery Channel) @ 19 minutes 22 seconds

Climbers' Competition:
1. Juan Manuel Gárate (Quick Step-Innergetic): 64 points
2. Ivan Basso (CSC): 56
3. Fortunato Baliani (Ceramiche Panaria-Navigare): 52

Points Competition:
1. Paolo Bettini (Quick Step-Innergetic): 169 points
2. Ivan Basso (CSC): 158
3. José Gutiérrez (Phonak): 132

Before moving on to the 2007 Giro, there is some unfinished business, that May 23 arrest of Manolo Saiz. The arrest had no immediate effect upon the Giro except to cause riders and directors to all tell the press that they had no involvement with whatever it was that was going on. The Spanish federation said that it was shocked, shocked that there were accusations of doping.

Going into the Tour, once again the pall of a doping scandal hung over everything. After a months-long investigation centered on Dr. Eufemiano Fuentes involving hidden cameras, the Spanish Civil Guard had arrested five men who were accused of an assortment of doping crimes. Among the five were the aforementioned Saiz and José Ignacio Labarta, the assistant sports director of the Comunidad Valenciana squad. Immediately, the Liberty Insurance Company withdrew its sponsorship from Saiz' team.

The weekend before the start of the Tour is the traditional time for the National Championships, allowing the countries' various champions to ride the Tour wearing their newly acquired national flag jerseys. On the Sunday morning of the road race championships, Spanish daily *El País* leaked major details about the ongoing investigation, now called *Operación Puerto*, showing that the riders and the teams had a deep involvement in systematized doping. The Spanish riders—as usual feeling that doping was their business and outraged at the publicity the story showered upon their illicit practices—staged a strike and refused to ride the Spanish Road Championship. The riders weren't outraged that there were cheaters amongst them. The anger was at the publicity.

It seemed that the second through fifth place finishers of the 2005 Tour (Armstrong, the winner, was retired) were going to return in even better form than ever and fight an extraordinary struggle to be the first post-Armstrong Tour victor. And then on the Thursday evening before the Saturday, July 1 Tour start, the Tour organization gave dossiers to the team managers, documenting the growing case against the riders involved in the Spanish doping scandal.

The team managers and Tour organization met and decided that since the Pro Tour code of ethics said, "No team will allow a rider to compete while under investigation in any doping affair", the riders who were part of the inquiry would have to be excluded. Ullrich was in the team bus on the way to a Friday pre-Tour presentation when he was informed of his suspension by the team. CSC director Riis had to tell Ivan Basso that he would not be able to ride the Tour.

2007

The 2007 professional racing season did not start smoothly. First, the fight between the owners of the Grand Tours and the UCI continued. The UCI wanted to assert its control of racing while the racing organizers wanted to protect both their age-old prerogatives and profits.

Two teams were victims of this war: Astana and Unibet. Both had made large commitments in both manpower and treasure to fulfill the stiff requirements of being a Pro Tour team. Yet the Grand Tour organizers refused to grant the two teams automatic entrance to their races as the UCI Pro Tour rules mandated. The organizers argued that Unibet was a gaming company and laws in many countries forbade the firm's advertising.

That left Unibet with its roster of powerful riders unable to race the most important races, including the Giro. To finesse the dispute in proper Italian style, Astana, now with Paolo Savoldelli, the 2002 and 2005 Giro winner (and an Italian), was granted a Giro wild-card.

While both sides threatened to fight to the death, neither wanted to ruin the racing season. So, as they had since 2005, they both threw verbal barbs and continued business almost as usual.

The bigger cloud hanging over racing was the unsettled allegations of *Operación Puerto* and the never-ending problems with dope. The 2006 Tour had been hit with yet another scandal when the winner, Floyd Landis, tested positive for synthetic testosterone. At the start of the 2007 Giro, the Tour had not yet been able to announce the winner of the 2006 Tour since Landis, aggressively asserting his innocence, was using all the appeals-process machinery at his disposal. He said that by July 2007, he had spent a million dollars fighting to keep his victory. In 2010, he gave up the fight, not only admitting that he had doped, but accusing Lance Armstrong and his team of a systematized doping program as well.

With the exception of having been excluded from the 2006 Tour, Basso appeared to have skated past the scandal. In this writer's opinion, the judge examining the *Puerto* case was trying to ignore as much of the case as he could and investigate as little as would appear seemly. He ended up shelving the investigation, saying that at the time, while it appeared that doping had occurred, nothing that had happened was against Spanish law. He also did all he could to keep authorities in other countries from examining the evidence to see if their laws had been broken.

CONI tried to investigate Basso, but since they couldn't get their hands on the evidence, they had to pronounce Basso able to sign for a team and ride in October, 2006. This non-exoneration clearance was all Johan Bruyneel needed to sign Basso to the Discovery team.

The other Pro Tour teams erupted in fury because they had all agreed to avoid signing Puerto riders until the case was closed and the riders found innocent.

The *Puerto* inquiry didn't quite die. The big break came in early April 2007 when German prosecutors were able to match up Jan Ullrich's DNA with blood bags seized from Fuentes. In late April it was revealed that an Italian prosecutor had his hands on blood bags that were thought to contain Basso's blood. From then on, Basso's defenses came apart. Knowing what was coming, Basso requested and was granted release from his Discovery contract.

On May 7, 2007, faced with too much evidence, Basso confessed to being involved with Fuentes, but steadfastly refused to admit that he had ever doped. He said he had planned to dope in the 2006 Tour, but that so far, all of his wins were clean. Skeptical observers wondered why he had been paying Fuentes tens of thousands of euros since 2004. And how did he climb the Colle San Carlo so fast?

The Giro barred the 50 or so riders implicated in the scandal from riding. This meant Tyler Hamilton, Michele Scarponi and Jorg Jaksche would not be able to start.

The race organizers had to get a handle on the doping and not just for reasons of common decency. In the wake of the *Puerto* scandal the television audience for the Vuelta fell thirty percent. When Comunidad Valenciana and Liberty Seguros pulled out of the sport, they took contracts with them that were worth $20,000,000 over their lifetime. Sales of racing related books and DVDs plummeted. It was absolutely vital to the economic health of pro racing that the cheating be brought under control.

At the end of April, former Telekom *soigneur* Jef D'Hont alleged that during the mid-1990s Telekom team doctors administered EPO to the riders as part of a team-wide doping program. The usual denials were given. But the wall of silence finally started to fall. Telekom riders from that era—Erik Zabel, Rolf Aldag, Brian Holm, and Udo Bölts—came forward and confessed. They said that with the pressure to beat other presumably doped riders, they had to use the needle or risk losing their jobs.

On Friday, May 25 (while the 2007 Giro was being raced), 1996 Tour de France winner and CSC team owner Bjarne Riis held a press conference and came clean. The man who had the nickname of "Mr. 60 percent" for his rumored high hematocrit, admitted that he had used EPO, hormones and cortisone in his campaign to win the Tour. D'Hont said that Riis had run his hematocrit up to 64 percent. Riis' incredible dominance in the 1996 Tour now became understandable.

Riis' confession left an important question unanswered. How could Riis, famous for his hands-on, close and careful management of his riders, not know about Basso's relationship with Fuentes and not wonder about Basso's extraordinary performance in the 2006 Giro, especially in light of his own dope-fueled performances?

The race that was announced in Milan, as usual, favored the specialist climbers with some challenging ascents including Monte Zoncolan and Tre Cime di Lavaredo.

In celebration of the 200th anniversary of Giuseppe Garibaldi's birth, the Giro used several of the stages to celebrate the great man's place in Italian history. The presentation of the teams was to be aboard the aircraft carrier *Garibaldi* and the first stage was to start on Caprera, an island next to Sardinia and Garibaldi's burial place. The name of the master guide book handed out to the Giro teams and the press each year, by the way, is the *Garibaldi*.

The race route began with a team time trial on Caprera, followed by three stages on Sardinia, the Giro's first visit there in sixteen years. After crossing to Salerno for the start of stage four, the race headed directly north. From about stage twelve, with its inclusion of the Izoard climb, the race would be between the mountain goats.

As the highest-placed rider from the 2006 Giro starting the 2007 edition, Gilberto Simoni, at 35 years old, was the odds-on favorite. He again found himself in the uncomfortable position of having a gifted young teammate who could steal the team leadership. Riccardo Riccò showed both confidence and power in the spring, having won two stages and the points classification in Tirreno–Adriatico.

The race started with that team time trial. The course's serpentine roads and high winds caused several teams to use normal road bikes instead of time trial machines. There were several crashes, the most notable being Popovych, who fell just before the end of the stage. While he suffered no serious injury, his team was forced to wait for him and lost almost a minute.

Di Luca's Liquigas team won the stage. Young Enrico Gasparotto was the first of his team to cross the line, earning him the first *maglia rosa*. Di Luca was visibly angry as the team finished, screaming at Gasparotto who was supposed to ease up to let his leader be first. The press, enjoying the *polemica*, tried to drive a wedge between Gasparotto, who at first said it was the team's intention to let him have the lead, and Di Luca, who publicly shrugged the entire thing off.

The next day Gasparotto apologized for his error ("Can I come down off my cross now?") and finished well behind Di Luca. This let Di Luca take the Pink Jersey on the basis of placings.

With the transfer back to the mainland after stage three, the logistics of the Garibaldi celebration infuriated the riders and their teams' support staff. The pre-race presentation on the aircraft carrier had turned out to be a hot, tiring day in the sun. The badly handled journey to the mainland caused some riders to get their bikes too late to take a training ride on the rest day that came after stage three. A day without riding in the middle of a stage race can make a rider's legs go blocky and powerless.

Stage four, starting in Salerno was the first stage to really offer any insight into the Giro contenders' form. After following the Amalfi Road around the Sorrento peninsula, the route headed inland to end with a finish at the top of Montevergine di Mercogliano. The stage started out at a leisurely pace, but half way through, a light rain started, making the well-used oily road as slippery as ice. A mass crash was the result, leaving many of the riders, including Di Luca and the once-again *maglia rosa* Gasparotto, bruised and some with broken bikes. The easy pace continued a bit longer, allowing the pack to re-group. Up front, Saunier Duval began to drive the pace hard, looking for a stage win for Riccardo Riccò.

As the final climb began, Liquigas displayed its power by running a perfect leadout train and sending off Danilo Di Luca for the stage win and the Pink Jersey with Riccò just off his wheel. The other contenders who tried to stay with Di Luca all agreed that at that moment, Di Luca was the best. Cunego said that he expected to have his full form in the third week and Simoni complained the stage left him exhausted. After his well-executed ride Di Luca said he had no intention of wasting any energy defending the jersey.

The General Classification after stage four. The first four riders are members of Di Luca's Liquigas team:

1. Danilo Di Luca
2. Franco Pellizotti @ 26 seconds
3. Andrea Noè @ 35 seconds
4. Vincenzo Nibali @ same time
5. Andy Schleck @ 53 seconds

Stage six gave Di Luca what he was looking for, a rider on a strong team (to keep escapes and attacks under control) who would keep his Pink Jersey warm, but would reliably suffer in the high mountains and return the cherished garment at the proper time.

It was an undulating stage that took the riders to Spoleto in the heart of hilly Umbria, tailor-made for a group of riders to ride away from a disinterested pack. A break of non-contenders dutifully escaped and Liquigas maintained a pace intended to let them go. Two riders survived to the end and divided the spoils. Luis Felipe Laverde took the stage win and Marco Pinotti of the T-Mobile squad, who didn't contest the sprint, got the Pink Jersey. Pinotti figured he would be able to ride in pink until the end of stage ten.

Stage eight, a trip over the Apennines via the Futa Pass into Emilia-Romagna gave the T-Mobile men a workout defending Pinotti's lead. A 27-man break containing Riccò escaped. Riccò was an unwelcome member of the break. The other members of the escape, including world champion Paolo Bettini, knew the pack would chase down a serious Classification contender. The break began to attack Riccò, doing everything they could to make him go back to the pack. At the same time, Riccò's two-way radio stopped working. He made the choice to drop back and now Saunier Duval had to join T-Mobile to keep the fast-moving group from getting too far up the road. In the end the gap was 4 minutes 19 seconds, small enough to let Pinotti keep his lead with a 28-second margin over Liquigas rider Andrea Noè. Pinotti said that his team, at this point down to six riders, could not sustain that kind of effort again.

The stage eight *fuga di bidone* had turned several good riders into Classification contenders, among them David Arroyo, Marzio Bruseghin, Francisco Vila, Andrea Noè, José Luis Rubiera and Emanuele Sella.

Stage ten finished outside Genoa at the top the Santuario Nostra Signora della Guardia. On the Santuario's slopes that reached a fourteen percent gradient, Di Luca made a test attack and then eased. Piepoli, the smallest man in the peloton, jumped four kilometers from the finish. No one could ride with "The Flying Trullo" (nicknamed for the ancient cone-shaped dwellings of his native Puglia), who finished alone. Di Luca finished eighteen seconds back and Simoni and Riccò were just behind him. Pinotti was right, keeping the lead after stage ten was beyond him. The new leader, Andrea Noè, at 38 years 4 months, was the oldest *maglia rosa* in the history of the Giro, beating Jens Heppner, 37 years 5 months in 2002, who had been the previous oldest wearer of the Pink Jersey. Up until then Aldo Moser, also slightly more than 37, had been the oldest Giro leader when he took over the Pink Jersey in 1971.

The new General Classification:
1. Andrea Noè
2. Marzio Bruseghin @ 1 minute 8 seconds
3. David Arroyo @ 1 minute 15 seconds
4. Francisco Vila @ 1 minute 38 seconds
5. Evgeni Petrov @ 1 minute 48 seconds

Stage twelve, with its ascents of the Colle d'Agnello—the 2007 *Cima Coppi*—and the Izoard signaled that the Giro had reached the high mountains. Simoni's riders did the pace-making during the kilometers leading up to the Agnello and on the slopes of the mountain itself. After Riccò had done his work, Piepoli set a fiendish pace. Popovych and

Savoldelli had been among several involved in a big finish line crash the day before and were too sore to keep up with Piepoli and dropped back.

On the Izoard, Piepoli and Simoni smashed the lead group with a series of hammer blows. Di Luca went over the top alone with Simoni and surprising Astana *gregario* Eddy Mazzoleni (who had been given his freedom when Savoldelli faded on the Agnello) only 15 seconds back. There was a small regrouping on the descent. Di Luca won the uphill sprint into Briançon, and with that stage victory, retook the lead.

The new General Classification:
1. Danilo Di Luca
2. Marzio Bruseghin @ 1 minute 3 seconds
3. David Arroyo @ 1 minute 16 seconds
4. Andy Schleck @ 1 minute 25 seconds
5. Francisco Vila @ 1 minute 39 seconds

An uphill individual time trial in stage thirteen brought a surprise. Bruseghin—who had won only one other race in his entire pro career, the 2006 Italian Time Trial Championship—took the stage and reduced Di Luca's lead to 55 seconds. That stage eight *fuga di bidone* was looking more interesting all the time.

Stage fourteen from Cantù, north of Milan, headed north into the mountains before ending in Bergamo. Since the final climb crested 40 kilometers from the finish and stage fifteen was considered the year's toughest stage, the top riders were expected to take it easy. If it were the Tour, where the riders usually ride not to lose, this would probably be the expected outcome. But this was the Giro, where riders are often more willing to take chances on a throw of the dice. So it was with stage fourteen, one of the finest days of racing in Giro history.

Early in the stage a group of eleven high-quality riders, including Paolo Bettini, Pietro Caucchioli, Iban Mayo and José Luis Rubiera escaped. Back in the peloton on the final kilometers of the first climb, the 26-kilometer Passo San Marco, Garzelli's Acqua & Sapone team ratcheted up the speed. Di Luca's men countered. Over the crest, Acqua's Massimo Codol took off on the technical descent and was quickly caught by Savoldelli, Garzelli and Mazzoleni. Soon thereafter Simoni went after the escapees and eventually they all hooked up. Di Luca (who had tarried to get a jacket for the cold descent), Bruseghin and Cunego had been caught napping. Three previous Giro winners, Garzelli, Savoldelli and Simoni, were off the front and chasing the eleven original breakaways.

At the base of La Trinità-Dossena, the trio caught the Bettini group, so the strength of the current World Champion was added to the power of the runaway Giro winners. The pursuit was really on. Cunego's and Di Luca's teams kept the break's lead within a minute. Simoni was daring on the descents, driving the break like a man possessed.

In the town of Bergamo he attempted a last-minute flyer, but Garzelli, always a quick sprinter, took the stage. Chasing hard, Di Luca was able to close within 38 seconds of Simoni.

Bruseghin, who stayed with his team captain Cunego, lost no time on Di Luca. While always respectful of Simoni, who had just taken 50 seconds away from him, Di Luca also noted that he had to increase his lead over Bruseghin with the Verona time trial coming up. The riders were exhausted, having spent the day redlined after a time trial. And the next day held the Tre Cime di Lavaredo. Who brought the biggest tank of gas to the Giro?

The General Classification stood thus:
1. Danilo Di Luca
2. Marzio Bruseghin @ 55 seconds
3. Andy Schleck @ 1 minute 57 seconds
4. Damiano Cunego @ 2 minutes 40 seconds
5. Gilberto Simoni @ 2 minutes 46 seconds

On a wet Sunday the riders met to contest a fearsomely difficult day with four major passes ending on the Tre Cime di Lavaredo. Simoni would be expected to attempt a *coup de grace* on the steepest sections.

Simoni certainly planned to take the Giro that day. On the first major climb of the day, the San Pellegrino, Simoni sent Riccò and Piepoli ahead. The team's David Cañada was already up the road in an earlier break. They were eventually joined by Pérez-Cuapio and Ivan Parra, neither of whom contributed to the break. The quartet blasted by the earlier escape and was about four minutes ahead of the pack.

Back in the peloton, the Astana team's leadership changed hands. Since Savoldelli was out of contention and Mazzoleni was riding beautifully, Mazzoleni got more than the freedom to win stages, he became Astana's protected General Classification rider.

On the next climb, the Passo Giau, Savoldelli upped the pace and shelled all of Di Luca's and Cunego's teammates from the *maglia rosa* group. Among the dropped riders were Stefano Garzelli and Marzio Bruseghin, who now ceased to be threats.

On the descent of the Giau, Savoldelli, who had been dropped but managed to regain contact, attacked and took Mazzoleni with him. By the bottom of the pass they were almost a minute and a half ahead of the small group of chasers which contained Di Luca, Cunego, Andy Schleck and Simoni.

Beginning the final ascent, Mazzoleni's gap to Di Luca had grown to 3 minutes 30 seconds. He was the virtual leader. Mazzoleni faded a bit on the steeper section of the mountain and Di Luca was able to dig deep enough to again save his lead and drop Simoni.

This left the Giro General Classification still tight, but now there was a new man looking for the Pink Jersey. Di Luca worried that Mazzoleni, a *gregario di lusso* who had always ridden in the service of others, was the superior time trialist and therefore the real dangerman:

1. Danilo Di Luca
2. Eddy Mazzoleni @ 1 minute 51 seconds
3. Andy Schleck @ 2 minutes 56 seconds
4. Gilberto Simoni @ 3 minutes 19 seconds
5. Damiano Cunego @ 3 minutes 23 seconds

During the rest day after the Tre Cime stage, winter came to the Giro and came hard. Many riders wanted to cancel or modify the coming stage but Giro organization went ahead, saying that difficult stages are fully in keeping with the Giro's history.

Stage sixteen had lots of climbing, but with the final mountain crest coming 27 kilometers before the finish and stage seventeen having Monte Zoncolan, the contenders chose to keep their guns quiet.

Garzelli paid the price for his stage fourteen exploit by losing almost seventeen and a half minutes on the Tre Cime stage. Being so far behind in the General Classification, he wasn't chased as he made an audacious move 50 kilometers from the end. First bridging up to a break and then attacking them on the day's penultimate descent over wet and dangerous roads, he held them all off on the final sixteen flat kilometers. That made a total of six career Giro stage victories for Garzelli and his first ever won solo.

Stage seventeen was expected to be the Giro's denouement with its hilltop finish atop Monte Zoncolan. Respecting the challenge, some riders had triple cranksets mounted. Even Di Luca, an excellent climber, had a compact cranks with a 34 tooth inner and a big 29 tooth cog in the back. Fearing that a stuck car might block the narrow road, team cars were forbidden and only motorcycles could follow the riders.

The contenders arrived at the base of the Zoncolan together. About half way up Simoni jumped so hard only Andy Schleck and Piepoli could take the pace, and on the final kilometer, with Piepoli doing the pacesetting, Schleck finally had to yield. Simoni won the stage, his second victory on top of the big mountain. Cunego tried with all his might to drop Di Luca, but Di Luca was having another superb day, losing only a half-minute to Simoni on Simoni's favorite turf.

That left the General Classification thus:

1. Danilo Di Luca
2. Andy Schleck @ 2 minutes 24 seconds
3. Gilberto Simoni @ 2 minutes 28 seconds
4. Damiano Cunego @ 3 minutes 29 seconds
5. Eddy Mazzoleni @ 3 minutes 36 seconds

Going into the final time trial Di Luca was generous in his words regarding his former teammate, Simoni, saying he hoped that Simoni would be able to stand with him on the final podium. Simoni was equally kind, expressing high regard for Di Luca and almost feeling bad that he had to attack Di Luca to win the Giro.

Simoni wasn't able to save his podium place. On a wet and dangerous ride that had many of the best riders throttling back a bit to stay safe, Savoldelli won the stage while Mazzoleni rode well enough to take third place overall. Di Luca, acknowledged by all the riders as the strongest and best rider that year, had won the 2007 Giro d'Italia.

He was also the first rider from south of Rome to win the Giro. He called himself a *terrone*, an abusive term for Southern Italians. Di Luca had refused to wear an earphone to take direction from his director, preferring to rely on his own tactical instincts. Even though he was usually isolated in the high mountains and subjected to repeated merciless attacks, he rode his own race and controlled each and every danger.

Simoni's Saunier Duval team was blessed with an extraordinary run of good luck. Not one of its riders had a flat tire during the 2007 Giro.

Final 2007 Giro d'Italia General Classification:

1. Danilo Di Luca (Liquigas) 92 hours 59 minutes 39 seconds
2. Andy Schleck (CSC) @ 1 minute 55 seconds
3. Eddy Mazzoleni (Astana) @ 2 minutes 25 seconds
4. Gilberto Simoni (Saunier Duval-Prodir) @ 3 minutes 15 seconds
5. Damiano Cunego (Lampre) @ 3 minutes 49 seconds

Climbers' Competition:

1. Leonardo Piepoli (Saunier Duval-Prodir): 79 points
2. Fortunato Baliani (Ceramiche Panaria-Navigare): 46
3. Danilo Di Luca (Liquigas): 45

Points Competition:

1. Alessandro Petacchi (Milram): 185 points
2. Danilo Di Luca (Liquigas): 130
3. Paolo Bettini (Quick Step-Innergetic): 120

Tests later revealed that four riders had displayed suspiciously low hormone levels, mimicking those of prepubescent boys: Di Luca, Eddy Mazzoleni, Gilberto Simoni and Riccardo Riccò. Doping was assumed, but never proven.

In October Di Luca was given a three-month suspension for his involvement with the 2004 Oil for Drugs scandal. Di Luca, as one of the above-mentioned four riders, had been accused of doping after the Monte Zoncolan stage of the 2007 Giro, but CONI exonerated him of that charge.

2008 The Grand Tour organizers, threatening to withdraw their races from the UCI calendar, forced the UCI into an agreement that would separate all of their events, including prestigious single-day races such as Paris–Roubaix and the Tour of Lombardy, from the Pro Tour. More control over the invitations was restored to the race promoters, freeing them of the requirement to invite all eighteen Pro Tour Teams to their races.

Zomegnan used this newfound freedom to change the way many teams approached the Giro. Those squads with a history of making the Tour de France their primary goal, using the Giro only as a training race to prepare for the Tour, were not invited. RCS Sport wanted to improve the quality of the race, and by making sure that everyone on the line was hungry for victory, that goal had a better chance of being fulfilled.

On May 4, about a week before the Giro's start, RCS Sport gave the cycling world a shock. Astana was given a last-minute invitation to ride because team director Johan Bruyneel had assured the Giro organization that he would send his "A" team to the Giro rather than a single good classification contender supported by a weak support squad as he had with his US Postal and Discovery Giro squads.

Alberto Contador, the 2007 Tour de France champion, had won both the Castilla y León and País Vasco stage races in the spring of 2008. Expecting little racing during the Giro and the Tour because his team was so far invited to neither, he had decided to take a rest. Called from his beach vacation, Contador, along with the rest of the Astana team, hurried to Palermo for the first stage, a team time trial. While the entry of Astana was good news for Contador, Andreas Klöden and Levi Leipheimer, it was a cruel blow to the smaller NCS-Medical team which had been carefully preparing (and spending money) for their Giro entry. Since there could only be 22 teams, NCS' invitation was withdrawn.

The results of the first stage, a 23.6-kilometer team time trial in Palermo, Sicily, were surprising. Team Slipstream, an American Continental team (a ranking below the Pro Tour status enjoyed by the big teams) won, making Christian Vande Velde the first American to wear pink since Andy Hampsten. Astana, shaking off the cobwebs, lost only 29 seconds. The day's results spelled trouble for Denis Menchov, Riccardo Riccò and Gilberto Simoni, whose teams each lost about a minute.

The next day had an uphill sprint finish in Agrigento. Riccò, who had targeted stage two, uncorked an irresistible sprint for the win. Vande Velde couldn't stay with the leaders at the final rush to the line and had to give up his *maglia rosa* to Franco Pellizotti, who had never worn pink. Pellizotti said that this was his year to capture the big prize because hanging over him was the knowledge that his team, Liquigas, had signed Ivan Basso, who would surely be the Liquigas team leader in 2009 after serving his suspension.

As the race crossed over to the mainland, Pellizotti nursed his narrow 1-second lead over Vande Velde while Di Luca remained close at 7 seconds.

Over the first few stages of the Giro the riders grew ever more angry with the difficult transfers and late arrivals to their hotels, the ferry ride from the island of Sicily having been particularly mismanaged. Some riders said that they had yet to be in bed before midnight. To appease the growing fury of the peloton, stage six was shortened from 265 kilometers down to 232.

Early in this long sixth stage, a *fuga di bidone* containing former Paris–Roubaix winner Magnus Backstedt and Italian Road Champion Giovanni Visconti pulled itself free, finishing 11 minutes 34 seconds ahead the peloton. This put young Visconti in the lead with Matthias Russ of Gerolsteiner in second place with the same time. Matteo Priamo of the CSF-Navigare squad won the stage, the first of several wins for this, uh, amazing team in this Giro.

The General Classification stood thus:

1. Giovanni Visconti
2. Matthias Russ @ same time
3. Daniele Nardello @ 1 minute 22 seconds
4. Alan Pérez Lezaun @ 4 minutes 42 seconds
5. Francesco Gavazzi @ 5 minutes 34 seconds
6. Matteo Priamo @ 9 minutes 7 seconds

The riders were aware that the twin Astana threats, Contador and Klöden were staying hidden and riding as economically as possible. World Champion Bettini said he thought Contador was looking better with each day.

Stage seven had a hilltop finish in Pescocostanzo after a leg-softening day crossing the Apennines. The contenders finished together, about three minutes behind the day's successful breakaway. Di Luca, Contador, Menchov, Leipheimer, Simoni, Pellizotti and Riccò remained clustered within two minutes of each other. Suffering like a dog, Visconti managed to hang on to the lead.

The next day brought the Giro to Tivoli, on the outskirts of Rome, with a "sting in the tail" uphill finish. This is the sort of stage that suits light, explosive sprinter types like Davide Rebellin and Paolo Bettini, but they were denied this time. The ever-surprising Riccò beat the specialists at their own game to win his second stage this Giro. With the high mountains still to be ridden, observers wondered if "The Cobra" were burning his matches too soon. Halfway through the stage Alberto Contador crashed, fracturing his elbow. He remounted and finished with the field.

Stage nine went up the western coast to land the race in Tuscany for its first rest day. The General Classification showed that, excepting the first three riders who were leading by virtue of their breakaway successes, the race remained tight:

1. Giovanni Visconti
2. Matthias Russ @ 34 seconds
3. Gabriele Bosisio @ 5 minutes 53 seconds
4. Danilo Di Luca @ 7 minutes 27 seconds
6. Riccardo Riccò @ 7 minutes 33 seconds
8. Alberto Contador @ 7 minutes 56 seconds

After the rest day the Giro moved to Le Marche for a 39.4-kilometer individual time trial. Starting on the coast in Pesaro, the entire route to Urbino was a long, hard, uphill drag with patches of ten and twelve percent gradient. Lampre's Marzio Bruseghin put himself into contention by winning the stage, while Contador showed his form by finishing only 8 seconds slower. Riccò (who crashed on the wet roads), Di Luca and Pellizotti each lost over two minutes, significant losses in an otherwise close race.

The next stages were for the sprinters as Visconti grimly held on to the lead. His ownership of the Pink Jersey was expected to end when the Giro hit the high mountains and end it did on stage fourteen.

The 2008 Giro's final chapter began in Verona. The fourteenth stage started in the city of Romeo and Juliet and headed almost due north into the Dolomites with two fearsome ascents to be conquered, the Passo Manghen and the hilltop finish at Alpe di Pampeago. Emanuele Sella took off early with a small group and then left the other breakaways behind on the Manghen. He stayed away till the end to win what looked like a beautiful solo victory. Contador, riding for what *La Gazzetta* called "Fortress Astana" had a less than perfect day, losing nearly a half-minute to Menchov, Pellizotti and Riccò. Although the lead passed to stage seven winner Gabriele Bosisio, Contador remained the first of the contenders. The Italian bookmakers still showed Di Luca as the odds-on favorite to win the Giro, but Di Luca, bleeding little dribs and drabs of time all over Italy, was not the rider he had been in 2007.

The General Classification stood thus:

1. Gabriele Bosisio
2. Alberto Contador @ 5 seconds
3. Marzio Bruseghin @ 28 seconds
4. Riccardo Riccò @ 1 minute 2 seconds
5. Danilo Di Luca @ 1 minute 7 seconds

On Sunday came stage fifteen, *il tappone*, with the Pordoi, San Pellegrino, Giau and Falzarego passes and a hilltop finish on the Marmolada.

Sella was on fire, taking off with a small group at only the fifth kilometer. As the race unfolded, he slowly shed his fellow breakaways until the final climb where he dropped his last two companions and sped away for his second spectacular mountain victory. Close behind him, the small group of contenders was fighting hard. Riccò dug deep twice before getting away. Neither Contador nor Menchov could stay with the Cobra and conceded about fifteen seconds. Yet, Contador had acquitted himself well. He had withstood serious punishment and at the end of the day was the owner of the Pink Jersey.

The new General Classification:
1. Alberto Contador
2. Riccardo Riccò @ 33 seconds
3. Danilo Di Luca @ 55 seconds
4. Marzio Bruseghin @ 1 minute 18 seconds
5. Denis Menchov @ 1 minute 20 seconds

While there was much celebration over the wonderful exploits of the intrepid riders, the recent racing gave the observant sports fan much to worry about—for example, stage fifteen's second place, Domenico Pozzovivo (CSF) ascended the Marmolada at a staggering 1,840 vertical meters per hour. The Giro's best climbers were climbing as fast as Marco Pantani in his prime. Something seemed wrong. No, something was wrong.

The next day, Monday, saw the eagerly awaited thirteen-kilometer super-steep timed hill-climb to the Plan de Corones. Pellizotti was the surprise stage winner. For all the difficulty the stage posed, the top rankings of the General Classification remained mostly unchanged. This race still had a marvelous equipoise with six riders within three minutes of the leader.

Stage nineteen crossed the mountains just northeast of Milan, taking in the Vivione and the Presolana before the hilltop finish on Monte Pora. On the slick, wet descent of the Vivione, Di Luca escaped with teammate Savoldelli. They quickly carved out a one-minute lead over the group containing the major contenders. On the Presolana, Di Luca dropped Savoldelli and pressed on alone with a 105-second lead.

Back in the Contador group Simoni, who had been having trouble maintaining contact, was dropped for good. On the Monte Pora ascent, as Di Luca looked like he was riding into pink, Contador finally reacted and attacked. The best riders were able to claw their way back to him. Now Riccò jumped hard twice. The second acceleration was successful and Riccò motored away from the others in search of Di Luca, who was too far gone to be caught.

The day's racing tightened up the standings a bit more. Riccò was just a few seconds away from the lead and Di Luca was now in the hunt for a second Giro victory:

1. Alberto Contador
2. Riccardo Riccò @ 4 seconds
3. Danilo Di Luca @ 21 seconds
4. Marzio Bruseghin @ 2 minutes 0 seconds
5. Franco Pellizotti @ 2 minutes 5 seconds

Riccò, who had a gift for saying the wrong thing, was furious that he had missed having the lead by only four seconds. He lashed out at Sella for working with Contador. Of course Sella was working for his own interests. Riccò then blamed his bike and finally said that he would be in the lead except for the stage ten Urbino time trial.

Stage twenty, the penultimate stage, was the final day in the mountains. Even though two of the Giro's most difficult climbs, the Gavia and the Mortirolo were scheduled for the day, the summits came too far from the finish to greatly affect the outcome. Sella rocketed to his third mountain stage win. The riders were growing weary and after Simoni's stage nineteen disaster where he lost over twelve minutes, Di Luca had his own catastrophe, losing over four minutes. Riccò tried to distance himself from Contador, who was growing stronger with every stage. His attacks came to naught and the gap remained at four seconds. Riccò now blamed his team, saying that if he had Astana behind him, he would be in the lead. That left things to be settled in the final stage, a 28.5-kilometer individual time trial into the heart of Milan.

Contador was the fastest of the contenders, cementing his victory, which was, as in the style of Franco Balmamion, done without winning a single stage. Given his time trial skills, some thought Bruseghin had an outside chance at snatching victory, but he said that the ferocity of the 2008 Giro had left him spent.

Final 2008 Giro d'Italia General Classification:
1. Alberto Contador (Astana) 89 hours 56 minutes 49 seconds
2. Riccardo Riccò (Saunier Duval-Scott) @ 1 minute 57 seconds
3. Marzio Bruseghin (Lampre) @ 2 minutes 54 seconds
4. Franco Pellizotti (Liquigas) @ 2 minutes 56 seconds
5. Denis Menchov (Rabobank) @ 3 minutes 37 seconds

Climbers' Competition:
1. Emanuele Sella (CSF Group-Navigare): 136 points
2. Vasil Kiryienka (Tinkoff Credit Systems): 63
3. Fortunato Balliani (CSF Group-Navigare): 48

Points Competition:
1. Daniele Bennati (Liquigas): 189 points
2. Emanuele Sella (CSF Group-Navigare): 138
3. Riccardo Riccò (Saunier Duval-Scott): 131

ॐ

I wrote earlier that the racers were flying up the mountains at speeds that raised more than a few eyebrows. The aftermath of the 2008 Giro provided a sad explanation. Sella, who won three mountain stages and the King of the Mountains prize, was found with a third generation of EPO, called CERA, in his system in an out-of-competition test in July. Two months later Riccò, who had insinuated that other racers were doping, was thrown out of the Tour de France after being positive for the same EPO/CERA. His teammate Leonardo Piepoli confessed that he too, had been guilty of the same offense, although he later withdrew the admission. Andreas Klöden made a badly veiled accusation against the CSF team that it had a team doping program. CSF's manager threatened legal action but, of course, didn't follow through.

It was rumored that this third generation of EPO had been widely used throughout the peloton in the 2008 Giro because the riders believed there was no test for it, which was true in May. Given that CSF had another rider who was not allowed to start the Giro because of a positive for steroids, one can reasonably conclude that some teams either continued to run institutionalized doping programs or looked the other way as their riders performed so spectacularly that the only explanation was doping.

In 2008 the Tour had its doping control performed by the French Anti Doping Agency (AFLD). After the Tour was over it was found that several riders had submitted suspicious urine samples. The AFLD went back and tested their blood samples and found that the third place rider, Bernhard Kohl, and the rider who had won both time trials, Stefan Schumacher, were both positive for EPO/CERA. That immediately raised the question of retesting Giro samples for EPO/CERA, whose existence at the time wasn't known by the dope testers.

The UCI was handling the Giro's testing and said re-checking would serve no purpose. On that day I am sure the angels wept.

2009 On December 13 the Giro presented a route celebrating its one-hundredth anniversary. Starting with a team time trial in Venice, the Giro headed almost immediately into the hills with mountaintop finishes in stages four and five. With important challenges this early, a rider wouldn't have the luxury of riding into form for the final week. Also, with key stages coming so early it would be difficult for a racer to attempt the Giro/Tour double because it would mean holding peak form from the beginning of May until the end of July.

Tossed in the middle of the race was the longest individual time trial in seventeen years, 60.6 kilometers. Basso said this would be the key to the race. A total of six hilltop finishes made a route that would be a constant, ongoing war. The final time trial, starting and ending at the Roman Forum, was a spectacular finishing touch. It was the first time the Giro hadn't finished in Milan since 1989.

The list of riders planning to contest the Centennial Giro made it look like one of the better fields in the race's history. Ivan Basso (having served his suspension), Danilo Di Luca, Carlos Sastre, Gilberto Simoni, Damiano Cunego, Levi Leipheimer, Denis Menchov, Thor Hushovd and Alessandro Petacchi all planned to attend the Giro. And there was one more rider.

With rumors swirling everywhere, seven-time Tour winner Lance Armstrong announced on September 9, 2008, that he was returning to professional cycling, joining his former director Johan Bruyneel's Astana squad, with victory in the 2009 Tour de France his ultimate goal.

The reaction to Armstrong's return was mixed. Some welcomed it, feeling that cycle racing and the cycle trade would get a shot in the arm. Tour boss Christian Prudhomme seemed indifferent, saying Armstrong would be welcome if he complied with all of the new anti-doping protocols. Underlying the negative reactions was the feeling that Armstrong had never dispelled the allegations of doping that followed him starting with his first Tour victory in 1999. The German television networks, who were in the midst of negotiating new Tour broadcasting rights, said that they were "not amused" with Armstrong's plans and that Armstrong belonged to an earlier generation, that he was a piece of the past that they did not want to see again.

To counter these feelings, Armstrong announced he would ride the Tour with total transparency. All of his blood values and tests would be posted online for all to see. Armstrong later reneged on that promise, saying that doing so would be expensive and complicated.

Meanwhile, Angelo Zomegnan made several trips to Texas, eventually persuading Armstrong to ride the Giro. Zomegnan brought more than the argument that Armstrong's career remained incomplete without a Giro win: Zomegnan is alleged to have brought a big bag of money. A rumored $3,000,000 in start money was said to have helped seal the deal.

Over the winter Cunego and Simoni, at the instigation of their wives, finally made real peace. Cunego was targeting the Tour and said that he would help Simoni win the Giro, even though they were on different teams. Cunego sensed that Armstrong and his friend Basso would work together and there had to be a countervailing force to their potentially powerful combination.

Armstrong's training was set back when he crashed in the first stage of the Vuelta a Castilla y León and broke his collarbone. It may have slowed him a bit, but three days after surgery requiring a five-inch steel plate and twelve screws to repair the break, he was back on the trainer. In early May he came in second to teammate Levi Leipheimer in the American Tour of the Gila stage race.

A few days before the Giro's start it came out that the Astana riders hadn't been paid by the Kazakh oligarchs backing the team for so long that the UCI's required bank reserve covering two-month's salary had been or was about to be used. Noises were made that Armstrong might take over the team, but all that was almost forgotten in the spectacle of a Venice start to the centenary Giro.

Garmin-Slipstream had targeted the first stage, a 20.5 kilometer team time trial on the Venice Lido, hoping to repeat their 2008 time trial victory that put Christian Vande Velde in the lead. Instead, American squad Team Columbia won, beating Garmin by 6 seconds and putting sprinter Mark Cavendish in pink. Armstrong said because his conditioning was behind schedule, Levi Leipheimer would be the team's designated leader. Sounded nice, but Armstrong was the first of his Astana team to cross the line. If Astana had won (they were third by 13 seconds), Armstrong would have been wearing the *maglia rosa*.

The next day reminded the world again that Armstrong was probably the finest stage racer of the age, even if he lacked his previous Tour-winning horsepower. As the pack raced through a technically difficult set of circuits around the city of Trieste, Armstrong had a teammate take him to the front to stay out of trouble. It was a canny move. A crash shortly before the end delayed all but about 50 of the riders. Between having a team that could ride a good time trial and avoiding the crash, Armstrong was now the second-best-placed Classification contender in the race. Some of his competitors were already a minute or more in arrears

A few chosen riders and their General Classification standings:
1. Mark Cavendish
8. Christian Vande Velde @ 20 seconds
10. Lance Armstrong @ 27 seconds
18. Levi Leipheimer @ 40 seconds
27. Denis Menchov @ 52 seconds
45. Ivan Basso @ 1 minute 7 seconds

Stage four had a mountaintop finish at San Martino di Castrozza, due north of Padua. On the lower reaches of the final ascent, Basso's Liquigas team was pulling the peloton, but couldn't drop any of the contenders. With about 350 meters to go Danilo Di Luca hit the gas and then closer to the finish, he did it again. His speed was irresistible and he came across the line with both hands off the bars. *Wunderkind* Thomas Lövkvist was the new leader with Di Luca two seconds back.

The next day was a short 125-kilometer day in the Dolomites and again it had a summit finish. At two kilometers from the top of Alpe di Siusi there were seven riders left, including Basso, Di Luca, Leipheimer, Menchov and Carlos Sastre. Near the finish Sastre tried to bolt but Menchov countered with Di Luca on his wheel. Even Di Luca had to give up, allowing Menchov to come in alone. Di Luca took the lead with Lövkvist five seconds behind.

The day had wrecked the chances of several Giro hopefuls. Simoni lost a not-catastrophic 47 seconds. Damiano Cunego came in 32nd at 2 minutes 39 seconds and Armstrong was a further 19 seconds back. Stefano Garzelli's General Classification hopes were certainly shattered with a *giornata no* that cost him 5 minutes 24 seconds.

The General Classification was thus:
1. Danilo Di Luca
2. Thomas Lövkvist @ 5 seconds
3. Michael Rogers @ 36 seconds
4. Levi Leipheimer @ 43 seconds
5. Denis Menchov @ 50 seconds

Then came two long days in the saddle. Stage six was 248 kilometers over mountainous terrain and stage seven was 244 kilometers of which 200 were a long slow uphill slog in cold rain that left the overall standings unchanged.

The Astana riders had removed the logos from their racing kits of the Kazakh sponsors who hadn't been paying the team. They were now two months in arrears and the UCI gave the team clearance to finish the Giro, but unless some solution were found, the team would lose its license.

Stage nine, a downtown Milan circuit race, was planned to be a Giro showpiece. Each of the 15.4-kilometer laps around the Castello Sforzesco and Piazzale Loreto (where the Giro had started in 1909) had 25 corners. On the first lap a crash occurred and the riders started slowing down, riding four laps at only 32 kilometers per hour. Finally the pack came to a halt at the finish line and Di Luca took a microphone to explain to the crowd that because the peloton felt the course with trolley tracks and parked cars was unsafe, they couldn't race it at full speed.

After restarting, an occasional rider would try to lift the speed, indicating the peloton wasn't unanimously behind the strike. When that would happen other riders would go to the front and snuff out the racing. Slowly the rate increased until the final laps were contested at full speed. Several racers pointed to Armstrong as the instigator of the strike, saying it was he who had complained several days earlier that this stage and the one previous to it were unsafe. Zomegnan was furious, having agreed earlier in the day to neutralize the stage and not let it count towards any of the classifications. He felt the slow-down was a betrayal. Furthermore, he argued that many races are filled with similar perils, such as Amstel Gold, but they weren't the objects of strikes. Right or wrong, the day was ruined.

During the rest day, Ivan Basso and Franco Pellizotti apologized for the riders' actions. Basso said, "Sometimes you just get nervous and decisions made during the race are not always right." On the other side Gilberto Simoni and Lance Armstrong remained unrepentant.

The Giro organization was not the only unhappy player in this drama. Riders on the Lampre team had worked hard to stifle all attempts at igniting the racing. Lampre team management told Marzio Bruseghin, one of the most visible actors in the strike, to find a new employer for 2010. Basso said that no matter what had happened during the Milan stage, the riders were ready to race. He was certainly right about that.

Stage ten was originally intended to be an homage to the Giro's epic past by replaying the 1949 stage seventeen with its ascents of the Maddalena, Vars, Izoard, Montgenèvre and Sestriere that Coppi won so magnificently. Between landslides that closed some roads and a strange conflict between French and Italian radio frequencies that kept the Giro from going into France (both the Giro and the Tour regularly cross borders), the stage had to be redesigned. It still went from Cuneo to Pinerolo and was actually eight kilometers longer than the 1949 version, but in 2009 it went over the Moncenisio, Sestriere and Pra' Martino climbs. It had neither the punch nor the romance of retracing Coppi's epic ride.

Halfway through the 262-kilometer alpine stage, Garzelli escaped on the Moncenisio. He increased his lead as he went through Sestriere (2009's *Cima Coppi*), still alone, and continued into an energy-sapping headwind. Eventually two chasers, Andriy Grivko and Giovanni Visconti caught him, putting off the inevitable. The fast-moving *maglia rosa* group caught them on the lower slopes of the final climb, the Pra' Martino. Franco Pellizotti tried to make himself scarce and indeed managed to go over the Pra' Martino with a few seconds' lead but was caught on the descent.

Di Luca used the descent to get a small gap and held it to the end. Pellizotti, Menchov and Sastre followed Di Luca in 10 seconds later while Leipheimer and Basso lost a half-minute. Writers were impressed by Di Luca's well-rounded prowess and his willingness to spend watts as if he were riding a Classic instead of a demanding Grand Tour.

The General Classification at this point:

1. Danilo Di Luca
2. Denis Menchov @ 1 minute 20 seconds
3. Michael Rogers @ 1 minute 33 seconds
4. Levi Leipheimer @ 1 minute 40 seconds
5. Franco Pellizotti @ 1 minute 53 seconds

Held on the Ligurian coast, the stage twelve 60.6-kilometer individual time trial was technically challenging with two ascents, prompting most riders to use conventional road bikes rather than their special time trial bikes.

Menchov won in commanding fashion, leading at all check points; Di Luca lost almost a two minutes as well as the overall lead to the Russian. Leipheimer, who was only twenty seconds slower than Menchov, moved into third place. Forty seconds now separated the top three riders.

Stage fourteen's short, sharp final ascent into San Luca (Bologna) should have been a perfect launch point for Di Luca. He tried, but he didn't have the punch to put any distance into his rivals. Di Luca was upset that the Liquigas team, which had promised to be aggressive, left the job of riding at the front entirely to his LPR team. Pellizotti answered that Liquigas was riding for its own interests and that's what happens in racing.

Stage sixteen was 237 kilometers of relentless climbing and descending with a finish atop Monte Petrano. Leipheimer had promised to use the stage's difficulty as an opportunity to take the lead, feeling that with the day's heat, the stage's length and climbs, some riders would crack. Because the evening before had been so hot, many riders slept poorly. Italians commonly shun air conditioning because they believe the cold, dehumidified air will make them sick.

An early break with Cunego, Popovych and Michele Scarponi managed to stay together until the penultimate mountain, the Catria. Further back, all of the Classification men stayed together with Menchov's team riding tempo at the front of the peloton. Popovych took off on the descent. Back in the pack, Leipheimer got a flat and had to get paced back up just as the race was getting set for what everyone knew would be a rocket-fast race to the finish.

At the base of Monte Petrano, Liquigas raised the pace. Not happy with that, Carlos Sastre's Cervélo teammate Simon Gerrans went by the Liquigas men and went still faster. Then the expected occurred. Sastre attacked and was quickly brought back by the other contenders. Then Sastre went again. That was it. With a little over eight kilometers to the summit, Carlos Sastre was flying away, much as he had on l'Alpe d'Huez to win the 2008 Tour.

Menchov and Di Luca, feeling that the race was between them, and that Sastre was too far down on time to chase, stayed together while Sastre soared up the mountain and passed all the breakaway riders.

Further back, perhaps as a result of his post-puncture chase, Leipheimer was in crisis. Armstrong, who had been staying with the front group, went back and paced Leipheimer to the finish.

After over seven hours of racing, Sastre won the stage by 25 seconds over Menchov, who managed to gap Di Luca by a single second. For Leipheimer, the day was a disaster. He lost almost three minutes and dropped down to sixth place while Sastre moved up to third. Several riders, including Leipheimer, said stage sixteen was the hardest day of racing they had ever endured. Sastre maintained he had come to the Giro to win, an unlikely outcome with so few stages left suited to his skills.

The General Classification after stage sixteen:
1. Denis Menchov
2. Danilo Di Luca @ 39 seconds
3. Carlos Sastre @ 2 minutes 19 seconds
4. Franco Pellizotti @ 3 minutes 8 seconds
5. Ivan Basso @ 3 minutes 19 seconds

Stage seventeen was a relatively short day, only 83 kilometers to Block Haus. The original plan had been to go an additional five and a half kilometers to the summit of Passo Laricano, but road damage during the winter altered plans. The riders looking to topple Menchov knew this was one of their last chances to gain time on the powerful Russian. Much was made of the fact that the race would pass through Di Luca's hometown of Pescara and Di Luca himself said that a good showing in front of his fellow Abruzzese would be gratifying.

Di Luca's LPR team assumed their usual front position and whipped up the peloton's speed as the Block Haus slope began to rise. Sastre's

Cervélo riders took over and sped things up a bit more, trying to set things up for another solo excursion on their team leader's part.

But it wasn't Sastre or Di Luca who broke free, it was Pellizotti with Armstrong in hot pursuit. Armstrong couldn't close the gap and had to return to the chasers but Pellizotti was well and truly gone. He came in alone, with a 42-second gap.

With ten kilometers to go Di Luca blasted off and a grim-faced Menchov immediately reacted, glomming on to his wheel. All the way to the top Di Luca worked to free himself of his shadow, to no avail. Garzelli dragged himself up to the duo. This being a Giro of seconds, Di Luca and his fans were deeply disappointed when Garzelli won the sprint for second place, taking the valuable 12-second time bonus. Di Luca, who took third, had to be content with the 8 seconds he earned when he opened a gap on an exhausted Menchov in the sprint. At the awards ceremony, angry Di Luca fans booed and whistled Garzelli. Sastre had been unable to respond to the attacks and lost almost two minutes. The race was a two-man fight.

The General Classification now:
1. Denis Menchov
2. Danilo Di Luca @ 26 seconds
3. Franco Pellizotti @ 2 minutes 0 seconds
4. Ivan Basso @ 3 minutes 28 seconds
5. Carlos Sastre @ 3 minutes 30 seconds

All eyes looked to the nineteenth stage with its finish near the top of Mount Vesuvius. Eight kilometers from Vesuvius' summit, Sastre teed off an attack by Basso and launched himself skyward. This time he had his good legs back and the rest were either uninterested in pursuing him or just couldn't. Three kilometers later Di Luca gave it another shot, taking Menchov and Pellizotti with him. Menchov, looking only to stay with Di Luca and preserve his lead, hung on as Di Luca relentlessly attacked. But it was Pellizotti who was able to escape, closing to within 21 seconds of Sastre at the line. Di Luca beat Menchov for third, reducing their gap to just 18 seconds.

Di Luca planned to use stage twenty's intermediate sprint time bonus and the final sharp uphill finish to try to close in on Menchov before the time trial. Menchov ruined the plans for the intermediate sprint when he surprised Di Luca's team with an early flier. Only quick thinking on teammate Petacchi's part kept Menchov from grabbing the full 6 seconds in play, but Menchov had still gained 2 valuable seconds. On the uphill finish to Anagni, Belgian Classics specialist Philippe Gilbert ended Silence-Lotto's winless Giro with a strong attack one and a half kilometers from the finish. Di Luca went to the Rome 14.4-kilometer individual time trial with a 20-second deficit. Menchov was regarded as the markedly superior time trialist and at this point, barring misfortune, the Giro belonged to the Russian.

The Giro selected a magnificent backdrop for the final stage of the centenary Giro, sending the riders by the Roman Forum, the Vatican and the Coliseum. The weather wasn't good, with on-and-off rain. Di Luca set off on a road bike and appeared to be out of the saddle most of his ride. At the first checkpoint, he was ahead by 5 seconds but that pace was too much and by mid-point he slowed. Di Luca was losing the Giro.

Or was he? With less than a kilometer to go, Menchov went sliding behind his bike on the wet cobbles. He was up and on a new bike in a flash. He ended up gaining another 21 seconds that day, saving his Giro.

The 2009 Giro was one of the most extraordinarily hard fought and exciting races I have ever had the privilege to watch. The duel between Menchov and Di Luca will go down as one of the great ones in cycling history. Di Luca fought every step of the way for every second he could get. He lost because, as he generously said, "In the end, the best guy won."

There were no doping positives in the 2009 Giro. Only the most naïve would believe that this meant that the entire peloton was clean: a VAM of 1838 for the Colle del Gato in stage eight, for example, gave reason for concern. In fact, disgraced racer Bernhard Kohl said that the current use of the "Biological Passport" (a record of an athlete's biological markers used to detect variations that might give away use of banned substances) by the UCI made doping easy.

Final 2009 Giro d'Italia General Classification:
1. Denis Menchov (Rabobank) 86 hours 3 minutes 11 seconds
2. Danilo Di Luca (LPR Brakes-Farnese Vini) @ 41 seconds
3. Franco Pellizotti (Liquigas) @ 1 minute 59 seconds
4. Carlos Sastre (Cervélo) @ 3 minutes 46 seconds
5. Ivan Basso (Liquigas-Doimo) @ 3 minutes 59 seconds

Climbers' Competition:
1. Stefano Garzelli (Acqua & Sapone-Caffe Mokambo): 61 points
2. Danilo Di Luca (LPR Brakes-Farnese Vini): 45
3. Denis Menchov (Rabobank): 41

Points Competition:
1. Danilo Di Luca (LPR Brakes-Farnese Vini): 170 points
2. Denis Menchov (Rabobank): 144
3. Franco Pellizotti (Liquigas-Doimo): 133

2010

Indeed, 2009 was a fairy tale too good to be true. While Menchov fended off questions about his involvement with the Humanplasma blood bank in Vienna, the other riders on the final podium were not as lucky. In July of 2009 it was announced that Di Luca had come up positive for EPO in two of the Giro stages. He was slapped with a two-year suspension and a €280,000 fine.

During the week before the 2010 Giro's start, the UCI announced that several riders had problems with their biological passports. Franco Pellizotti was accused of irregular blood values dating back to a sample given before the start of the 2009 Tour de France. The "Dolphin of Bibbione" and his team maintained that while the UCI's experts may have thought they found clear evidence of doping, Pellizotti's experts found the variations to be normal. Normal or not, being under investigation for doping, Pellizotti was pulled from his Liquigas' team roster and was replaced by a rider who had been preparing to ride the Tour of California, Vincenzo Nibali. Nibali, seventh in the 2009 Tour, would join Ivan Basso in making Liquigas the most powerful team at the Giro.

Since Menchov had decided to pass on the 2010 Giro to concentrate on the Tour, the Giro was missing its entire 2009 podium. The Giro didn't give an invitation to Riccardo Riccò's Flaminia team, preferring to see if the climber, just off his suspension, could stay out of trouble for a year. The field had stars nonetheless. Alexandre Vinokourov, who had just won both Liège–Bastogne–Liège and the Giro del Trentino after serving a two-year suspension for blood doping, was in formidable condition. World Champion Cadel Evans had his own Classic win that spring, the Flèche Wallonne. 2008 Tour de France winner Carlos Sastre was also back for another shot at pink.

Showing the thinness of Italian stage racing talent that could avoid doping penalties, the best Italian hopes were Basso, Nibali and Garzelli. The 2010 Giro would be 38-year-old Gilberto Simoni's farewell race.

The Giro's first three days were in the Netherlands, where the riders would have to deal with powerful winds that blow in from the North Sea as well as narrow roads filled with obstructions the Dutch use to slow down traffic. After a transfer to Italy for a stage four team time trial, the Giro would build to a crescendo in the Dolomites. The list of famous climbs must have made the *scalatori* salivate: Monte Grappa, Monte Zoncolan, Plan de Corones (as a time trial), the Mortirolo, Gavia and Tonale. This would be a race for climbers who could survive the mean streets of Holland.

Bradley Wiggins (fourth in the 2009 Tour) of the new, swaggering, wealthy and supremely British Team Sky took the first Pink Jersey after winning the stage one time trial in Amsterdam. Evans was 2 seconds slower while Vinokourov was just 5 seconds off the pace.

No one was surprised by the carnage the next two days of racing on Dutch roads caused. Wiggins was delayed by a crash in the second stage, gifting the *maglia rosa* to Evans who was in pink for the first time since 2002.

The next day Evans was slowed by fallen riders, having come across nearly the entire Sky team scattered across the road. Weirdly, they had chosen to ride deep dish carbon wheels in the brutal North Sea winds. Once Evans was back on his bike, he was without teammates and had to chase alone. When Vinokourov heard that Evans and other contenders were delayed by crashes he told his team to ramp up the pace. Not sporting perhaps, but certainly effective.

So effective, in fact, that Vinokourov took the lead. Wiggins, part of that Sky team catastrophe, suffered a four-minute loss. Before his wheels touched Italian soil, the Great British Hope was effectively out of the race.

The first day of racing in Italy was a 33-kilometer uphill drag of a team time trial into Cuneo. Evans' weaker BMC team didn't suffer the shellacking that was expected to kill his Classification hopes, but they did lose about a minute and a half. Keenly aware that recent Giri and Tours had been affairs in which seconds were pearls beyond price, Evans said, "You're talking to someone who lost the [2007] Tour de France by 23 seconds." In the 2008 Tour Carlos Sastre beat Evans by 58 seconds.

Liquigas performed so well in the rainy stage that when they were done the General Classification podium was all Liquigas. Vincenzo Nibali was the new *maglia rosa* and Basso was second at 13 seconds. Battered by Vinokourov's desperate pulls at the front, the Astana team fell apart in the last kilometers, costing the Kazakh precious seconds.

Liquigas riders were in the pole position while Vinokourov was down 33 seconds, Evans at 1 minute 59 seconds and Carlos Sastre a further 14 seconds behind. That was Wednesday. The next two days would be for the sprinters and breakaway artists with Saturday having the potential to turn the race upside down when the race went over the *strade bianche* of Chianti country.

And turn it upside down it did. Through the winds, fog, rain and eventually mud, the riders blitzed away at full gas, covering 52.5 kilometers the first hour. As the stage progressed, Vinokourov kept the pressure on the pack. The pivotal moment came about 30 kilometers before the end when nearly the entire Liquigas team crashed. Just as the *maglia rosa* and his team were hitting the deck,

Vinokourov slogs through the mud.

the German Milram squad was starting to up the pace. Vinokourov threw more gas on the fire and the riders started to come unglued. The rain turned the final kilometers on dirt roads into a muddy agony that brought the best bike handlers to the front. Climbing to the finish line at Montalcino were Evans, Cunego, Vinokourov and David Arroyo. Evans muscled his way to the front and led out the sprint, which he won.

Most of the shattered peloton started coming in a minute later. Nibali lost two minutes. After the long (222 kilometers) cold, wet ride, many riders were glassy-eyed with exhaustion.

Vinokourov's payoff for his hyper-aggression was the Pink Jersey while Evans moved into second place, 1 minute 12 seconds behind.

Stage eight drove the riders south from Chianciano Terme in Umbria to a foggy hilltop finish at Terminillo which left the times between the contenders relatively unchanged.

After stage eight the General Classification stood thus:
1. Alexandre Vinokourov
2. Cadel Evans @ 1 minute 12 seconds
3. Vincenzo Nibali @ 1 minute 33 seconds
4. Ivan Basso @ 1 minute 51 seconds
5. Marco Pinotti @ 2 minutes 17 seconds

At 262 kilometers, stage eleven was the year's longest. Everyone knew the Apennine stage was going to be filled with aggression and so it was. From the gun, the attacks came and after only twenty kilometers a big 54-man group forged a gap. The group was potent with Bradley Wiggins and several members of his Sky team, Carlos Sastre, David Arroyo with four of his team along and Richie Porte and two of his Saxo squad. What probably affected the days racing most was that Liquigas, the Giro's strongest team, had four in the break including two well-placed riders, Valerio Agnoli and Robert Kiserlovski.

Vinokourov, Evans, Nibali and Basso all missed the move. The fast moving break, whose members had plenty of reason to cooperate, built a seventeen-minute lead. Liquigas played poker and waited for Vinokourov's Astana and Evans' BMC team to take up the chase. They couldn't or wouldn't. Most of the Astana riders were ill (three had to drop out of the race at the end of the day) and Evans' team didn't have the horsepower to chase down a break like this. Eventually Liquigas aided the chase which had Garzelli, Vinokourov, Evans and Basso also pulling the pack.

The *fuga di bidone* rolled into L'Aquila with almost thirteen minutes in hand. Both Wiggins and Sastre had earlier suffered what seemed to be time losses large enough to eliminate them from contention, but after stage eleven their hopes had new life. Neo-pro Richie Porte was the new leader with journeyman David Arroyo second at 1 minute

42 seconds. Vinokourov and Evans were down ten and eleven minutes respectively.

As soon as the riders were off their bikes the angry finger pointing began. Liquigas director Roberto Amadio had miscalculated badly. Cunego lamented that he didn't learn about the break and its potential to wreck havoc until it was too late.

Stage eleven was so difficult that 41 riders finished after the time cutoff of 39 minutes and had to get special dispensation to continue racing. At that time the points leader was American Tyler Farrar. He was among the day's late arrivals and, following a newly instituted rule, was handed a 25-point penalty, giving the points lead to Frenchman Jérôme Pineau. The rule was intended to keep sprinters from riding slowly in the mountains and keeping their prizes even after the judges had shown special mercy to those who would otherwise be eliminated.

Locking the barn door after the horses had bolted, vigilance was the order of the day in stage twelve. Vinokourov even made a play for the stage win and the bonus seconds, but Italian Champion Filippo Pozzato won. Pozzato's victory, the first individual stage win of the year by an Italian, ended an embarrassing episode for Italian racing. Never had Italy had to wait so long for one of her countrymen to win a Giro stage. Until 2010, the longest Italian winless drought was in 1973 when Gianni Motta finally won stage six.

The showdown in the Dolomites began that Saturday with stage fourteen. It was a flattish run-in to the Monte Grappa ascent with a technical descent before the finish in Asolo. Liquigas had promised to make the day hard for everyone else and they lived up to their words. From the beginnings of the Grappa ascent, Liquigas riders set a fiendish pace. The result was a quartet of Basso, Nibali, Evans and Michele Scarponi cresting the top with Vinokourov slightly gapped.

Nibali, one of the finest descenders in professional cycling, schooled the others in how to push the limits of tire adhesion and took the stage. Porte was a casualty of the Liquigas set-piece and Arroyo was the new *maglia rosa*.

For the next stage Zomegnan had put on his Sunday-best. He started with three leg-softening passes: the Chianzutan, Duran and Valcalda followed by a finish atop Monte Zoncolan.

Liquigas repeated the process. They blasted away at the bottom of Monte Zoncolan and quickly battered the peloton into little pieces.

Scarponi made a blistering attack and it was over for everyone but Evans and Basso. Basso did the pacesetting, spinning a low gear and riding faster than Evans could go.

Basso, who had been riding as almost a *gregario di lusso* for Nibali, now asserted his leadership of the team, cruising into Asolo 1 minute 19 seconds ahead of Evans and 2 minutes 26 seconds in front of Vinokourov. Arroyo raced up the mountain fast enough to retain his lead, but it was looking like he was renting the Pink Jersey from Basso.

After Monte Zoncolan the General Classification looked like this:
1. David Arroyo
2. Richie Porte @ 2 minutes 35 seconds
3. Ivan Basso @ 3 minutes 33 seconds
4. Carlos Sastre @ 4 minutes 21 seconds
5. Cadel Evans @ 4 minutes 43 seconds
6. Alexandre Vinokourov @ 5 minutes 51 seconds

After the second rest day the riders faced the *cronoscalata* (timed hill-climb) up to the Plan de Corones. Stage winner Stefano Garzelli used a tiny 34 x 29 gear. Since he was a half-hour behind in the General Classification standings, Garzelli's win had no effect upon the race, But Evan's second place did. He was able to pull 28 seconds closer to Basso and 94 seconds nearer to Arroyo. Instead of blowing up the race, the steep hill-climb tightened things still further:
1. David Arroyo
2. Ivan Basso @ 2 minutes 27 seconds
3. Richie Porte @ 2 minutes 36 seconds
4. Cadel Evans @ 3 minutes 9 seconds

Friday's stage nineteen was the penultimate day of hard mountain racing with a climb to Aprica then a loop to take in the Trivigno and Mortirolo passes before a return to Aprica for a hilltop finish.

Basso used his Liquigas team to soften the peloton's legs and on the Mortirolo, Basso set a pace that only Scarponi and teammate Nibali could match. The three stayed clear on the wet, dangerous technical descent of the Mortirolo (Nibali and Scarponi had to wait for the slow-descending Basso) while the others tried to form an effective chase. Trying to get up to the trio, Arroyo descended with suicidal desperation, but they were too far up the road. Arroyo, Evans, Vinokourov, Carlos Sastre and John Gadret were clearly shattered and unable to mount an effective, united chase. As Basso pulled the others up the final climb to Aprica, he extended his lead over the Evans group until it was 3 minutes 5 seconds.

Scarponi won the stage but Basso was in pink with Arroyo at 51 seconds. At four minutes, Evans looked to have little chance against Basso.

Bad weather threatened the planned final mountain stage with a Gavia Pass crossing, but as the sun rose on Saturday it was announced that the Gavia, the year's *Cima Coppi*, would be ascended from the easier north side on the way to a hill-top finish at the top of the Tonale.

Gilberto Simoni was riding his last Giro, and looking to go out in a blaze of glory, broke away on the Gavia with Swiss rider Johann Tschopp. Tschopp was unsentimental and dropped Simoni near the Gavia's top and continued on to a solo stage victory.

Near the end of the final ascent Evans managed to rip himself clear of Basso, but only by nine seconds. Scarponi stayed with Basso and gained time on Nibali. With the final time trial in Verona the sole remaining stage, a single second separated Nibali and Scarponi:

1. Ivan Basso
2. David Arroyo @ 1 minute 15 seconds
3. Vincenzo Nibali @ 2 minutes 56 seconds
4. Michele Scarponi @ 2 minutes 57 seconds
5. Cadel Evans @ 3 minutes 47 seconds

The 15-kilometer time trial in Verona was too short to change the standings, but Evans was able to gain 20 seconds and Nibali predictably out-rode Scarponi.

Final 2010 Giro d'Italia General Classification:
1. Ivan Basso (Liquigas-Doimo) 87 hours 44 minutes 1 second
2. David Arroyo (Caisse d'Epargne) @ 1 minute 51 seconds
3. Vincenzo Nibali (Liquigas-Doimo) @ 2 minutes 37 seconds
4. Michele Scarponi (Androni Giocatolli-Diquigiovanni) @ 2 minutes 50 seconds
5. Cadel Evans (BMC) @ 3 minutes 27 seconds

Climbers' Competition:
1. Matthew Lloyd (Omega Pharma-Lotto): 56 points
2. Ivan Basso (Liquigas): 41
3. Johann Tschopp (Bouygues Telecom): 38

Points Competition (now a red jersey):
1. Cadel Evans (BMC): 150 points
2. Alexandre Vinokourov (Astana): 128
3. Vincenzo Nibali (Liquigas): 116

Stung by accusations of incompetence in ferreting out dopers, UCI boss Pat McQuaid announced there had been a change in how the racers' blood values evolved during this Giro and that hemoglobin levels in the riders' blood were going down over the three weeks of the race, as they should, indicative to him of fewer blood transfusions.

At 39.707 kilometer per hour, this was by far the fastest Giro in history, beating the previous record, 2003's extraordinary 38.928. The changing nature of the Giro might explain why the race was so fast. The rising importance of the Giro coupled with its more international peloton has meant an end to the *piano* days of yore. Damiano Cunego said the race is far harder than it was when he won in 2004 and that even though his power numbers were as good as they have ever been, he said another Giro win for him was out of the question.

Professional coach Hunter Allen did an analysis of power outputs of one of his clients who rode both the Giro and the Tour and found that there was no question that the Giro was the harder of the two races.

2011 To celebrate the 150th anniversary of Italy's unification, the 2011 Giro route started in Turin, Italy's first capital. With even more climbing than the last few editions, Alberto Contador expected the 2011 Giro to be the hardest Grand Tour he had ever ridden.

Contador had more problems than just steep mountains. After being found positive for the banned drug Clenbuterol in the 2010 Tour de France, he was exonerated by the Spanish cycling federation and cleared to race. The federation had come under intense political pressure from all corners of Spain, even from the Spanish Premier, to accept Contador's explanation that he had eaten a contaminated piece of beef. Unhappy with the Spanish Federation's ruling, the UCI filed an appeal with the Court for Arbitration of Sport, which put off a final decision until 2012.

Initially planning to ride a low-key Giro in support of teammate Vincenzo Nibali before going on to his major objective, the Tour, Basso was having trouble finding good form and felt that riding both races was beyond him and pulled out of the Giro.

There were still plenty of good riders starting, given the Giro had been granted an exemption from the UCI's 200-rider limit. Zomegnan invited 23 teams of nine for a total of 207, using his five wild cards to bring in five smaller teams with strong Italian connections. The startlist included four former winners: Garzelli, Di Luca, Contador and Menchov. Nibali's name was on everyone's lips as the rider most likely to give Contador trouble.

And again, there was another doping scandal, this time centered in Mantua, with what appeared to be convincing evidence that some riders from the Lampre, BMC and Movistar teams had taken EPO, testosterone, corticoids, human growth hormone and engaged in blood doping. Former world champion Alessandro Ballan and hard-guy Marzio Bruseghin were pulled from their teams' startlists and at the Giro's start, another 30 people were waiting to hear if the Italian prosecutor would bring them to trial.

Decades after it should have, the UCI finally adopted a rule prohibiting the injections of medicines or any other substances without a clear-cut medical necessity. Even the possession of items that could be used in injections created the presumption of guilt under the new rule. There being no power granted to any official organization for searches, the rule was toothless.

It was time to race. Starting at Venaria Reale near Turin, one of the royal palaces of the House of Savoy (the first rulers of unified Italy), the day's route was 19.3 flat kilometers of team time trialing into Turin. Well-drilled HTC-Highroad beat Radio Shack by 10 seconds, and according to plan, 35-year-old Marco Pinotti was given the job of leading the team across the finish line, thereby earning him the year's first *maglia rosa*. Contador's Saxo squad gave up 30 seconds while Menchov's Geox and Garzelli's Acqua & Sapone teams lost about a minute.

The events of stage three, with its successful break giving David Millar the lead, cast a pall over what was looking to be a sparkling Giro. With about 40 kilometers to go, Belgian Wouter Weylandt crashed horribly while descending the technical Passo del Bocco. Paramedics were unable to revive the racer who was airlifted to a hospital and pronounced dead before the stage was over. The riders weren't told about the tragedy until the stage's finish.

The next day's stage was neutralized with Weylandt's team, Leopard-Trek, crossing the finish line together. That evening the team announced its withdrawal from the race.

2010's trip across Tuscany's *strade bianche* had been a rousing success, creating a brutal day of exciting, selective racing. Not one to miss a chance to spice up the competition, Zomegnan included nineteen kilometers of white roads in stage five's hilly trip across Tuscany into Umbria, finishing it off with a trip up the stiff climb to Orvieto. It worked. Swiss rider Martin Kohler stormed away from the peloton when the stage was only twelve kilometers old and managed to build a gap that at one point grew to nearly thirteen minutes. With twenty kilometers to go, Pieter Weening and John Gadret raced after the Swiss buccaneer, catching him ten kilometers later. Weening still had lots in the tank and shortly after making contact with Kohler, went off in his own search of glory. It was a close thing. When he crossed the line with both arms in the air, the pack was only 8 seconds behind. *Maglia rosa* Millar had a dreadful day, crashing and suffering from allergies. He lost nearly three minutes and the Pink Jersey, which migrated to Weening.

Several riders complained about the *strade bianche*, a not uncommon occurrence when Grand Tour organizers add anything beyond glass-smooth pavement to a race route. Zomegnan answered Di Luca's complaint by recalling the wonderful ride Di Luca had on the unpaved Colle delle Finestre in the 2005 Giro, "Maybe that was a long time ago for him, I don't know." Zomegnan understood that his customers were the *tifosi*, who had plenty of other forms of entertainment if the Giro were insufficiently enthralling, while the racers, with their fruit-fly short careers, care little for the long-term health of the sport. Otherwise they would never have fought so bitterly against dope-testing and in favor of race radios (by which team directors control their riders and deaden racing's spontaneity).

Stage seven's finish atop Montevergine di Mercogliano wasn't steep enough to create a selection. In fact, all the contenders along with Weening, finished in the front group that came millimeters from catching lone escapee and stage winner Bart de Clercq.

But stage nine's two ascents up Sicily's Mount Etna, with an average slope of six percent and patches of eleven and twelve was another kettle of fish. The day before Contador had sent a shudder up the peloton's collective spine when he had grabbed a five-second gap on the field, chasing and nearly catching stage eight winner Oscar Gatto.

At the start of the second ascent of the volcano, a break devoid of hope was three minutes up the road. 2005's revelation José Rujano had announced his ambitions for a high final placing and erupted off the front of the peloton, looking for more than just a stage win.

Then, with less than seven kilometers remaining, Alberto Contador attacked in the big ring with Scarponi for company. Seeing the intensity of the acceleration, Nibali wisely decided to ride to the top at his own speed. Contador set a pace that was too hot for Scarponi who realized that in trying to hold the Spaniard's wheel he had gone too deep, forcing him to return to the chasing group.

Contador caught Rujano and as Contador flew by, the little Venezuelan managed to grab his wheel. Contador was in no mood to pull the reborn climber along, but it took several blistering attacks before he could shake his stubborn follower, and then, just barely.

Contador crossed the line alone with Rujano only 3 seconds back. The rest of the hopefuls? Garzelli, Nibali, Roman Kreuziger and Scarponi were about a minute back. It was a masterful display that left the others open-mouthed in admiration and wondering if there was any way to overcome a rider with this strength.

After stage nine, the General Classification stood thus:
1. Alberto Contador
2. Kanstantsin Sivtsov @ 59 seconds
3. Christophe Le Mével @ 1 minute 19 seconds
4. Vincenzo Nibali @ 1 minute 21 seconds
5. Michele Scarponi @ 1 minute 28 seconds

During the rest day, the Giro transferred to Termoli for three stages up the Adriatic coast before the high mountains. Contador wanted someone else to take the *maglia rosa*, someone with a good team who could relieve his squad of policing the peloton and enduring the presentation ceremonies after each stage when they preferred being in the hotel resting. Yet who could be expected to dutifully croak when the air got thin and hand the lead back to the Spaniard? Christophe Le Mével looked to be in just such a hunt in the eleventh stage, but teams hungry for a stage win caught the fleeing Frenchman just as the stage's finish line was in sight. Mark Cavendish took two of the three Adriatic stages and then, with the Dolomites looming, headed for the airport along with five other sprinters.

Stage thirteen had four major passes with a finish atop Austria's Grossglockner. The big men held their fire until the Grossglockner started to hurt. Euskaltel had hopes that Igor Anton might do well and drove the peloton hard. Anton gave it a go, as did Rujano and the relentless Scarponi, and nearly all had to yield to Contador. Only Rujano could hold his wheel. Contador worked with him to the summit and then let Rujano take the stage, because despite his ambitions, at this point Rujano was no Classification threat.

Stage fourteen, or to be exact, the descent off the penultimate climb, Monte Crostis, spelled trouble. As it came closer to Giro time and the riders personally examined the route, many began to question the safety of the narrow road with its steep and dangerous-looking dropoffs. Safety nets were installed, but the team managers were not appeased given that only motorcycles and not team follow cars were going to be allowed on the road, despite this being the same scheme employed on the Zoncolan. At nine in the evening before the day of

Contador gifts stage thirteen to Rujano.

the stage, the UCI ruled that the Crostis had to be eliminated. Not because it was unsafe, but because the follow cars would not be with the riders for 37 kilometers, and that endangered the sporting fairness of the race. This infuriated Zomegnan who found it strange to change from safety to sporting fairness as the reason to eliminate the mountain. He continued to insist the original route was safe, fair and spectacular.

The Tualis was hurriedly added in replacement, but as the riders were well into the stage it was learned that a crowd of angry *tifosi* were gathering on the Tualis to protest the Crostis' elimination. In an abundance of caution, that climb was also eliminated. That still left the Zoncolan (which also barred follow cars, but allowed service motorcycles) to separate the men from the boys.

On the Zoncolan's final kilometers Anton escaped while the cool and collected Contador was content to sit on now second-place Nibali until the right moment. And then Contador lit up the hill (riding a special bike with 36 x 32 gearing), finishing a half-minute behind Anton. The *tifosi* thought Contador and his Saxo team boss Riis were among those who had requested the Crostis be eliminated and booed the Spaniard as he finished the stage.

The General Classification stood thus:
1. Alberto Contador
2. Vincenzo Nibali @ 3 minutes 20 seconds
3. Igor Anton @ 3 minutes 21 seconds
4. Michele Scarponi @ 4 minutes 6 seconds
5. John Gadret @ 5 minutes 23 seconds

Before the second rest day there was another big day in the mountains, this time with the Piancavallo, Cibiana, Giau, Marmolada and Gardeccia passes. Looking to replicate his 2009 King of the Mountains win, Stefano Garzelli took off from the day's break on the Giau with Mikel Nieve chasing. Garzelli scooped up the double KOM points that the Giau's status as the *Cima Coppi* conferred, and then pressed on to the Marmolada with a very determined Nieve in hot pursuit.

Back in the remnants of the pack, Contador attacked and found himself with the race's best riders at the start of the descent of the Giau. Nibali—arguably the peloton's best descender since Savoldelli—left the *maglia rosa* group behind and by the time he was on Marmolada, was within 45 seconds of Garzelli. On the Marmolada, Nibali was caught and then again dropped, but yet again regained contact after performing an insane descent, made more dangerous with rain.

Garzelli's dream of winning the *tappone* was shattered when Nieve went by him on the climb to Gardeccia and continued on for the stage win. Garzelli was consoled by his near unassailable lead in the climbers' competition. Riding with economy and tactical finesse, Contador waited until the stage's final kilometers before attacking the remnants of his chasing group. He pushed himself hard, but at the stage's end he could only gain 6 seconds on Scarponi. Later Contador said the Gardeccia stage was the hardest day of racing in his life.

With a much-needed rest day next, the General Classification stood thus:

1. Alberto Contador
2. Michele Scarponi @ 4 minutes 20 seconds
3. Vincenzo Nibali @ 5 minutes 11 seconds
4. John Gadret @ 6 minutes 8 seconds
5. Mikel Nieve @ 7 minutes 3 seconds

The first stage of the final week was a 13-kilometer *cronoscalata* to the Nevegal ski station. Contador raced up the narrow defile between the hordes of fans and increased his lead over Scarponi to nearly five minutes. With Contador's superb form making it unlikely that the others could take the lead, attention was now focused on the fight for second place with Scarponi sitting on a 47-second lead over Nibali.

Contador was riding confidently, not bothering to fight for small scraps of time. At stage nineteen's Macugnaga hilltop finish, Contador was racing for the line a few seconds ahead of Nibali when he caught Paolo Tiralongo, who had gone on a flyer. The two spoke a few words and then Contador pulled Tiralongo before easing to let his former Astana *gregario* take the stage win. It was an act of both stunning bravado as well as generosity to a rider who had labored in previous seasons to help the Spaniard.

Before the final stage, a 26-kilometer Milan time trial (truncated because of a shortage of police), Contador was sitting on a fat five and a half minute lead, prompting him to announce that he would ride the stage carefully and avoid any chance of crashing. Nibali expressed displeasure over the stage shortening, noting this was his last chance to wrest second place from Scarponi. In any case, Scarponi did well enough to keep his second place, and Contador's easy ride secured his second Giro and sixth Grand Tour victory. The old Spanish national anthem from the days of Franco was accidently played, irritating the Spanish Sports Council enough to file a formal complaint. Some people just don't know how to win.

Contador joined Miguel Induráin as the only Spaniards to win two Giri until February 6, 2012. On that day the Court of Arbitration for Sport ruled in favor of the UCI, which had appealed the Spanish Cycling Federation's decision to clear Contador of the doping charge. Contador was suspended for two years, dating back to the positive in the 2010 Tour. Among other races, he was stripped of his 2010 Tour and 2011 Giro championships. Michele Scarponi became the winner of the 2011 Giro d'Italia.

There was a chorus of complaints from the riders that the long, difficult stages and eight summit finishes made the race too hard, with some of them arguing, as 1923 Tour winner Henri Pélissier did nearly a century ago, that overly long stages make for slow and dull racing. The riders also complained that in looking to visit as many of Italy's twenty regions as possible, there were too many long and tiring transfers. Zomegnan was apologetic about the transfers but was fierce in his defense of the route's difficulty, arguing there was lots of high-speed racing. At 38.758 kilometers per hour, the 2011 Giro was fully in line with the speeds of the previous decade's Giri and the racing was as exciting as it could be, given Contador's dominating form.

2011 Giro d'Italia General Classification before Contador's disqualification:

1. Alberto Contador (Saxo) 84 hours 5 minutes 14 seconds
2. Michele Scarponi (Lampre) @ 6 minutes 10 seconds
3. Vincenzo Nibali (Liquigas) @ 6 minutes 56 seconds
4. John Gadret (Ag2r) @ 10 minutes 4 seconds
5. Joaquin Rodriguez (Katusha) @ 11 minutes 5 seconds

Final 2011 Giro d'Italia General Classification after Contador's disqualification:

1. Michele Scarponi (Lampre) 84 hours 11 minutes 24 seconds
2. Vincenzo Nibali (Liquigas) @ 46 seconds
3. John Gadret (Ag2r) @ 3 minutes 54 seconds
4. Joaquin Rodriguez (Katusha) @ 4 minutes 55 seconds
5. Roman Kreuziger (Astana) @ 5 minutes 18 seconds

Climbers' Competition:

1. Stefano Garzelli (Acqua & Sapone): 67 points
2. ~~Alberto Contador (Saxo): 58~~
2. José Rujano (Androni Giocattoli): 43
3. Mikel Nieve (Euskaltel): 39

Points Competition:
 1. Alberto Contador (Saxo): 202 points
 1. Michele Scarponi (Lampre): 122
 2. Vincenzo Nibali (Liquigas): 121
 3. José Rujano (Androni Giocattoli): 107

Zomegnan didn't survive the carping about his 2011 route. Before the Giro was over rumors were flying that he would be replaced and in July his ouster was confirmed. While Zomegnan's autocratic ways allowed for plenty of justifiable criticism, the combination of his artful management and the internationalized field brought by the Pro Tour resulted in the Giro's becoming a truly great race. The long *piano* days of slow riding with an insane final hour of racing are gone. In 2010, no one who rode the Giro finished in the Tour's top ten. In 2011, Alberto Contador was so exhausted from the Giro, he could only manage fifth place in the Tour.

Michele Acquarone, the new race director for RCS Sport, said he would avoid Zomegnan's confrontational style, but also showed the Giro was not going to be watered down when it was revealed that 2012's penultimate day would include the Tonale, Aprica, Teglio, Mortirolo and Stelvio ascents. Already the riders were complaining. The *polemiche* have started. There's nothing like the Giro.

Glossary

All fields have their own jargon, and bicycle racing is no exception.

@: In English language race results, an asperand (or "at" sign) is used to denote the amount of time or number of points behind the winner. In the example below, Fausto Coppi won the race, taking 9 hours 19 minutes 55 seconds to complete the course. Gino Bartali was well behind him and crossed the finish line 11 minutes 52 seconds later. Martini was still further behind, finishing 19 minutes 14 seconds after Coppi. Cottur was with Martini but slightly behind him. The "s.t." means that he was given the same time as Martini. If a rider finishes close enough to a racer who is in front of him so there is no real gap, he will be given the same time as the first rider of that group. French or Spanish results will use often use "m.t." to denote same time. If no time is given, same time is assumed.

1. Fausto Coppi: 9 hours 19 minutes 55 seconds
2. Gino Bartali @ 11 minutes 52 seconds
3. Alfredo Martini @ 19 minutes 14 seconds
4. Giordano Cottur s.t.

a: In Italian race results "a" is the same as @.

Abandon: To quit a race.

Abbuono: Italian for time bonus. See Bonification.

Ammiraglia: Italian for a team follow car.

Arcobaleno: Italian for rainbow. See Rainbow Jersey.

Arrivo: Italian for the finish line.

Arrivo in salita: Italian for hilltop finish.

Attack: Generally a sudden acceleration in an attempt to break free of the peloton. On flat roads it is usually done by riding up along the side of the pack so that by the time the attacker passes the peloton's front rider, he is traveling too fast for the pack to easily react. In the mountains it is usually enough to accelerate from the front.

Autobus: French. See Grupetto and Time Limit.

Azzurri: Italian for the Men in Blue: the Italian national team wears blue jerseys.

Bell Lap: The last lap before the finish, when a bell is traditionally rung.

Bidon: Water bottle. Now made of plastic, early ones were metal with cork stoppers. Until 1950 they were carried on the handlebars, sometimes in pairs. Around 1950 riders started mounting bottle cages on the downtube. The trend to dispensing with the bar-mount cages started in the early 1960s and by 1970 they were a thing of the past. In the early 1980s, as a result of the sport of triathlon, builders started brazing bosses on the seat tube allowing mechanics to attach a second cage so that riders could again carry two bottles.

Bonification: Time bonus (actually time subtracted) awarded to a rider. Stage races vary, and the Giro is always tinkering with its rules. Bonifications can be earned several ways: winning or placing in a stage, winning or placing in an intermediate sprint, being among the first riders over a rated climb.

Bonk: To completely run out of energy, often called hunger knock. Sometimes a rider will forget to eat, or think he has enough food to make it to the finish without stopping to get food. The result can be catastrophic as the rider's body runs out of glycogen, the stored chemical the muscles burn for energy. Famously, José-Manuel Fuente didn't eat during the long stage fourteen in the 1974 Giro. He slowed as his body's ability to produce energy came to a crashing halt. Merckx sped on and took the Pink Jersey from the Spaniard who had shown such terrible judgment. It's happened to many great riders including Induráin and Armstrong, but not always with such catastrophic results. The French term is une fringale.

Break: Short for breakaway.

Breakaway: One or more riders escaping from the front of peloton, usually as the result of a sudden acceleration called an "attack". Riders will work together sharing the effort of breaking the wind hoping to improve their chances of winning by arriving at the finish in a smaller group. This can also be called a "break". Some riders do not possess the necessary speed to contest mass sprints and therefore try very hard to escape the clutches of the peloton well before the end of the race. Franco Bitossi was a master of the lone break even though he possessed a fearsome sprint. Sometimes a break will escape and no team will take responsibility to chase it down. See Chapatte's Law and Fuga di Bidone.

Bridge: To bridge a gap. To go from one group of cyclists to a break up the road.

Bunch: When preceded by "the", usually the peloton. Far less often a group of riders can be "a bunch".

Cadence: The speed at which the rider turns the pedals.

Caravan: The long line of vehicles preceding and following the racers.

Category: In European stage racing, it is a designation of the difficulty of a mountain climb. This is a subjective judgment of the difficulty of the ascent, based upon its length, gradient and how late in the stage the climb is to be ridden. A medium difficulty climb that comes after several hard ascents will get a higher rating because the riders will already be tired. The numbering system starts with "four" for the easiest that still rate being called a climb and then with increasing severity they are three, two, one. In the Giro the hardest climbs are usually rated Category one although it has happened that a climb is so difficult it has been classified as "Special".

Chairman Bill McGann: A harmless drudge.

Chapatte's Law: Formulated by former racer and Tour commentator Robert Chapatte, it states that in the closing stages of a race a determined peloton will chase down a break and close in at the rate of one minute per ten kilometers traveled. If a break is three minutes up the road the peloton will need to work hard for 30 kilometers to catch it. American television race commentator Paul Sherwen regularly uses Chapatte's Law to come up with his often accurate predictions of when a break will be caught.

Cima Coppi: The highest point in the Giro.

Classic: Any of seven one-day races whose history and prestige will make the career of its winner. They are: Milan–San Remo, Tour of Flanders, Gent–Wevelgem, Paris–Roubaix, Flèche Wallonne, Liège–Bastogne–Liège and the Tour of Lombardy. Only Rik van Looy has won them all. Some writers include a few other races in their list of Classics: Omloop Het Nieuwsblad, Amstel Gold Race, Rund um den Henniger Turm, San Sebastian Classic, Paris–Brussels and Paris–Tours.

Classifiche Generali: Italian for General Classification.

Colle: Italian for a small climb.

Commissaire: A race official with the authority to impose penalties on the riders for infractions of the rules. A common problem is dangerous or irregular sprinting. The commissaire will usually relegate the offending rider to a lower placing.

CONI: Italian. An acronym for Comitato Olimpico Nazionale Italiano, the Italian Olympic Commitee. It is responsible for the development and management of sports in Italy.

Criterium: A bike race around and around a short road course, often a city block. Good criterium riders have excellent bike handling skills and usually possess lots of power to enable them to constantly accelerate out of the corners. The Dutch and the Belgians are the masters of the event.

Crono: Italian, short for time-trial. See Cronometro, Time Trial.

Cronometro: Italian for time trial. Cronometro individuale is individual time trial and cronometro a squadre is team time trial.

Cronoscalata: Italian for an individual timed hill climb.

Cyclamen Jersey: The purple jersey of the points leader in the Giro until 2010, when the points leader began wearing a red jersey.

Défaillance: French for a total mental or body collapse. See Bonk for more.

Directeur Sportif: The on-the-road manager of a bike team. Although French, it is the term used in English as well. Often shortened to DS.

Direttore Sportivo: Italian for directeur sportif.

DNF: Did not finish. Used in results to denote that the racer started but did not complete the race.

DNS: Did not start. Used in results to denote a racer who was entered in a race but failed to start. Often seen in results in stage races where the rider abandons after the completion of the previous stage. In the Tour it's NP for non-partant.

Domestique: French. See Gregario.

Drafting: At racing speed a rider who is only a few inches behind another bike does about 30 percent less work. Riding behind another rider in his slipstream is called drafting. This is the basic fact of bike racing tactics and why a rider can only with the greatest difficulty ride away from the others, no matter how strong he is. Only in the rarest of cases can a racer stay away from a determinedly chasing peloton. To make an escape work he needs the pack to be uninterested in chasing for some length of time so that he can gain a large enough time gap. Then, when the sleeping pack is aroused it does not have enough time to catch him no matter how fast it chases. Hugo Koblet's wonderful solo escape in the 1951 Tour is one of the rare instances when a solo rider outdid a determined group of elite chasers. A rider who drafts others and refuses to go to the front and do his share of the work is said to be "sitting on". There are a number of pejorative terms for a rider who does this, the best known is "wheelsucker".

Drop: When a rider cannot keep up with his fellow riders and comes out of their slipsteam, whether in a break or in the peloton, he is said to be dropped.

Echelon: When the riders are hit with a side wind they must ride slightly to the right or left of the rider in front in order to remain in that rider's slipstream, instead of riding nose to tail in a straight line. This staggered line puts those riders further back in the pace line in the gutter. Because they can't edge further to the side, they have to take more of the brunt of both the wind and the wind drag of their forward motion. Good riders then form a series of echelons so that all the racers can contribute and receive shelter. Italian is ventaglio.

Escape: When used as a noun it is a breakaway. When used as a verb it is the act of breaking away.

Feed zone: The specific point along a race route where the riders pick up food and drink. Racing etiquette generally keeps racers from attacking at this point, but there have been some famous initiatives that have started while the riders were having musettes (bags) of food handed up. In 1987 a plot to attack Jean-François Bernard who was then leading the Tour was executed by Charly Mottet and his Système U team. They informed Stephen Roche and Pedro Delgado of their plans so that they would have enough horsepower to carry it through, which they did.

Field: See Peloton.

Field Sprint: The race at the finish for the best placing among those in the peloton. The term is usually used when a breakaway has successfully escaped and finished the stage, and the peloton is reduced to fighting for the remaining lesser places.

The Story of the Giro d'Italia

Fixed gear: A direct drive between the rear wheel and the cranks. The rear cog is locked onto the rear hub so that the rider cannot coast. When the rear wheel turns, the crank turns. Because this is the most efficient of all possible drive trains, riders in the early days of cycle racing preferred fixed gears to freewheels. When mountains became part of racing in the early twentieth century, the riders had to mount freewheels so that they could coast down the descents; otherwise their velocity was limited by their leg speed. Track bikes use fixed gears.

Flahute: French slang for tough-guy bike racer, usually Belgian. A Flahute thrives on the cold-weather, rain, winds, slippery cobbles and sustained high speeds that characterize the Belgian Classics. A Flahute should expect to taste wet cow dung thrown up by the other riders' wheels as they race across barely usable farm country roads. Examples: Marcel Kint, Walter Godefroot, Roger de Vlaeminck, Rik van Looy and Rik van Steenbergen.

Flyer: Usually a solo breakaway near the end of a race.

Foratura: Italian for flat tire.

Fuga: Italian for breakaway.

Fuga di Bidone: Italian for a particular kind of successful break. A fuga di bidone generally escapes early in a stage and is initially innocent-looking, but because of inaction on the part of the peloton, a large time gap occurs that becomes dangerous to the main General Classification contenders. Often hidden in a fuga bidone is a quality rider who, as a result of the successful break, has risen high enough in the standings to contend for the overall victory. Stage eleven of the 2010 Giro d'Italia which finished in l'Aquila was a classic fuga di bidone. 54 men escaped at kilometer 20 and by the end of the stage were over twelve minutes ahead of the main field. In that break was journeyman Spanish rider David Arroyo who then became the maglia rosa once the race hit the Dolomites; he put up a tremendous, but ultimately unsuccessful fight to keep the Pink Jersey.

GC: General Classification.

General Classification: The ranking of the accumulated time or placings, whichever basis the race uses to determine its winner. Since 1913 both the Giro and the Tour have used time. See Stage Race.

Giri: Plural of giro.

Giro d'Italia: A three-week stage race held in Italy, traditionally in May. It was first run in 1909. Often referred to as, simply, the Giro.

Giudice di Gara: Italian for commissaire.

GPM: Italian, for Gran Premio della Montagna. In 1933 the both the Giro and the Tour started awarding points for the first riders over certain hard climbs, the winner of the competition being what the English-speaking world calls the King of the Mountains. The classification has lost some of its magic in recent years because of the tactics riders use to win it. Today a rider wishing to win the GPM intentionally loses a large amount of time in the General Classification. Then when the high mountains are climbed, the aspiring King can take off on long breakaways to be first over the mountains without triggering a panicked chase by the GC contenders. The leader of the GPM classification in the Giro wears a green jersey.

Gran Premio della Montagna: Italian, see GPM.

Grand Tour: There are three Grand Tours, each lasting three weeks: the Tour de France, the Giro d'Italia and the Vuelta a España.

Green Jersey: Worn by the leader of the GPM classification.

Gregario: Italian. Because bicycle racing is a sport contested by teams and won by individuals, a man designated to be the team leader has his teammates work for him. These men have been called domestiques in France and the English-speaking world since Tour founder Henri Desgrange used it as a term of contempt for Maurice Brocco, whom he believed was selling his services to aid other riders in the 1911 Tour. Italians use a word for soldier, gregario. Today the terms have lost any bad connotation and serve as acknowledgements of the true nature of racing tactics. Gregari (plural) will chase down competitors and try to neutralize their efforts, they will protect their team leader from the wind by surrounding him. When a leader has to get a repair or stop to answer nature, his gregari will stay with him and pace him back up to the peloton. They are sometimes called "water carriers" because they are the ones designated to go back to the team car and pick up water bottles and bring them back up to the leader.

Gregario di lusso: A domestique of such high quality that he could be the captain of his own team. When Herman van Springel, who nearly won the 1968 Tour de France, raced for Eddy Merckx, he was a gregario di lusso.

Giornata no: Italian. A day in which a racer has no strength or energy. French is un jour sans (a day without).

Gruppetto: Italian. In the mountains the riders with poor climbing skills ride together hoping to finish in time to beat the time limit. By staying together in a group, they hope that if they don't finish in time they can persuade the officials to let them stay in the race because so many riders would otherwise be eliminated. It doesn't always work. Often the group lets a particularly experienced racer who knows how to pace the Grupetto lead them in order to get in just under the wire. This risky strategy minimizes the energy the riders have to expend. The French term is Autobus. The Grupetto is also sometimes called the Laughing Group.

Gruppo: Italian, literally, "group". In road racing it is the peloton. When they are all together without any active breakaways, it is gruppo compatto. When referring to the bicycle, gruppo means the core set of components made by a single manufacturer, such as a Campagnolo Gruppo.

Hilltop finish: When a race ends at the top of a mountain, riders with the greater climbing skills have the advantage. It used to be that the finish line was far from the last climb, allowing the bigger, more powerful riders to use their weight and strength to close the gap to the climbers on the descents and flats.

The Story of the Giro d'Italia

Hook: To extend an elbow or thigh in the way of another rider, usually during a sprint, to impede his progress while he is attempting to pass. Often it is said that a rider "threw a hook".

Intermediate sprint: To keep the race active there may be places along the race course where the riders will sprint for time bonuses or other prizes (premiums, or primes—pronounced "preems").

ITT: Individual time trial. See time trial.

Jump: A rider with the ability to quickly accelerate his bike is said to have a good "jump".

Kermesse: A lap road race much like a criterium but the course can be longer, as long as 10 kilometers.

King of the Mountains: See GPM.

KOM: King of the Mountains. See GPM.

Laughing Group: See Grupetto.

Maglia Rosa: Italian, see Pink Jersey.

Maglia Iridata: Italian, see Rainbow Jersey.

Massaggiatore: Italian for soigneur.

Massed Start Road Race: All the riders start at the same time. This is different from a time trial where the riders are set off individually at regular time intervals.

Mechanical: A problem with the function of a racer's bicycle, usually not meaning a flat tire. Sometimes there have been rules in place that prevent a rider's changing bikes unless a mechanical problem is present; mechanics have then manufactured mechanicals in sometimes successful attempts to fool the judges.

Minute Man: In a time trial the rider who starts a minute ahead. It's always a goal in a time trial to try to catch one's minute man.

Musette: A cloth bag containing food and drinks handed up to the rider in the feed zone. It has a long strap so the rider can slip his arm through it easily on the fly, then put the strap over his shoulder to carry it while he transfers the food to his jersey pockets.

Natural or nature break: Because races can take over seven hours, the riders must occasionally dismount to urinate. If the riders are flagrant and take no care to be discreet while they answer the call of nature they can be penalized. Charly Gaul lost the 1957 Giro when he was attacked while taking such a break, so he later learned to urinate while on the fly.

Off the back: To be dropped.

Paceline: Riders riding nose to tail saving energy by riding in each other's slipstream. Usually the front rider does the hard work for a short while, breaking the wind for the others, and then peels off to go to the back so that another rider can take a short stint at the front. The faster the riders go, the greater the energy saving gained by riding in the slipstream of the rider in front. When the action is hot and the group wants to move fast the front man will take a short, high-speed "pull" before dropping off. At lower speeds the time at the front is usually longer. See Echelon.

Palmarès: French for an athlete's list of accomplishments.

Parcours: The race course.

Partenza: Italian for race start.

Passista: Italian for rouleur.

Passista-Scalatore: A rouleur who can climb well, an all-rounder. Generally this is the type of rider who can win a stage race because he can do well on the flats and time trials and not lose time (and may even gain time) in the mountains. Examples: Fausto Coppi, Bernard Hinault, Lance Armstrong, Eddy Merckx, Giovanni Battaglin.

Passo: Italian for mountain pass. Plural is passi.

Pavé: French for cobblestone, and in English cycling is used to refer to a cobblestone road. Riding the pavé requires skill and power. Some riders such as the legendary Roger de Vlaeminck seem to almost glide over the stones knowing exactly what line to take to avoid trouble. De Vlaeminck, who won the Paris–Roubaix four times, rarely flatted in this race famous for its terrible cobbles.

Peloton: The main group of riders traveling together in a race. Breaks leave the front of it, dropped riders exit its rear. Synonyms: bunch, group, field, pack. Italian is plotone.

Piano: Italian for soft. It can mean slow or easy when riding. In the past, the Giro often had "piano" stages where the riders intentionally took it easy until the final kilometers leading up to the sprint.

Piazza: Italian. See Podium.

Pink Jersey: Worn by the rider who is currently leading in the General Classification in the Giro d'Italia. It was chosen because the sponsoring newspaper *La Gazzetta dello Sport* is printed on pink paper. In 1931 Learco Guerra was first rider to wear the Pink Jersey. Italian is maglia rosa.

Plotone: Italian for peloton.

Podium: The top three places, first, second and third. Many racers know that they cannot win a race and thus their ambition is limited to getting on the podium. In major races such as the Tour and the Giro, attaining the podium is such a high accomplishment that it almost makes a racer's career. Italian is piazza.

Points: The usual meaning is the accumulation of placings in each stage. The Giro awards the same number of points regardless of the stage's terrain. The Tour gives more points to the flatter stages so the winner of the points competition is a more likely to be sprinter. See General Classification. In the Giro the Points leader wears a red jersey, in the Tour he dons a green one.

Prologue: French. An introductory stage in a stage race that is usually a short individual time trial, normally under ten kilometers. The Giro has also used a team time trial format in the prologue.

Pull: A stint at the front of a paceline.

Queen Stage: The hardest, most demanding stage of a stage race; it is always in the high mountains. Italian is il tappone.

Purple Jersey: In the Giro a purple, or more specifically cyclamen, jersey was awarded to the leader of the points competition until 2010.

Rainbow Jersey: The reigning World Champion in a particular cycling event gets to wear a white jersey with rainbow stripes. The championships for most important events are held in the fall. A former World Champion gets to wear a jersey with rainbow trim on his sleeves and collar. If a World Champion becomes the leader of the Tour, Giro or Vuelta he will trade his Rainbow Jersey for the Leader's Jersey. Italian is maglia iridata.

Relegate: Italian and English (pronounced differently, of course) for a judge's decision to assign a lower place to a rider after a rule infraction. Sprinters who fail to hold their line in the final meters and endanger the other racers are generally given the last place of their group.

Rifornimento: Italian for taking on food and drink. Zona Rifornimento is Italian for the feed zone.

Ritiro: Italian for abandon

Road furniture: Concrete medians and barriers put in roads to slow traffic. The roads of northern Europe, in particular, are filled with road furniture and it can make bicycle racing there dangerous.

Rouleur: French for a rider who can turn a big gear with ease over flat roads and is the term most often used in English. Rouleurs are usually bigger riders who often suffer in the mountains. Italian is passista.

Same time: See "@".

Scalatore: Italian for one who climbs well.

Scattista: Italian for a climber who can explode in the mountains with a devastating acceleration. The most famous and extraordinary of these pure climbers were Charly Gaul and Marco Pantani.

Soigneur: Today a job with many duties involving the care of the riders: massage, preparing food, handing up musettes in the feed zone and sadly, doping. Usually when a doping scandal erupts the soigneurs are deeply involved. Italian is massaggiatore.

Sprint: At the end of a race the speeds get ever higher until in the last couple of hundred meters the fastest riders jump out from the peloton in an all-out scramble for the finish line. Teams with very fine sprinting specialists will employ a "lead-out train". With about five kilometers to go these teams will try to take control of the race by going to the front and stepping up the speed of the race in order to discourage last-minute flyers. Sometimes two or three competing teams will set up parallel pace lines. Usually the team's train will be a pace line organized in ascending speed of the riders. Each rider takes a pull and peels off; the next rider in line will be a quicker one who can keep increasing the speed. The last man before the team's designated sprinter is a speedy rider who will end up with a good placing by virtue of being at the front of the race in the final meters and having a good turn of speed himself.

Squadra: Italian for team.

Squalificato: Italian for disqualification. When Marco Pantani was found to have a high hematocrit near the end of the 1999 Giro, he was tossed from the race. He suffered a squalificato.

S.T.: Same time. See "@".

Stage race: A cycling competition of two or more separate races involving the same riders with the results added up to determine the winner. Today the victor is usually determined by adding up the accumulated time each rider took to complete each race, called a "stage". The one with the lowest aggregate time is the winner. Alternatively the winner can be selected by adding up the rider's placings, giving one point for first, two points for second, etc. The rider with the lowest total is the winner. The Giro used a points system between 1909 and 1912 because the judging was simpler and cheating could be reduced. Because points systems tend to cause dull racing during most of the stage with a furious sprint at the end, they are rarely used in determining the overall winner. Because points systems favor sprinters, most important stage races have a points competition along with the elapsed time category. In the Giro the time leader wears pink and the man ahead in points wears red. In the Tour de France the leader in time wears the Yellow Jersey and the points leader wears green. The race's ranking of its leaders for the overall prize is called the General Classification, or GC. A rider can win the overall race without ever winning an individual stage, as Carlo Oriani did in the 1913 Giro.

Stayer: A rouleur.

Strada bianca (pl. strade bianche): Italian "white roads", used to denote unpaved gravel roads.

Switchback: In order to reduce the gradient of a mountain ascent the road engineer has the road go back and forth across the hill. The Stelvio climb is famous for its 48 switchbacks as is l'Alpe d'Huez for its 21. In Italian the term is tornante.

Tappa: Italian for stage.

Il tappone: Italian for the Queen Stage of stage race. It is the hardest, most demanding stage and is always in the high mountains.

Team time trial: See time trial. Instead of an individual rider, whole teams set off along a specific distance at intervals. It is a spectacular event because the teams go all out on the most advanced aerodynamic equipment and clothing available. To maximize the slipstream advantage the riders ride nose to tail as close to each other as possible. With the riders so close together, going so fast and at their physical limits, crashes can occur. Some teams targeting an overall win practice this event with rigor and the result is a beautifully precise fast-moving team that operates almost as if it were one rider. Sometimes a team with a very powerful leader who is overly ambitious will be shattered by his making his turns at the front too fast for the others. Skilled experienced leaders take longer rather than faster pulls so that their teammates can rest.

Technical: Usually refers to a difficult mountain descent or time trial course on winding city streets, meaning that the road will challenge the rider's bike handling skills.

Tempo: Usually means riding at a fast but not all-out pace. Teams defending a leader in a stage race will often go to the front of the peloton and ride tempo for days on end in order to discourage breakaways. It is very tiring work and usually leaves the gregari of a winning team exhausted at the end of a Grand Tour.

Tifosi: Italian sports fans, sometimes fanatical in their devotion to an athlete or team. The term is said to be derived from the delirium of typhus patients.

Time Bonus: see Bonification

Time Limit: To encourage vigorous riding, the Grand Tours impose a cutoff time. If a racer does not finish a stage within that time, he is eliminated from the race. This prevents a racer's resting by riding leisurely one day, then winning the next. To calculate the time limit, they increase the stage winner's time by some percentage. Because it is the intention of the races to be fair, the rules are complex. On flat stages where the riders have less trouble staying with the peloton and the time gaps are smaller, the percentage added to the winner's time is smaller, and in the mountain stages it is higher. The faster the race is run, the higher the percentage of the winner's time allowed the slower riders. Riders who have unusual trouble can appeal to the commissaires for clemency.

Time trial: A race in which either an individual or team rides over a specific distance against the clock. It is intended to be an unpaced ride in which the individual or team is not allowed to draft a competitor. The riders are started at specific intervals, usually two minutes. In the Giro and the Tour the riders start in reverse order of their standing in the General Classification, the leader going last. Usually the last twenty riders are set off at three-minute intervals. If a rider catches a racer who started ahead of him the rules say that he must not get into his slipstream but must instead pass well to the slower rider's side. This is one of the more often ignored rules in cycling. The Giro's first time trial was in 1934.

Tornante: Italian for switchbacks.

Track: See Velodrome.

Trade team: A team sponsored by a commercial entity. Until the mid-1950s, cycle team sponsorship was limited to companies within the bicycle industry. Real change came in 1954 when Fiorenzo Magni's bicycle manufacturer, Ganna, fell into financial difficulty. Magni was able to supplement the shortfall by getting the Nivea cosmetic company to sponsor his team. The move was initially resisted but it is now the standard. Bicycle companies today usually do not have the monetary resources to finance big-time racing teams.

TTT: See Team Time Trial.

Transfer: Usually a Giro stage will end in a city one afternoon and start the next morning from the same city. When a stage ends in one city and the next stage starts in another, the riders must be transferred by bus, plane or train to the next day's starting city. This schedule is normally done so that both the finish and start city can pay the Giro organization for the privilege of hosting the Giro. The racers loathe transfers because this delays their massages, eating and resting.

UCI: The governing world body of cycling, the Union Cycliste Internationale.

Ultimo Kilometro: Italian for the final kilometer.

Velodrome: An oval bicycle racing track with banked curves. They can be sited either indoors or outdoors. Olympic tracks are usually 333⅓ meters around but indoor ones are smaller and have correspondingly steeper banking. Some road races like Paris–Roubaix have the riders ride onto the velodrome and finish the race with a couple of laps on the track. In the past, the Giro would regularly do this, often with the rider's time being clocked as he entered the velodrome. With a 200-man field in modern Giri this is impractical. The disappearance of velodromes is also a major factor in this trend.

Ventaglio: Italian, literally a fan, but in cycling slang it means echelon.

Virtual Pink Jersey: When a rider has a large enough lead on the Giro leader, so that if the race were to be ended at that very moment he would assume the leadership, he then is called the Virtual Pink Jersey.

Washboard: A rough riding surface with small bumps or irregularities. Like the pavé, riding on washboard requires a lot of power and puts the smaller riders with less absolute power at their disposal at a disadvantage.

White Jersey: In the 1930s Giri it was worn by the leader of the unsponsored class of riders, called independents. Today it is worn by the best rider under 25.

Yellow Jersey: Worn by the rider who is leading in the General Classification in the Tour de France.

Bibliography

Books marked * are highly recommended.

Abt, Samuel. *Up the Road: Cycling's Modern Era from LeMond to Armstrong*. Boulder, Colorado: VeloPress, 2005.

Armstrong, David. *Merckx: Man and Myth*. Silsden, England: Kennedy Brothers Publishing, undated.

*Bobet, Jean. *Tomorrow, We Ride*. Norwich, England: Mousehold Press, 2009.

Bergonzi, Pier and Elio Trifari. *Un Secolo di Passioni: Giro d'Italia 1909–2009*. Milan, Italy: RCS Libri spa, 2009.

Bergonzi, Pier and Giuseppe Castelnovi. *Giro d'Italia, Le storie e le foto più belle della leggenda rosa*. Milan, Italy: SEP Editrice, 2000.

Berto, Frank J. *The Dancing Chain*. San Francisco, California: Van der Plas Publications, 2009.

Duggan, Christopher. *A Concise History of Italy*. Cambridge, England: Cambridge University Press, 1994.

Brunel, Philippe. *An Intimate Portrait of the Tour de France: Masters and Slaves of the Road*. Denver, Colorado: Buonpane Publications, 1995.

*Buzzati, Dino. *The Giro d'Italia: Coppi Versus Bartali at the 1949 Giro d'Italia*. Boulder, Colorado: VeloPress, 1999.

Calamai, Franco. *Alfredo Martini, memorie di un grande saggio del ciclismo*. Milan, Italy: Edit Vallardi, 2008.

Cervi, Gino and Paolo Facchinetti. *Il Giro d'Italia: Strade Storie Oggestti di un Mito*. Bologna, Italy: Bolis Edizioni srl, 2009.

Castelnovi, Giuseppe and Marco Pastonesi. *Una Vita da Gregario*. Milan, Italy: SEP Editrice, 2004.

Conti, Beppe: *100 Storie del Giro, 1909-2009*. Torino, Italy: Graphot Editrice, 2008.

Conti, Beppe and Gian Paolo Ormezzano. *Il Giro e L'Italia, un storia d'amore*. Ancarano (TE), Italy: Editoriale Diemme srl, 2007.

Cornand, Jan. *57th Giro d'Italia: Tour of Italy 1974*. Keighley, U.K.: Kennedy Brothers Publishing, 1974.

————. *58th Giro d'Italia: Tour of Italy 1975*. Keighley, U.K.: Kennedy Brothers Publishing Ltd., 1975.

————. *59th Giro d'Italia: Tour of Italy 1976*. Keighley, U.K.: Kennedy Brothers Publishing Ltd., 1976.

Duker, Peter. *61st Tour of Italy 1978*. Keighley, U.K.: Kennedy Brothers Publishing Ltd., 1978.

Fignon, Laurent. *We Were Young and Carefree*. London: Yellow Jersey Press, 2010.

Fotheringham, William. *A Century of Cycling*. St. Paul, Minnesota: MBI Publishing, 2003.

*————. *Fallen Angel: The Passion of Fausto Coppi*. London: Yellow Jersey Press, 2009.

Fretwell, Peter and A.Gadenz. *55th Giro d'Italia: Tour of Italy 1972*. Keighley, U.K.: Kennedy Brothers Publishing Ltd., 1972.

————. *56th Giro d'Italia: Tour of Italy 1973*. Keighley, U.K.: Kennedy Brothers Publishing Ltd., 1973.

Godaert, Janssens, Cammaert. *Tour Encyclopedie* (7 volumes). Ghent, Belgium: Uitgeverij Worldstrips, 1997.

*L'Équipe. *The Official Tour de France Centennial 1903–2003*. London: Weidenfeld & Nicolson, 2004.

Henderson, N.G. *Continental Cycle Racing*. London: Pelham Books, 1970.

————. *Fabulous Fifties*. Silsden, England: Kennedy Brothers Publishing, Ltd. Undated.

Howard, Paul. *Sex, Lies and Handlebar Tape: The Remarkable Life of Jacques Anquetil, the First Five-Times Winner of the Tour de France*. Edinburgh, Scotland: Mainstream Publishing, Ltd., 2008.

Kirkpatrick, Ivonne. *Mussolini, A Study in Power*. New York: Avon Books, 1964.

*Lazell, Marguerite. *The Tour de France, An Illustrated History*. Buffalo, New York: Firefly Books, 2003.

*Maertens, Freddy. *Fall From Grace*. Hull, U.K.: Ronde Publications, 1993.

Martin, Pierre. *The Bernard Hinault Story*. Keighley, U.K.: Kennedy Brothers Publishing Ltd., 1982.

————. *Tour 80*. Keighley, U.K.: Kennedy Brothers Publishing Ltd., 1980.

————. *Tour 82*. Keighley, U.K.: Kennedy Brothers Publishing Ltd., 1982.

————. *Tour 83*. Keighley, U.K.: Kennedy Brothers Publishing Ltd., 1983.

————. *Tour 84*. Keighley, U.K.: Kennedy Brothers Publishing Ltd., 1984.

————. *Tour 85*. Keighley, U.K.: Kennedy Brothers Publishing Ltd., 1985.

————. *Tour 88*. Keighley, U.K.: Kennedy Brothers Publishing Ltd., 1988.

————. *Tour 90*. Keighley, U.K.: Kennedy Brothers Publishing Ltd., 1990.

*Mulholland, Owen. *Uphill Battle*. Boulder, Colorado: VeloPress, 2003.

Negri, Rino. *Parla Coppi*. Trent, Italy: Alta Anaunia Editrice, 1971.

*Nye, Peter. *Hearts of Lions*. New York: W.W. Norton Company, 1988.

*Ollivier, Jean-Paul. *Maillot Jaune*. Boulder, Colorado: VeloPress, 2001.

Pastonesi, Marco. *Gli Angeli di Coppi*. Portogruaro (VE), Italy: Ediciclo Editore srl, 2006.

Picchi, Sandro. *Il Giro d'Italia, Storia Illustrata* (2 Volumes). Florence, Italy: Ponte alle Grazie Editori srl, 1992.

Pratolini, Vasco. *Al Giro d'Italia*. Milan, Italy: La Vita Felice, 2001.

*Rendell, Matt. *The Death of Marco Pantani, A Biography*. London: Phoenix, 2007.

Roche, Stephen. *My Road to Victory*. London: Stanley Paul & Co., 1987.

Ronchi, Manuele and Gianfranco Josti. *Man on the Run: The Life and Death of Marco Pantani*. London: Robson Books, 2005.

Sánchez, Javier García. *Induráin: A Tempered Passion*. Norwich, U.K: Mousehold Press, 2002.

Serantoni, Ildo. *Felice Gimondi: The Story of a Man who was also a Champion in Life*. Milan, Italy: SEP Editrice, 2005.

Seray, Jacques. *1904, the Tour de France Which Was to Be the Last*. Boulder, Colorado: Buonpane Publications, 1994.

Sergent, Pascal. *Paris–Roubaix*. London, U.K.: Bromley Books, 1997.

*Sykes, Herbie. *The Eagle of the Canavese: Franco Balmamion and the Giro d'Italia*. Norwich, England: Mousehold Press, 2008.

*———. *Maglia Rosa: Triumph and Tragedy at the Giro d'Italia*. London, U.K: Rouleur Ltd., 2011.

*Thompson, Christopher S. *The Tour de France: A Cultural History*. Berkeley and Los Angeles, California: University of California Press, 2006.

Vanwalleghem, Rik. *Eddy Merckx, the Greatest Cyclist of the 20th Century*. Boulder, Colorado: VeloPress, 2000.

*Voet, Willy. *Breaking the Chain*. London: Yellow Jersey Press, 2002.

*Walsh, David. *From Lance to Landis: Inside the American Doping Controversy at the Tour de France*. New York: Ballantine, 2007.

Wilcockson, John. *Marco Pantani: The Legend of a Tragic Champion*. Boulder, Colorado: VeloPress, 2005.

*Witherell, James. *Bicycle History, A Chronological Cycling History of People, Races and Technology*. Cherokee Village, Arkansas: McGann Publishing, 2010.

*Woodland, Les. *The Crooked Path to Victory*. San Francisco, California: Cycle Publishing, 2003.

*———. *Tourmen: The Men Who Made the Tour de France*. Cherokee Village, Arkansas: McGann Publishing, 2010.

*———. *The Yellow Jersey Companion to the Tour de France*. London: Yellow Jersey Press, 2003.

Magazines: Various issues of *Velonews, Procycling, Cycle Sport, Bicisport, Bicyclist*

Websites
www.memoire-du-cyclisme.net
www.letour.fr
www.bikeraceinfo.com
www.cyclingnews.com
www.velonews.com
www.gazzetta.it (the website of *La Gazzetta dello Sport*)
www.wikipedia.com
and others

McGann

Conversations, letters and e-mails over the years with the following generous people, not in any particular order: Owen Mulholland, John Mulholland, Larry Theobald, Les Woodland, James Witherell, Fiorenzo Magni, Giorgio Albani, Greg LeMond, Brian Robinson, Marcel Tinazzi, Felice Gimondi, Joe Lindsey, Steve Lubanski, Celestino Vercelli, Paolo Guerciotti, Valeria Paoletti, Antonio and Mauro Mondonico, Faliero Masi, Rene Moser, Derek Roberts, Franco Bitossi, Pier Bergonzi, Italo Zilioli, Ferdy Kübler, Freddy Maertens, Jac van Meer. Thank you all so much.

Memories of stories told to me over the years of my career by the many people in the bike industry whom I have had the good fortune to meet.

Index